Uncovering Ways of War

A volume in the series

CORNELL STUDIES IN SECURITY AFFAIRS

edited by Robert J. Art, Robert Jervis, *and* Stephen M. Walt

A full list of titles in the series appears at the end of the book.

Uncovering Ways of War

U.S. INTELLIGENCE AND FOREIGN MILITARY INNOVATION, 1918–1941

THOMAS G. MAHNKEN

Cornell University Press

ITHACA AND LONDON

First published 2002 by Cornell University Press

Printed in the United States of America

Library of Congress Cataloging-in-Publication Data

Mahnken, Thomas Gilbert, 1965–
Uncovering ways of war: U.S. intelligence and foreign military
innovation, 1918–1941 / Thomas G. Mahnken.
p. cm.—(Cornell studies in security affairs)
Includes bibliographical references and index.
ISBN 0-8014-3986-8 (cloth : alk. paper)
1. Military intelligence—United States—History—20th century.
2. Military art and science—Effect of technological innovations
on—History—20th century. I. Title. II. Series
UB251.U5 M44 2002
355.3'432—dc21
2001006788

Cornell University Press strives to use environmentally responsible
suppliers and materials to the fullest extent possible in the publishing
of its books. Such materials include vegetable-based, low-VOC inks
and acid-free papers that are recycled, totally chlorine-free,
or partly composed of nonwood fibers. For further information,
visit our website at www.cornellpress.cornell.edu.

Cloth printing   10   9   8   7   6   5   4   3   2   1

To my parents

Contents

Tables and Figures

Acknowledgments

This book would have been impossible without the help of a teacher, a professor, and a mentor; I owe all three an enduring intellectual debt. In high school, Mrs. Rose Sleigh taught me the craft of expository writing. In college, Walter McDougall sparked in me an enduring interest in history and diplomacy. In graduate school, Eliot Cohen kindled my passion for strategic studies. His dedication to the profession of teaching, concern for his students, and devotion to the highest academic standards are unparalleled.

A great number of people assisted me during this book's long gestation. Roger W. Barnett, Alvin Coox, Captain James FitzSimonds, USN, Aaron Friedberg, Michael Handel, Timothy Hoyt, Robert Jervis, Michael Mandelbaum, John Maurer, Bruce Parrott, Chip Pickett, Stephen Rosen, Andrew Ross, Abram Shulsky, Ronald Spector, and Thomas Welch all gave me valuable comments on portions of the manuscript. I benefited greatly from insights of Thomas C. Hone regarding the development of British and Japanese carrier aviation and of Mark R. Peattie and David C. Evans regarding the Japanese navy. I am especially indebted to Andrew W. Marshall, the director of the Office of Net Assessment in the Department of Defense, a civil servant in the best sense of the word. I had the honor to serve in his office for two years, an experience that taught me more about the theory and practice of strategic assessment than I could have learned anywhere else.

Archivists are the unsung heroes of historical scholarship. I thank Richard A. Van Doenhoff, John E. Taylor, and Barry Zerby of the Military Reference Branch of the National Archives; Evelyn Cherpak of the Naval Historical Collection at the Naval War College; Gina Akers, Kathy Lloyd, and John Hodges of the Naval Historical Center; Hannah Zeidlik of the U.S. Army Center of Military History; David Keough and Pamela Cheney of the U.S. Army Military History Institute at Carlisle Barracks, Penn.; Carol Leadenham of the Hoover Institution Archives, Stanford, Calif.; and the staff of the U.S. Naval Institute, Annapolis, Md., for their assistance in researching this book.

I had the good fortune to serve as a national security fellow at the John M. Olin Institute for Strategic Studies at Harvard University during the 1995–1996 academic year. The directors of the institute— Samuel P. Huntington, Stephen P. Rosen, and Michael C. Desch— gave me encouragement, advice, and support throughout my tenure in Cambridge. I also benefited from comments from my colleagues at Harvard, including Colin Elman, Geoffrey Herrera, Christopher Layne, Jeffrey Legro, Laura Miller, Jeffrey Taliaferro, Brian Taylor, Bradley Thayer, Pascal Vennesson, and Lieutenant Colonel Rick Villalobos, USAF. In addition, this book could not have been completed without the generous support of the Lynde and Harry Bradley Foundation and the Northrop-Grumman Corporation.

My civilian and military colleagues in the Department of Strategy and Policy at the U.S. Naval War College have been a constant source of inspiration. I cannot think of a more challenging and stimulating environment in which to teach and study strategy. I am particularly grateful to George Baer, Alberto Coll, John English, William Fuller, David Kaiser, Bradford Lee, Thomas Nichols, and Steven Ross, as well as my military teaching partners—Colonel William Goodwin, U.S. Army; Colonel B. C. Bell, U.S. Marine Corps; and Captain James Harrington, U.S. Navy—for the advice and support they have offered during my time in Newport.

Last but not least, I would like to thank my wife, Deborah, for her patience, understanding, and support throughout this long journey.

Portions of chapter 3 appeared in "Gazing at the Sun: The Office of Naval Intelligence and Japanese Naval Innovation, 1918–1941," *Intelligence and National Security* 11, no. 3 (July 1996). Portions of chapter 4 appeared in "Uncovering Foreign Military Innovation," *Journal of Strategic Studies* 22, no. 4 (December 1999).

THOMAS G. MAHNKEN

Newport, Rhode Island

Uncovering Ways of War

[Introduction]

Military Intelligence
in an Interwar Period

"A soldier . . . in peacetime is like a sailor navigating by dead reckoning. You have left the terra firma of the last war and are extrapolating from the experiences of that war. The greater the distance from the last war, the greater become the chances of error in this extrapolation. Occasionally there is a break in the clouds: a small-scale conflict occurs somewhere and gives you a "fix" by showing whether certain weapons and techniques are effective or not; but it is always a doubtful fix. . . . For the most part you have to sail on in a fog of peace until at the last moment. Then, probably when it is too late, the clouds lift and there is land immediately ahead; breakers, probably, and rocks. Then you find out rather late in the day whether your calculations have been right or not."[1]

As Sir Michael Howard notes, discerning the shape of future wars is one of the most challenging tasks that soldiers and statesmen perform. Long periods of peace often witness dramatic shifts in military balances that become apparent only in wartime. The emergence of new ways of war compounds the challenge of measuring power. The result is often a gulf between prewar expectations and wartime reality.

Warning political and military decision makers of the development of new weapons by potential adversaries is one of the central tasks of any intelligence organization. The record shows, however, that intelligence services have had at best mixed success. In some cases, they completely missed the advent of new technology and doctrine. In others, they collected accurate information but failed to understand its significance.

In this book, I examine why intelligence organizations often fail to detect the development of innovative technology and doctrine by ally and adversary alike. I argue that preconceptions about the character

---

1. Michael Howard, "Military Science in an Age of Peace," *Journal of the Royal United Services Institute for Defence Studies* 119, no. 1 (March 1974): 4.

and conduct of war, ethnocentrism, and incomplete information frequently conspire to prevent observers from understanding new ways of war.

I explore these issues by assessing how well U.S. Army and Navy intelligence organizations understood innovation in the Japanese, German, and British armed forces between 1918 and 1941. The years between the two world wars witnessed both a considerable shift in the balance of power in Europe and Asia and the emergence of new ways of war, including carrier aviation, amphibious operations, and combined-arms armored warfare. These innovations—and American perceptions of them—form the core of this book.

These cases are characteristic of the problems that intelligence organizations face as they attempt to recognize military innovation. Consider Japan, which illustrates the difficulties associated with assessing a rising power. At the beginning of the period, Japanese technology lagged behind that of other major states. Military observers correctly viewed Japanese training and combat skills as inferior to those of European and American militaries. Within two decades, however, Japan grew into a first-class military power. Tokyo developed the ability to design and manufacture modern weapons domestically. Indeed, it fielded some unique weapons, such as the Type 93 *Long Lance* oxygen-propelled torpedo. The Japanese army and navy also devised operational concepts designed to offset the advantages of their technically sophisticated adversaries. The United States devoted considerable resources to monitoring Japan, but all too often Japanese secrecy and preconceptions about the character and conduct of war skewed U.S. assessments. The cultural distance that separated the two states further complicated intelligence collection and analysis. In some cases, the Japanese managed to conceal the development of new ways of war from American observers. In others, American intelligence professionals discounted what turned out to be accurate information because of their ingrained assumptions about war. Detecting weapons and doctrine that differed considerably from that which the U.S. armed forces employed proved particularly difficult.

U.S. assessments of Germany during the 1920s and 1930s illustrate the problems associated with rapid shifts in military power. Much of Germany's military activity, including the development of tanks and aircraft, occurred under the cloak of secrecy. Hitler's rise to power and Berlin's subsequent rearmament represented a dramatic discontinuity, as the German armed forces expanded, adopted operational concepts, and fielded formations substantially different from those of their American counterparts. The U.S. Army nonetheless did an excellent job of understanding German concepts of combined-arms armored warfare. A close relationship with the German armed forces, together with the insights of talented attachés, allowed the United States to gather information on some of Germany's most closely held secrets. American intelligence enjoyed less success in its attempts to understand German air doctrine. Even though U.S. intelligence collected information indicating that the *Luftwaffe* planned to emphasize support of ground forces, attachés in Berlin and the Army Air Corps leadership believed that Germany was intent on building a strategic air force. U.S. intelligence organizations had even greater difficulty understanding Berlin's development of advanced technology, such as ballistic and cruise missiles.

British innovations posed a third challenge. The British armed forces had a long and well-deserved reputation for prowess on the battlefield. During the interwar period, however, economic weakness and the failure to take full advantage of new warfare areas eroded British military power. U.S. intelligence gathering in Britain yielded mixed results. On the one hand, American attachés did a good job of tracking technology and doctrine that had already proved effective. The Army, for example, looked to Britain for insight on tank technology and armored doctrine. However, American observers often viewed the development of armored warfare through the lens of World War I. Moreover, U.S. Army and Navy attachés paid little attention to Britain's development of radar, a tendency that tight British security abetted. It was not until the British literally handed radar technology to the United States that attachés began systematically to collect information on British radar.

Earlier studies of U.S. intelligence in the years between the two world wars have portrayed Army and Navy intelligence as neglected and ineffective. Alvin Coox has characterized U.S. intelligence organizations during the period as "complacent, chauvinistic, and arrogant,"[2] and David Kahn has gone so far as to state that "intelligence had little to do with American assessments of Germany and Japan before December 1941."[3] Scholars have also argued that intelligence regarding foreign militaries had little influence on the development of U.S. weapons and doctrine. Ernest May has concluded that U.S. forces during World War II "were designed virtually without analysis of intelligence about potential enemies."[4] Stephen Peter Rosen, for his part, has

2. Alvin D. Coox, "The Rise and Fall of the Imperial Japanese Air Forces," *Aerospace Historian* 27, no. 2 (June 1980): 75.

3. David Kahn, "The United States Views Germany and Japan in 1941" in *Knowing One's Enemies: Intelligence Assessment Before the Two World Wars,* ed. Ernest R. May (Princeton, N.J.: Princeton University Press, 1984): 476.

4. May, "Capabilities and Proclivities" in *Knowing One's Enemies,* 535.

argued that decisions about new weaponry in the interwar period were made with little intelligence input.[5]

This book challenges both propositions. First, I show that despite limited personnel and funds, U.S. Army and Navy intelligence did an excellent job of detecting attempts by Japan, Germany, and Great Britain to develop new ways of war. U.S. intelligence services were at least partially successful in six of the nine cases this book explores. Second, in several significant cases, intelligence regarding foreign developments influenced U.S. technology and doctrine. Information gathered in Germany and Great Britain helped shape the doctrine and organization of American tank forces, and observation of Japanese landing operations in China influenced the design of American landing craft.

Three patterns emerge from this book. First, intelligence agencies are more inclined to monitor the development of established weapons than to search for new military systems. Second, intelligence agencies pay more attention to technology and doctrine that have been demonstrated in war than to those that have not seen combat. In other words, one should expect intelligence organizations readily to identify incremental changes to weapons whose value has been demonstrated in war. Intelligence organizations should experience more difficulty detecting new or unique systems. Finally, it is easier to identify innovation in areas that one's own services are exploring than those they have not examined, are not interested in, or have rejected. As a result, intelligence organizations should more frequently detect foreign developments that mirror those of their own armed forces than those that differ substantially from them.

5. Stephen Peter Rosen, *Winning the Next War* (Ithaca: Cornell University Press, 1991): 187.

[1]

Intelligence and Military Innovation

The wartime debut of novel military technology and doctrine often yields dramatic results on the battlefield. It is also a common source of surprise. Prussia's mastery of the railroad, rifle, and telegraph allowed it, the least of the European great powers, to defeat Denmark, Austria, and France between 1964 and 1871 and to unify Germany under its control. At the beginning of World War II, Nazi Germany's development of armored warfare and tactical aviation delivered a string of unexpected lightning victories against Poland, Norway, Denmark, Belgium, Luxembourg, the Netherlands, and—most dramatically—France. Imperial Japan's use of carrier aviation, naval surface warfare tactics, and amphibious landings allowed it not only to cripple the U.S. fleet at Pearl Harbor, but also to seize American, British, and Dutch possessions in Asia in just five months. During the 1973 Arab-Israeli War, Egypt's innovative use of surface-to-air missiles and anti-tank guided munitions inflicted on Israel its worst battlefield defeat. The use of stealth and precision-guided munitions by the United States in the 1991 Gulf War yielded a rapid victory that shocked participant and observer alike.

While technological surprise is a common phenomenon, it has not been systematically studied.[1] The development of new ways of war frequently spans years or decades and almost always yields enough information to allow an intelligence service to identify and to characterize new weapons and doctrine. A good intelligence organization should be able to obtain enough information not only to warn of the existence of new ways of war, but also to develop an appropriate response.[2] Why, then, do intelligence organizations succeed in detecting new ways of war in some cases and fail in others?

---

1. The only systematic study of the phenomenon is Michael I. Handel, "Technological Surprise in War," *Intelligence and National Security* 2, no. 1 (January 1987).
2. Ibid., 41.

This book argues that expectations about the character and conduct of war drawn from combat experience and organizational culture, combined with incomplete and often inaccurate information, often prevent intelligence organizations from recognizing the emergence of new ways of war. Intelligence agencies are more inclined to monitor the development of established weapons than to search for new military systems. It is also easier for them to detect technology and doctrine that have been demonstrated in war than weapons and concepts that have not seen combat. As a result, intelligence agencies readily identify incremental changes to weapons whose value has been demonstrated in war. They experience greater difficulty identifying new or unique systems. Finally, intelligence organizations often pay greater attention to innovations in areas that their own services are exploring than to those that they have not examined, are not interested in, or have rejected. One would therefore expect the agencies to monitor foreign developments that mirror those of their own armed forces more closely than those that differ substantially.

EXPECTATIONS DRAWN FROM COMBAT EXPERIENCE

Attempts to understand innovative technology and doctrine must often contend with ingrained assumptions about the character and conduct of war. These expectations have many sources, including wartime experience, professional training, and cultural and organizational norms. These factors tell the observer what to look for and how to interpret the observations. Data that confirm expectations are readily accepted, and contrary evidence is rejected or ignored.[3] Preconceptions tend to form quickly, doggedly resist change, and persist even after they have been discredited.[4]

Research in the field of cognitive psychology has demonstrated that preconceptions have a particularly pervasive influence on the analysis of ambiguous information, such as initial indications of the development of new technology and doctrine. In fact, the greater the ambiguity, the greater the impact of expectations in reaching a judgment. Preconceived notions about war may have a particularly pervasive influence on attempts to understand new combat methods. Intelligence analysts are often among the first to look at a new weapon or concept, when the

3. Robert Jervis, *Perception and Misperception in International Politics* (Princeton, N.J.: Princeton University Press, 1976): 143.
4. Richards Heuer, *Psychology of Intelligence Analysis* (Washington, D.C.: Center for the Study of Intelligence, 1999).

evidence is likely to be fragmentary. It is at this stage that preconceptions form. The analyst then often follows the problem as additional evidence is collected and the picture comes into focus. But preconceptions tend to endure, despite contradictory evidence. The acquisition of information in small increments abets this tendency.[5]

Cognitive research shows that people learn most from firsthand experience, from events early in life, and from events that have important consequences.[6] It is therefore hardly surprising that combat experience provides one of the most compelling sources of expectations about the character and conduct of war. The "lessons" of wars influence how a nation trains and equips its own armed forces as well as how it measures the military power of others. Ingrained assumptions about war may also hinder the recognition of innovation in peacetime, particularly during periods of technological and doctrinal ferment. They may prevent military services—including intelligence organizations—from identifying new military practices. As Richard Betts puts it, "Generational views of strategic reality, annealed in experience of earlier war, are not sensitive to fragmentary, inconclusive, or theoretical indicators of innovation."[7] European armies in the late nineteenth and early twentieth centuries, for example, failed to comprehend that the machine gun and quick-firing artillery had rendered close-order infantry attacks and cavalry charges obsolete.[8] This failure contributed to the bloody stalemate that characterized World War I on the western front.

Analogies to the past may obscure the novelty of emerging technology and doctrine by focusing on similarities to what has gone before.[9] As a result, one would expect intelligence organizations to identify evolutionary refinements of past practices more readily than radically new ones. Incomplete and ambiguous information abets this tendency. When intelligence organizations acquire only fragmentary

5. Richards J. Heuer Jr., "Do You Really Need More Information?" *Studies in Intelligence* 23, no. 1 (spring 1979): 15–25. See also Amos Tversky and Daniel Kahneman, "Judgment under Uncertainty: Heuristics and Biases" in *Benefit-Cost and Policy Analysis*, eds. R. Zeckhauser, A. C. Harberger, R. H. Haveman, L. E. Lynn, W. A. Niskanen, and A. Williams (Chicago: Aldine, 1975): 68–80.

6. Jervis, *Perception and Misperception*, 239.

7. Richard Betts, *Surprise Attack: Lessons for Defense Planning* (Washington, D.C.: The Brookings Institution, 1982): 115.

8. Michael Howard, "Men against Fire: Expectations of War in 1914," *International Security* 9, no. 1 (summer 1984): 42–55; Edward L. Katzenbach, "The Horse Cavalry in the Twentieth Century," in *The Use of Force: Military Power and International Politics*, eds. Robert J. Art and Kenneth N. Waltz Lanham, Md: University Press of America, 1988: 152–71

9. Jervis, *Perception and Misperception*, 220.

information on foreign military developments, they tend to view foreign activity through the lens of their own experience. Only when they possess relatively complete and accurate information do they recognize innovation.

The way an analyst receives information also influences its evidentiary weight irrespective of its true value.[10] As the Office of Naval Intelligence (ONI) warned prospective attachés in 1930, "The character and paramount importance of certain information very easily may bias an informant and excite his imagination out of all proportion to the actual conditions."[11] Vivid, concrete data—accurate or inaccurate—have a much greater impact than pallid, abstract data because the former come to mind much more readily.[12] Personal experiences are more compelling than what one reads. Certain types of intelligence, such as that gathered firsthand (by participating in combat operations or observing military exercises, for example), are likely to be especially persuasive.

Combat experience creates expectations about not only the dominant form of warfare, but also the military competence of combatants. A country's battlefield performance establishes expectations about its future effectiveness. Yet the military power of states, and the military effectiveness of their armies, may change considerably between wars. Assessing the military effectiveness of forces that have not seen combat for some time is particularly difficult. Indeed, after Winston Churchill concluded that Mussolini would attack England, he advised General Ismay of the need to engage Italian naval and air forces at the outset of the conflict "in order that we can see what their quality really is, and whether it has changed at all since the last war."[13]

To the extent that past performance creates expectations about future capabilities, estimates of a state's military power will become more inaccurate over time. Furthermore, one would expect intelligence organizations to underestimate the capabilities of rising powers and to overestimate those of declining ones.[14] The failure of the U.S. intelligence

10. Richard Nisbett and Lee Ross, *Human Inference: Strategies and Shortcomings of Social Judgment* (Englewood Cliffs, N.J.: Prentice-Hall, 1980): chap. 3.

11. E-9-a 20313, "The Duties of Naval Attaches," May 1930, *Naval Attaché Reports, 1921–1939*, Box 820, Record Group 38, National Archives (hereafter referred to as NA), 33.

12. Heuer, "Biases in Evaluation of Evidence," *Studies in Intelligence* (Winter 1981): 32–33.

13. Winston S. Churchill, *Their Finest Hour* (Boston: Houghton Mifflin Company, 1949): 126–27.

14. See, for example, Aaron L. Friedberg, *The Weary Titan: Britain and the Experience of Relative Decline, 1895–1905* (Princeton: Princeton University Press, 1988), *passim*.

community and the vast majority of academics to anticipate the decline of the Soviet economy and the collapse of the Soviet Union is but one of the most recent and dramatic examples of a perennial problem.[15]

The lessons of past wars serve as a cognitive anchor that prevents military organizations from appreciating fully the magnitude of change. Although views of warfare may adjust somewhat to the appearance of new technology and doctrine, they are unlikely to keep pace with it.[16] The result is a widening gap between perception and reality. As the U.S. naval constructor David W. Taylor noted in 1910, "If we could have a war lasting several years with a battle every month, the experience gained would of course be conclusive. . . . But when there is but a single battle, or two at most, the elements of chance may very well entirely obscure the result as regards technical matters."[17] The magnitude of this divergence depends on the amount of time that passes between wars and the degree of technological and doctrinal dynamism in the interwar period. During periods of frequent interaction, one would expect military organizations to resemble one another. In periods of less interplay, they may display considerable variety.[18]

ORGANIZATIONAL CULTURE

Professional and cultural norms are the source of another set of preconceptions. Edgar H. Schein defines organizational culture as:

15. These charges, together with rebuttals, are contained in Bruce D. Berkowitz and Jeffrey T. Richelson, "The CIA Vindicated: The Soviet Collapse *Was* Predicted," *The National Interest* no. 41 (fall 1995); Lirsten Lundberg, *The CIA and the Fall of the Soviet Empire: The Politics of "Getting it Right,"* Kennedy School of Government Case Program C16–94–1251.0 (1994); Douglas MacEachin, *CIA Assessments of the Soviet Union: The Record Versus the Charges,* Central Intelligence Agency, Center for the Study of Intelligence Monograph 96–001 (May 1996); William Odom, "Academe and Soviet Myth," *The National Interest* no. 31 (spring 1993).

16. Anchoring occurs when the mind uses a natural starting point as a first approximation to a judgment. The mind modifies this starting point as it receives additional information. Typically, however, the starting point serves as an anchor that reduces the amount of adjustment, and the final estimate remains closer to the starting point than it should be. Tversky and Kahneman, "Anchoring and Calibration in the Assessment of Uncertain Quantities," *Oregon Research Institute Research Bulletin* 12 (1972).

17. David W. Taylor, response to Sir William H. White, "Notes on the Armaments of Battleships," in *Transactions of the Society of Naval Architects and Marine Engineers* 18 (1910): 26.

18. John A. Lynn, "The Evolution of Army Style in the Modern West, 800–2000," *International History Review* 13, no. 3 (August 1996): 509–10.

the pattern of basic assumptions that a given group has invented, discovered, or developed in learning to cope with its problems of external adaptation and internal integration, and that have worked well enough to be considered valid, and, therefore, to be taught to new members as the correct way to perceive, think, and feel in relation to those problems.[19]

Culture, in organizations as in societies, offers a way to socialize members.[20] It helps determine the goals, tasks, and functions of the group, the best means to accomplish them, and criteria for measuring performance. It also influences how the organization distributes resources and rewards: behaviors that comply with the organization's culture flourish; those that run contrary to it perish.[21]

A military organization's culture may prevent its members from recognizing the emergence of unorthodox technical or doctrinal solutions to military problems. Preconceptions regarding the conduct of war may instead cause observers to see foreign technology and doctrine as a mirror image of their own. Preconceptions may also lead them to highlight military experiences that reinforce their doctrinal assumptions and to ignore those that are unconventional. For example, Jeffrey Legro has argued that the Royal Navy's emphasis on the battleship led British naval officers to discount the threat posed by German submarines. To the extent that the British anticipated a challenge to their commerce, they saw it as coming from surface raiders, not submarines.[22]

The culture of an intelligence service may skew its assessment of foreign military developments in a number of ways. Ernest May has shown how assumptions drawn from French doctrine caused the Deuxième Bureau to overestimate the number and composition of German armored units prior to the fall of France in 1940.[23] Mark Russell Shulman has argued that the U.S. Navy's approach to war at sea shaped how the Office of Naval Intelligence gathered and assessed intelligence in the period from its founding in 1882 to the entry of the United States into World War I. He concludes that the prevalence of Alfred Thayer Mahan's theories of sea power led ONI to suppress intelli-

19. Edgar H. Schein, "Coming to a New Awareness of Organizational Culture," *Sloan Management Review* 25, no. 2 (winter 1984): 3.

20. Ann Swidler, "Culture in Action: Symbols and Strategies," *American Sociological Review* 51 (April 1986): 277.

21. Schein, "Coming to a New Awareness of Organizational Culture," 9, 11.

22. Jeffrey W. Legro, *Cooperation under Fire: Anglo-German Restraint during World War II* (Ithaca: Cornell University Press, 1995): 75.

23. Ernest R. May, *Strange Victory: Hitler's Conquest of France* (New York: Hill and Wang, 2000): 353.

gence showing the promise of other approaches to war at sea.[24] Scott Alan Koch has focused on how "intelligence doctrine" influenced U.S. Army estimates of German rearmament under Hitler.[25] He concludes that the Army's tradition of seeking battles of annihilation, combined with a penchant for quantitative measurement, prevented it from comprehending fundamental changes in the character of warfare that occurred between the two world wars.[26] Finally, John Ferris has noted the role of organizational culture in British estimates of the Japanese army prior to World War II. In his view, Britain underestimated the effectiveness of the Japanese army not because of racial stereotypes, but because intelligence officers measured it by the yardstick of a European war.[27]

Although such cases are compelling, unless an organization's culture has an unlimited ability to suppress or to distort discrepant information, at some point its preconceptions should collapse beneath the weight of contradictory evidence, forcing both intelligence organizations and decision makers to recognize approaches to warfare much different from their own. In other words, one would expect organizational culture to exert greater influence on intelligence assessment when analysts possess incomplete and inconsistent information than when they enjoy access to sources that are consistent and credible.

A TAXONOMY OF SURPRISE

Intelligence services have a mixed record of detecting new technology and doctrine. In some cases, secrecy and preconceptions about war have prevented them from identifying new ways of war. In other cases surprise was partial: intelligence agencies detected new ways of war

24. Mark Russell Shulman, "The Rise and Fall of American Naval Intelligence, 1882–1917," *Intelligence and National Security* 8, no. 2 (April 1993): 221–22.

25. Koch contends that "Four recurring ideas are dominant: (1) intelligence means quantification and identification, (2) war is essentially a problem of industrial production and management of logistics, (3) the course of any wars in which the United States became involved would be basically the same, and (4) the United States would go to war only under narrowly defined circumstances and for reasons enjoying broad popular support." Scott Alan Koch, "Watching the Rhine: U.S. Army Military Attache Reports and the Resurgence of the German Army, 1933–1941" (Ph.D. dissertation, Duke University, 1990): 20.

26. Ibid., 240.

27. John Ferris, "Worthy of Some Better Enemy?: The British Estimate of the Imperial Japanese Army, 1919–1941, and the Fall of Singapore," *Canadian Journal of History* 28, no. 2 (August 1993): 230–231.

but failed to comprehend their significance because of the uncertainty inherent in new and untested weapons and doctrine. In still other cases, agencies succeeded in both detecting and identifying new approaches to combat before the onset of war.

Surprise

Intelligence organizations often fail to detect the emergence of new ways of war. During World War I, for example, the British army's use of tanks surprised the Germans, and the German army's use of poison gas surprised the British.[28] During World War II, the German navy surprised the British with its use of submarines to attack merchant vessels at night on the surface, even though Admiral Dönitz had discussed the tactic in a book published prior to the war.[29]

One cause of the failure to detect new technology and doctrine is secrecy. Most militaries try to conceal their development of new technology and doctrine, at least to some degree. In the case of particularly sensitive capabilities, security may be extensive. In some cases, a military is able to develop a weapon system behind an impenetrable cloak of security. The United States, for example, failed to detect Britain's program to develop radar prior to World War II. More recently, the Soviet Union surprised the U.S. intelligence community by fielding an automated system designed to launch its nuclear arsenal in time of war.[30]

A state may also try to deceive others regarding its capabilities.[31] The most common form of peacetime deception involves exaggerating or downplaying a state's military capabilities. In the 1950s, for example, Nikita Khrushchev sought to exaggerate the size of Soviet strategic bomber and ballistic missile forces to deter the West. The German army, by contrast, hid its efforts to rearm in violation of the Versailles Treaty after World War I to forestall British and French retaliation.[32]

28. Handel, "Technological Surprise in War," 9–13.

29. Ibid., 3–4.

30. William J. Broad, "Russia Has Computerized Nuclear 'Doomsday' Machine, U.S. Expert Says," *New York Times*, October 8, 1993, p. A6.

31. Donald C. Daniel and Katherine L. Herbig, *Strategic Military Deception* (New York: Pergamon Press, 1982); John Gooch and Amos Perlmutter, eds., *Military Deception and Strategic Surprise* (London: Frank Cass and Company, 1982); Richards J. Heuer Jr., "Strategic Deception and Counterdeception: A Cognitive Process Approach," *International Studies Quarterly* 25, no. 2 (June 1981); Barton Whaley, *Codeword BARBAROSSA* (Cambridge: The MIT Press, 1973).

32. Barton Whaley, *Covert German Rearmament, 1919–1939: Deception and Misperception* (Frederick, Md.: University Publications of America, 1984).

Weapon systems produced on a small scale or to meet a unique operational requirement pose a particular challenge.[33] These programs are often difficult to identify because of their small size and *ad hoc* nature. The United States, for example, failed to detect Japan's development of shallow-running torpedoes in the months leading up to the attack on Pearl Harbor.[34] Had ONI spotted this development, it might have taken the air threat to the U.S. Pacific Fleet's anchorage more seriously. Similarly, U.S. Army intelligence failed to detect Japan's training to conduct jungle warfare as it prepared to invade Southeast Asia and the western Pacific islands.

All too often, intelligence services fail to spot new ways of war because they aren't looking. In some cases, assumptions about war cause them to focus on existing warfare areas at the expense of potentially revolutionary technology and doctrine. In 1935, for example, the U.S. military attaché in Berlin learned that the German air force was interested in airborne operations from his assistant, who had gleaned the information from a student at the German General Staff School, the *Kriegsakademie.* However, because Germany possessed no parachute units at the time, the attaché considered the idea to be of purely theoretical interest and instructed his assistant not to accord it a high priority.[35] Instead, the officer was to concentrate his efforts on German infantry, artillery, cavalry, armor, and combat engineer units. It was not until the fall of France and the Low Countries in 1940 that the Army tasked its intelligence assets with collecting information on German airborne operations and forces. Army and Navy intelligence paid remarkably little attention to Britain's development of radar and to Germany's development of ballistic and cruise missiles during the same period.

In other cases, preconceived notions of technological superiority blind an intelligence organization to foreign developments. Information indicating that an adversary has achieved a technological breakthrough may contradict the deeply held beliefs of experts. This is particularly true when the adversary has developed a capability that the observing country has yet to master. As R. V. Jones, the father of technical intelligence, wrote, "In my own experience, while there have been times when the experts alone were right, there have been important occasions when the other forms of intelligence have been right

33. Handel, "Technological Surprise in War," 13–16.
34. Roberta Wohlstetter, *Pearl Harbor: Warning and Decision* (Stanford, Calif.: Stanford University Press, 1962): 369–70.
35. Robert Hessen, ed., *Berlin Alert: The Memoirs and Reports of Truman Smith* (Stanford: Hoover Institution Press, 1984): 121.

[13]

and the experts wrong."[36] British intelligence, for example, long discounted the possibility that Germany might be pursuing radar, even
though the British scientific community had already proved that it
was feasible.[37] In fact, Berlin's radar research and development program had begun in 1934; by the outbreak of World War II, it had deployed navigation radar on several surface ships, was deploying an
early warning radar system, and was in the late stages of developing
an anti-aircraft fire control radar. Until intelligence conclusively
proved the existence of the "Freya" air defense radar in early 1941,
however, there was widespread disbelief within the British armed
forces that Germany had deployed radar systems. The British also believed that the Germans had not developed radar countermeasures,
known as "chaff." This led the British to refrain from using chaff
against Germany in the incorrect belief that doing so would prevent
the German armed forces from emulating them.[38] Similarly, during
World War II the German army believed—incorrectly—that only it
possessed nerve gas. It therefore underestimated the Allies' ability to
retaliate against a chemical attack.[39]

Although development of increasingly sophisticated collection
methods, such as airborne and space-based sensors, has reduced the
possibility of technological surprise, it has not eliminated it altogether.
During the 1950s, for example, the Soviet Union attempted to develop
an intercontinental cruise missile. The United States did not learn of the
program—later canceled—even after the Soviet Union flight-tested
the missile.[40] In the 1960s, the U.S. intelligence community produced
muddled estimates of the Soviet ballistic missile defense and of multiple independently targeted reentry vehicle programs. In the 1970s, it
underestimated Soviet sea-based ballistic missile development. In the
1980s, it lagged in forecasting improvements in Soviet missile accuracy.
Nor did it learn much about Soviet nuclear warhead designs and
chemical and biological weapon programs.[41]

36. R. V. Jones, "The Scientific Intelligencer," *Studies in Intelligence* 3 (fall 1962): 42.
37. F. H. Hinsley, *British Intelligence in the Second World War* 2, *Its Influence on Strategy and Operations* (New York: Cambridge University Press, 1981): 244–45.
38. Jones, *The Wizard War: British Scientific Intelligence, 1939–1945* (New York: Coward, McCann & Geoghegan, 1978): 189–90.
39. Legro, *Cooperation under Fire*, 186, 189.
40. Steven Zaloga, "Most Secret Weapon: The Origins of Soviet Strategic Cruise Missiles, 1945–1960," *Journal of Slavic Military Studies* 6, no. 1 (June 1993): 271.
41. Loch K. Johnson, *Secret Agencies: U.S. Intelligence in a Hostile World* (New Haven, Conn.: Yale University Press 1996): 187, 200.

Partial Surprise

Although intelligence organizations are in some cases totally surprised by the advent of some new way of war, in other cases surprise is partial. In these instances intelligence organizations may detect new ways of war but fail to understand their significance. Israel was surprised by Egypt's use of AT-3 *Sagger* anti-tank guided missiles (ATGMs) at the beginning of the 1973 Arab-Israeli War. Israeli intelligence knew of the weapon's existence and understood its performance characteristics.[42] Indeed, the Israeli army had encountered an earlier Soviet ATGM, the AT-1 *Snapper,* during the 1967 war. Israel even had an analogous weapon, the French SS-10, in its inventory. However, Israeli intelligence failed to anticipate that the Egyptian army had developed novel tactics for employing ATGMs, which took a heavy toll on the Israeli tank corps.

The emergence of new technology is another source of surprise. Intelligence services frequently fail to investigate unproven technologies. British intelligence learned of the German missile program by chance in 1939, but did not begin a concerted effort to collect information on it until December 1942.[43] The U.S. intelligence community had difficulty understanding the scope and pace of Soviet intercontinental ballistic missile programs during the 1950s.[44] From the late 1970s through the 1980s it experienced difficulty understanding advanced Soviet research and development programs, including the Soviet program to develop ground-based laser and high-energy space-based anti-satellite weapons.[45]

The culture of an intelligence service frequently skews its assessment of foreign military developments. During the late 1930s, U.S. Army intelligence tended to view the development of the *Luftwaffe* through the lens of Army Air Corps doctrine, which emphasized strategic bombing over close air support. This resulted in a serious misestimation of German air power. British intelligence tended to attribute to Germany the same doctrine of the bomber offensive as that of the Royal Air Force.

42. Ephraim Kam, *Surprise Attack: The Victim's Perspective* (Cambridge, Mass: Harvard University Press, 1988): 18.

43. Jones, *The Wizard War,* 332.

44. Donald P. Steury, ed., *Intentions and Capabilities: Estimates on Soviet Strategic Forces, 1950–1983* (Washington, D.C.: Center for the Study of Intelligence, 1996): 55–138.

45. Ibid., 411–91; Michael Dobbs, "Deconstructing the Death Ray," *Washington Post,* October 17, 1999: p. F1; on Soviet research and development in these fields, see Zaloga, "Red Star Wars," *Jane's Intelligence Review* (May 1997): 205–8.

This led the British to hold false notions of German strategy.[46] Similarly, U.S. naval intelligence viewed Japanese naval surface warfare tactics as a mirror of those of the United States, ignoring signs that Japan had developed innovative technology and doctrine.

Organizational culture skewed U.S. intelligence assessments during the Cold War as well. Robert Bathurst has argued that the United States misinterpreted Soviet naval concepts because it viewed them as a mirror image of U.S. practice.[47] Not until the early 1980s did the U.S. intelligence community realize that the Soviet Union had developed concepts of naval warfare considerably different from those of the U.S. Navy.[48] Others believe organizational culture influenced assessments of Soviet nuclear forces and doctrine. Throughout much of the Cold War, the U.S. intelligence community and many American defense intellectuals assumed that Soviet nuclear doctrine and force posture mirrored that of the United States.[49] This belief led to an underestimation of the growth of the Soviet strategic nuclear arsenal, a pattern that persisted despite improvements in intelligence collection methods and analytical methodologies.[50]

Surprise Averted

Although intelligence organizations often fail totally or partially to detect the advent of new ways of war, the problem is not intractable. Indeed, intelligence services have in notable cases identified new weapons in time to devise suitable responses. A case in point is Britain's development of countermeasures after detecting Germany's use of radio navigation to increase the accuracy of its bomber force.[51] This book contains other examples, including the recognition by U.S. naval intelligence of

---

46. Legro, *Cooperation under Fire*, 132–33.

47. Robert B. Bathurst, *Intelligence and the Mirror: On Creating an Enemy* (London: Sage Publications, 1993): 94–96.

48. Director of Central Intelligence, "Soviet Naval Strategy and Programs Through the 1990s," NIE 11–15–82/D (March 1983), RG 263, NA.

49. Lawrence Freedman, *U.S. Intelligence and the Soviet Strategic Threat*, 2d ed. (Princeton: Princeton University Press, 1986): ch. 6.

50. Albert Wohlstetter, "Is There a Strategic Arms Race?" *Foreign Policy*, no. 15 (Summer 1974); Wohlstetter, "Rivals, but No 'Race'" *Foreign Policy*, no. 16 (Fall 1974); Wohlstetter, "How to Confuse Ourselves," *Foreign Policy* 20 (fall 1975). The team of experts that George Bush commissioned as CIA director to review intelligence estimates regarding the Soviet Union found evidence of mirror-imaging as well. See "Soviet Strategic Objectives: An Alternative View, Report of Team B" in Donald P. Steury, comp., *Estimates on Soviet Military Power, 1954 to 1984: A Selection* (Washington, D.C.: Central Intelligence Agency, 1994): 328–35.

51. See Jones, *The Wizard War*, ch. 33.

Japanese amphibious warfare doctrine and accurate assessments by U.S. military intelligence of British and German tank developments. The central question that this book addresses is: *Why do intelligence organizations succeed in detecting new ways of war in some cases and fail in others?*

This book argues that intelligence organizations are most likely to recognize foreign military innovation under three conditions. First, they are most likely to identify innovation when the information, even when slight and ambiguous, fits with their predispositions. Second, they find demonstrations of new warfare areas on the battlefield or in realistic war games more convincing than theoretical pronouncements. Finally, it is easier to identify innovation in areas that one's own services are exploring than in those that they have not examined, are not interested in, or have rejected. As a result, intelligence organizations more frequently identify foreign developments that mirror those of their own armed forces than those that differ substantially from them.

[2]

U.S. Military Intelligence
in the Interwar Period

Historians have frequently criticized the performance of U.S. military intelligence in the years that separated the two world wars. Nathan Miller has characterized the period as "a time of dissolution and decay for American intelligence."[1] Similarly, Harry Howe Ransom has charged, "Intelligence clearly was neglected in the decades between the two world wars. . . . Both army and navy intelligence hobbled along in the 1920s and 1930s, rarely attracting the most promising officers and receiving only meager congressional appropriations."[2] Even such a respected scholar of intelligence as Christopher Andrew has written that "there was no American intelligence community until the Second World War."[3]

Nor have civilians been the only ones to criticize U.S. military intelligence before World War II. An official history of the Army's Military Intelligence Division (MID) completed immediately after World War II asserts that at the outbreak of the war:

> There was no intelligence on enemy air or ground order of battle; there was no detailed reference material on enemy forces such as weapons, insignia, fortifications, and documents; there was no detailed topographic intelligence for planning landing operations; there were insufficient facts—but plenty of opinion—on which to base strategic estimates; and there were no trained personnel for either strategic or combat intelligence.[4]

1. Nathan Miller, *Spying for America: the Hidden History of U.S. Intelligence* (New York: Paragon House, 1989): 209.

2. Harry Howe Ransom, *The Intelligence Establishment* (Cambridge, Mass.: Harvard University Press, 1970): 53–54.

3. Christopher Andrew, *For the President's Eyes Only: Secret Intelligence and the American Presidency from Washington to Bush* (New York: HarperCollins, 1995): 1.

4. Military Intelligence Division, War Department General Staff, A *History of the Military Intelligence Division, 7 December 1941–1942 September 1945,* U.S. Army Center of Military History (hereafter referred to as USACMH), 1946: 2.

This view, which has become the orthodox portrayal of U.S. intelligence prior to World War II, is at best incomplete, at worst inaccurate. During the 1920s and 1930s, the Army and Navy relied heavily on information supplied by attachés stationed across the globe. These officers gathered information on foreign armed forces by inspecting military and industrial facilities, observing exercises and battles, and eliciting information from the host country's military. These organizations did a surprisingly good job—given their limited funds and personnel—of monitoring foreign military developments.

THE OFFICE OF NAVAL INTELLIGENCE

The Office of Naval Intelligence, founded in 1882, is the oldest intelligence organization in the United States and five years older than its British counterpart, the Naval Intelligence Division.[5] Although the office published reports on an impressive range of subjects during the first three and a half decades of its existence, it was World War I that marked its emergence as a world-class intelligence organization. The office grew from sixteen officers and clerks in 1916 to 306 officers and eighteen civilians by the end of the war.[6] During the war, the office received information from its naval attachés abroad and developed a network to monitor the movement of German submarines. Given the scale of foreign intelligence activities in the United States, ONI's counterintelligence duties also expanded considerably.[7]

ONI's postwar demobilization mirrored reductions in the U.S. armed forces as a whole. By February 1920, the Navy had cut the size of the office to seventy officers; eight months later it was down to eighteen.[8] The office's manpower remained stable in the years immediately following the war. In 1926, for example, it contained sixteen officers

5. The standard works on the history of ONI are Jeffery M. Dorwart, *The Office of Naval Intelligence: The Birth of America's First Intelligence Agency, 1865–1918* (Annapolis, Md.: Naval Institute Press, 1979); Jeffery Dorwart, *Conflict of Duty: The U.S. Navy's Intelligence Dilemma, 1919–1945* (Annapolis: Naval Institute Press, 1983); James Robert Green, "The First Sixty Years of the Office of Naval Intelligence" (master's thesis, The American University, Washington, D.C., 1963); Rear Adm. A. P. Niblack, *The History and Aims of the Office of Naval Intelligence* (Washington, D.C.: Government Printing Office, 1920).

6. Niblack, *History and Aims*, 23.

7. Green, "The First Sixty Years," chap. 6; Packard, *A Century of U.S. Naval Intelligence*, 61–65.

8. Green, "The First Sixty Years," 73.

and twenty-two civilians.[9] Although that staffing was a sharp reduction from wartime levels, it still left ONI more than twice its prewar size. Such a posture was a sensible response to an environment in which the greatest menace to the United States lay not in Europe, which was recovering from the ravages of World War I, but in Asia, where Japan's growing power threatened U.S. possessions in the Western Pacific.

Throughout the 1920s and 1930s ONI was, in the words of the Navy's official history, "a small but well-organized administrative unit" with a peacetime complement of fifteen officers.[10] In addition to the director and assistant director, one officer was assigned to the Administrative Branch, six to the Intelligence Branch, three to the Public Relations Branch, and three to the Historical Branch. Intelligence officers were also assigned to naval districts, although the officers' primary concern was preventing foreign espionage. The staffs of the Atlantic, Pacific, and Asiatic fleets each included an intelligence officer who advised the fleet commander and collected and analyzed information regarding navies in the fleet's area of operations. The Fleet Marine Force also had a small intelligence office that produced, among other things, monographs on the Japanese Mandate Islands.

Until the late 1920s, the Director of Naval Intelligence (DNI) held the rank of captain; thereafter, he was a rear admiral. For some officers, appointment to DNI was the culmination of a career in intelligence. Four interwar DNIs, for example, had previous experience as naval attachés; another four later became attachés.[11] Others came to the job with no intelligence experience. ONI did not enjoy stability in its upper ranks: in the decade before the Pearl Harbor attack, the average tenure of the DNI was less than two years; during 1941, four officers commanded ONI.[12]

Intelligence duty did not enjoy high prestige within the Navy. Indeed, Captain Laurance Safford, himself an intelligence officer, be-

9. Comdr. L. W. Townsend, USN, "Naval Intelligence," lecture at the Army War College, Washington Barracks, D.C., January 5, 1926, E-9-a 19285, "Naval Intelligence," *Naval Attaché Reports, 1921–1939*, Box 818, Record Group (RG) 38, National Archives (hereafter referred to as NA), 2.

10. *United States Naval Administration in World War II, Chief of Naval Operations, Office of Naval Intelligence* 1, Operational Archives, Naval Historical Center (hereafter referred to as OA/NHC), 26–27.

11. Green, "The First Sixty Years," 107.

12. "The Reminiscences of Alan Goodrich Kirk," part 1, Oral History Research Office, Columbia University, 1962, OA/NHC, 183.

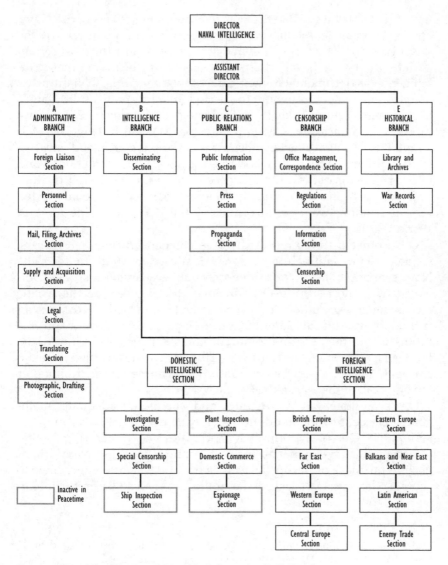

DIRECTOR NAVAL INTELLIGENCE

ASSISTANT DIRECTOR

A ADMINISTRATIVE BRANCH	B INTELLIGENCE BRANCH	C PUBLIC RELATIONS BRANCH	D CENSORSHIP BRANCH	E HISTORICAL BRANCH
Foreign Liaison Section	Disseminating Section	Public Information Section	Office Management, Correspondence Section	Library and Archives
Personnel Section		Press Section	Regulations Section	War Records Section
Mail, Filing, Archives Section		Propaganda Section	Information Section	
Supply and Acquisition Section			Censorship Section	
Legal Section				
Translating Section				
Photographic, Drafting Section				

DOMESTIC INTELLIGENCE SECTION

FOREIGN INTELLIGENCE SECTION

Inactive in Peacetime

Investigating Section	Plant Inspection Section	British Empire Section	Eastern Europe Section
Special Censorship Section	Domestic Commerce Section	Far East Section	Balkans and Near East Section
Ship Inspection Section	Espionage Section	Western Europe Section	Latin American Section
		Central Europe Section	Enemy Trade Section

Source: "Naval Intelligence," *Monthly Information Bulletin* 13, nos. 8 and 9 (February-March 1931).

Figure 1: Organization of the Office of Naval Intelligence, 1931

lieved that "Naval Intelligence was the dumping ground of the Navy, and assignment to Intelligence duties was generally considered the 'kiss of death.'"[13] Because command at sea represented the most certain path to promotion, naval officers saw shore duty, including that in intelligence, as detrimental to their careers.[14] Despite this, ONI attracted talented personnel throughout the period. Indeed, many of the Navy's best officers served in intelligence during the interwar period. Raymond A. Spruance was Assistant Director of Naval Intelligence, William F. Halsey naval attaché in Berlin, and Thomas C. Kinkaid naval attaché in Rome.[15] Alan Kirk, who served as naval attaché in London and later as Director of Naval Intelligence, went on to command the amphibious task force at Normandy. Charles Lockwood, who succeeded him in London, went on to command the U.S. submarine force in World War II.

Other officers served repeatedly in intelligence during their careers. Captain Henri Smith-Hutton's career is a case in point. In 1926, the Navy sent him to Japan for a three-year tour as a language student, followed by a short stint in ONI. In June 1930, he became the Asiatic Fleet's intelligence officer. Two years later, he returned to Tokyo as an assistant naval attaché. After his tour in Japan, he took command of a destroyer and then became communications officer aboard the Asiatic Fleet's flagship, the *Augusta*. In the spring of 1939, he returned to Tokyo as naval attaché, a post he held until the Japanese interned him after the outbreak of the war in the Pacific.[16]

ONI's mission was "to organize and operate an adequate intelligence Service, foreign and domestic, for the use of the Navy in peace and war."[17] One of the office's top priorities was monitoring foreign technological developments, including innovations the Navy might wish to purchase or to copy as well as threats the Navy might have to counter. Because ONI lacked the ability to analyze technical intelli-

13. Quoted in Gordon W. Prange, with Donald M. Goldstein and Katherine V. Dillon, *Pearl Harbor: The Verdict of History* (New York: McGraw-Hill, 1986): 288.

14. Green, "The First Sixty Years," 104.

15. Fleet Adm. William F. Halsey, USN, and Lt. Comdr. J. Bryan III, USNR, *Admiral Halsey's Story* (New York: McGraw-Hill, 1947); Gerald E. Wheeler, *Kinkaid of the Seventh Fleet: A Biography of Admiral Thomas C. Kinkaid, U.S. Navy* (Washington, D.C.: Naval Historical Center, 1995): chap. 5.

16. Reminiscences of Capt. Henri Smith-Hutton, USN (retired), U.S. Naval Institute Archives (hereafter referred to as USNI).

17. Office of Naval Intelligence, "Instructions for Attaches," *Naval Attaché Reports, 1921–1939*, Box 10, RG 38, NA, 13.

gence, it had to turn to the Navy's bureaus for help. It forwarded reports on foreign aeronautical developments to the Bureau of Aeronautics (BuAer).[18] Similarly, it sent reports to the Bureau of Ordnance (BuOrd), describing foreign guns, torpedoes, and fire control systems. Not surprisingly, however, the technical bureaus considered intelligence a low priority and often took months to respond.[19] Moreover, because the Navy's technicians were experts in American—rather than foreign—systems, their analyses of technological developments frequently reflected mirror-imaging.

ONI used information from naval attachés abroad and from intelligence officers afloat to compile massive monographs containing political, military, and economic information on countries of interest.[20] The monographs, updated as new information became available, were designed "so that, if war were imminent, copies . . . could be promptly placed in the hands of our commanding officers afloat to help them in making their operational plans to overthrow enemy naval power, to throttle his trade, to blockade his ports, and to conduct combined Army and Navy expeditions to invade his shores."[21] The Fleet Marine Force, for its part, maintained monographs on Japan's Pacific possessions.[22]

In 1915 ONI began to issue a series of *Information Bulletins.* In 1919 they were superseded by the *Monthly Information Bulletin,* a classified journal containing items drawn from attaché reports, reprints of newspaper stories, and analyses by the ONI staff. The bulletin devoted considerable attention both to the Royal Navy and to the Imperial Japanese Navy. Between January 1919 and June 1929, for example, the bulletin carried ninety-two articles on Great Britain and 122 on Japan. Reports on Britain generally focused on technical developments, because the Navy saw its British counterpart as a source of technological

18. Lecture by Comdr. R. A. Spruance, USN, at the Marine Corps School, Quantico, Va., March 22, 1929, E-9-a 19285, "Naval Intelligence," *Naval Attaché Reports, 1921–1939,* Box 818, RG 38, NA, 11.

19. Reminiscences of Rear Adm. Arthur H. McCollum, USN (retired), USNI, 146.

20. In 1940 the monographs were divided into eleven main sections: political forces, social forces, economic forces (finance), economic forces (industry), economic forces (commerce), cities and towns geography, communications, army, navy, air, and general summary. Packard, *A Century of U.S. Naval Intelligence,* 146.

21. "Naval Intelligence," 49.

22. Lt. Col. Robert L. Denig, Assistant Chief of Staff, F-2, 1st Lieutenant Stuart W. King, Assistant F-2, *Monograph of Japanese Mandate Islands,* prepared by the Intelligence Section of the Fleet Marine Force (1934), Box 57, Strategic Plans Division Files, Series III, OA/NHC.

innovation. Reports on Japan, by contrast, concentrated on shipbuilding, naval operations, and maneuvers. The journal also ran articles discussing the lessons of foreign wars and published a special issue devoted to Japan's war in China.[23]

The Navy's network of attachés collected the lion's share of naval intelligence. As Rear Admiral Albert B. Niblack put it, the Office of Naval Intelligence existed "largely for the benefit of, and for the support of, the naval attachés abroad."[24] Indeed, it was because of the naval attaché system that ONI was able to perform its duties with such a small staff.

By 1914, the United States had the fourth largest corps of naval attachés in the world, with eight officers abroad; only Britain, Brazil, and Russia had more.[25] By 1920, 149 U.S. naval officers had served as attachés in twenty-three foreign capitals: thirteen in Europe, two in Asia, seven in South America, and one in the West Indies.[26] Although World War I led to an expansion of the attaché corps, the armistice led to a reduction in the number of officers abroad. In 1921, for example, the attaché in Copenhagen covered all of Scandinavia; by 1925, responsibility for Scandinavia had shifted to Berlin. Still, while consolidation occurred in some areas, other areas saw expansion. In 1923, for example, the Navy dispatched attachés to both Lima and Havana.[27] In 1926, ONI had sixteen attachés and assistant attachés; five years later, there were eighteen.[28] As the threat of war grew, so did the size of the attaché corps. By 1938, it included twenty-seven attachés and assistant attachés, plus approximately thirty civilians and enlisted men abroad.[29] On the eve of Pearl Harbor, the attaché system included 133 officers and two hundred enlisted personnel.[30]

Naval attachés spent one to three years abroad, with an average tour lasting around two. An attaché was a staff member of the embassy or mission to which he was accredited but did not work for the U.S. ambassador. Instead, he reported to the Director of Naval Intelligence, who wrote his annual fitness report.[31] The attaché was in charge of the

23. "Notes on the Present Conflict in China," *Information Bulletin* 18, no. 1 (March 1939).

24. Niblack, *History and Aims*, 6.

25. Lt. William L. Sachse, "Our Naval Attaché System: Its Origins and Development to 1917," *U.S. Naval Institute Proceedings* 72, no. 5 (May 1946), 669.

26. Niblack, *History and Aims*, 5.

27. Green, "The First Sixty Years," 74.

28. Townsend, "Naval Intelligence," 2; "Naval Intelligence," 47.

29. *Naval Administration in World War II*, 524.

30. Green, "The First Sixty Years," 102.

31. Wheeler, *Kinkaid of the Seventh Fleet*, 121.

assistant naval attachés and office staff and supervised any naval officers assigned to the country for language studies.[32]

The mission of the naval attaché was to collect information on the navy of the country to which he was accredited. Because much of the mission concerned foreign naval technology, technical expertise was an asset. The Navy also periodically augmented its attachés with technical specialists. In 1929, for example, it assigned one naval construction corps officer, one radio and communications officer, and a submarine specialist as assistant naval attachés in Europe.[33] ONI monitored naval aviation developments as well, accrediting a number of naval aviators as "assistant naval attachés for air matters."

The Navy established programs to teach its officers Chinese, Japanese, and Russian. The Japanese language program, established in 1910, expanded a decade later to include the study of military and naval affairs. Students lived in Japan for three years of intense language training, followed by assignment to ONI or the Office of Naval Communications, which was responsible for Communications Intelligence (COMINT) operations. During the interwar period, sixty-five Navy and Marine Corps officers received language training in Japan.[34] Many later returned to Japan as attachés.

The spread of fascism in Europe, coupled with Japan's expansion in Asia, changed markedly the balance of power in Europe and Asia. As the international scene darkened, ONI expanded. Appropriations grew from $144,000 in 1931 to $249,000 in 1937.[35] The size of the office grew as well. At the time of the Pearl Harbor attack, ONI included 230 officers, 175 enlisted men, and three hundred civilian clerks and typists.[36] The British Naval Intelligence Division, by comparison, had only 161 officers, even though Britain had already been at war for two years. The Japanese equivalent to ONI, the Naval Staff's Third Bureau, had a mere twenty-nine officers.[37]

THE MILITARY INTELLIGENCE DIVISION

The Army established its intelligence organization, the Division of Military Information, in 1885 to collect "military data on our own and

32. ONI, "Instructions for Attaches," 3.
33. Spruance lecture, 9.
34. John Prados, *Combined Fleet Decoded: The Secret History of American Intelligence and the Japanese Navy in World War II* (New York: Random House, 1995): 8–10.
35. *Naval Administration in World War II*, 28.
36. Green, "The First Sixty Years," 102.
37. Prados, *Combined Fleet Decoded*, 70.

foreign services which would be available for the use of the War Department and the Army at large."[38] In April 1917, the Chief of Staff directed that an intelligence section be established within the War College Division. The following year, the Army separated the Military Information Committee from the Army War College and redesignated it the Military Intelligence Division.[39] No longer subordinate to the War College, MID developed rapidly as an intelligence organization.

After World War I MID, like the rest of the Army, shrank dramatically. Headquarters personnel dropped from a wartime high of 1,441 in 1918 to ninety by 1922 and reached a peacetime low of sixty-six in 1936. Even at its nadir, however, MID was roughly equal in size to its European counterparts. Its personnel strength was, for example, approximately the same as that of the French *Deuxième Bureau*, which employed seventy-five people during the 1930s.[40]

MID's mission was to conduct "those duties of the War Department General Staff which relate to the collection, evaluation, and dissemination of military information."[41] Monitoring foreign technology and doctrine was an important element of this mission. As Colonel James H. Reeves told a class of intelligence officers in 1927, MID was responsible for keeping "our teaching, training, and manufacturing establishments abreast of the military thought and progress of the world."[42] It provided the Army War College with a wealth of information on foreign armies.[43] It also supplied information to Army planners regarding foreign ground and air forces.

Although MID's organization changed many times throughout the interwar period, the division's organization in 1938, shown in Figure 2, is illustrative. At the time, the office employed sixty-nine people—eighteen active-duty officers, one officer each from the Reserve and Na-

38. Marc B. Powe, "The Emergence of the War Department Intelligence Agency: 1885–1918" (master's thesis, Kansas State University, 1975): 16–17.

39. John F. Votaw, "United States Military Attaches, 1885–1919: The American Army Matures in the International Arena" (Ph.D. dissertation, Temple University, 1991), 45.

40. Ernest R. May, "Capabilities and Proclivities" in *Knowing One's Enemies: Intelligence Assessment before the Two Wars*, ed. May (Princeton, N.J.: Princeton University Press, 1984): 525.

41. MID 2464–34/11, Assistant Chief of Staff, G-2, War Department General Staff, "Standing Instructions for Military Attaches," n.d. (received November 2, 1931) (hereafter referred to as 1931 *SIMA*), *Military Intelligence Division Correspondence, 1917–1941*, Box 1388, RG 165, NA, 1.

42. Col. J. H. Reeves, "Problems of the Military Intelligence Division," lecture, G-2 course no. 5, January 4, 1927, #332A-5, U.S. Army Military History Institute (hereafter referred to as USAMHI), 2.

43. William O. Odom, *After the Trenches: The Transformation of U.S. Army Doctrine, 1919–1939* (College Station: Texas A&M University Press, 1999): chap. 10.

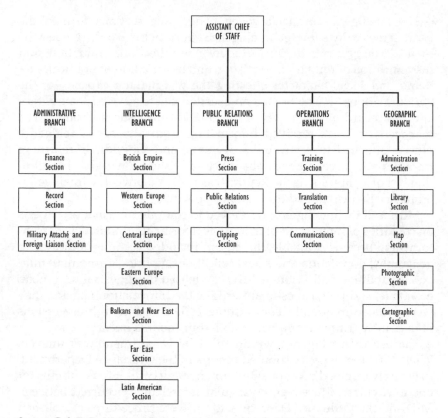

```
                          ASSISTANT CHIEF
                             OF STAFF


  ADMINISTRATIVE      INTELLIGENCE       PUBLIC RELATIONS      OPERATIONS         GEOGRAPHIC
     BRANCH             BRANCH              BRANCH              BRANCH             BRANCH


    Finance           British Empire         Press              Training        Administration
    Section              Section            Section             Section            Section


    Record            Western Europe     Public Relations      Translation          Library
    Section              Section            Section             Section            Section


 Military Attaché and  Central Europe       Clipping          Communications          Map
 Foreign Liaison Section  Section           Section             Section            Section


                      Eastern Europe                                            Photographic
                         Section                                                  Section


                   Balkans and Near East                                         Cartographic
                         Section                                                  Section


                        Far East
                        Section


                      Latin American
                        Section
```

Source: Col. E. R. Warner McCabe, Assistant Chief of Staff, G-2, "The Military Intelligence Division, War Department General Staff," lecture at the Army War College, January 4, 1938, OA/NHC.

Figure 2: Organization of the Military Intelligence Division, 1938

tional Guard, three enlisted men, and forty-six civilians. Besides handling finance and records, the Administrative Branch managed the attaché system, selected language students, and conducted liaison with foreign military attachés in the United States.[44] The Public Relations Branch handled the War Department's relations with the press and the public. The Operations Branch supervised the training of intelligence officers and managed the Army's intelligence reserve program. The Geographic Branch produced maps and conducted topographical and geological surveys.[45]

44. Col. E. R. Warner McCabe, "The Military Intelligence Division, War Department General Staff," lecture, G-2 course no. 5, January 4, 1939, USAMHI, 2.
45. 1931 *SIMA*, 4.

[27]

The Intelligence Branch's seven geographic sections formed the heart of the Army's foreign intelligence effort. In the words of one MID manual, the branch's duties included "the collection, evaluation, and dissemination of military information and information of political, economic and social character affecting the war-making capacity of the various nations."[46] The branch and section chiefs advised the military attachés regarding the types of information they should collect. The managers, in turn, received information from attachés, intelligence officers attached to Army units overseas, and individuals returning from duty or travel abroad. The office published a weekly "Distribution List of Military Attaché Reports" as well as a biweekly Intelligence Summary that circulated throughout the Army.[47]

MID used the intelligence it received to compile Information Digests on countries of interest. Kept in loose-leaf form and updated as new information became available, the digests included sections dedicated to geography, population and social conditions, politics, economics, military capabilities, and aviation. MID condensed the digests into combat, economic, and political estimates.[48] Like the Information Digests, they were updated frequently. For example, MID distributed three versions of its combat estimate of Japan within four months in early 1939.

The use of intelligence within the War Department was uneven. While MID regularly distributed reports to the Ordnance Department, they rarely received prompt attention. In many cases it took months for one to circulate. Moreover, no regular interchange occurred between MID and the Ordnance Department, nor were procedures established to follow up reports of interest. Finally, because the Army had little money for research and development, there were few opportunities for foreign intelligence to influence U.S. procurement.[49]

At the outbreak of World War I, the United States possessed the world's largest corps of military attachés, with fifteen officers accredited to nineteen embassies and legations.[50] The period of U.S. involvement witnessed a rapid expansion of the ranks of the attachés, reaching

46. MID 2461–34/64, Assistant Chief of Staff, G-2, "Standing Instructions for Military Attaches", October 16, 1939 (hereafter referred to as 1939 *SIMA*), *Military Intelligence Division Correspondence, 1917–1941*, Box 1388, RG 38, NA, 7.

47. Ibid., 9.

48. Ibid., 10–12.

49. Constance McLaughlin Green, Harry C. Thomson, and Peter C. Roots, *The Ordnance Department: Planning Munitions for War* (Washington, D.C.: Office of the Chief of Military History, Department of the Army, 1955): 209, 214–15.

50. Sachse, "Our Naval Attaché System," 669.

a high of 111 in December 1918.[51] The Army's postwar demobilization led to a predictable reduction in the size of the corps. By 1922, it had shrunk to thirty attachés, assisted by fourteen line officers and six air officers.[52] By 1929, it was down to twenty-two attachés and fifteen assistants.[53] Between 1933 and 1937, Congress capped the total number of military attachés at thirty-two.[54] Despite these constraints, the U.S. Army possessed the third largest attaché corps in the world in 1936, behind France and Great Britain but ahead of Italy, Germany, and the Soviet Union.[55]

As part of the postwar drawdown, the Army recalled attachés from Belgium, Czechoslovakia, Ecuador, Egypt, Hungary, the Netherlands, Sweden, and Switzerland. Many remaining officers were given responsibility for multiple countries. The military attaché in Germany, for example, also reported on developments in the Netherlands, Sweden, and Switzerland. The number of countries to which U.S. military attachés were accredited thus actually grew from twenty-five in September 1918 to a high of fifty-five in January 1922. Even in the lean years between 1933 and 1937, MID reported on forty-four countries.[56]

According to one primer published by MID, an attaché "should have tact, discretion and sound judgment, and the poise that comes from worldly experience." He should possess both "acute powers of observation" and "a scrupulous exactitude of memory."[57] The military attaché corps included some of the best officers in the Army, including John J. Pershing, Joseph E. Kuhn, Peyton C. March, Frank R. McCoy, and Sherman Miles, as well as others who served with competence if not acclaim. Although most served a single tour, some served repeatedly, often at different posts.[58] Miles, who was the Assistant Chief of Staff at the time of Pearl Harbor, had previously served as attaché to five countries.

51. Robert G. Angevine, "Gentlemen Do Read Each Other's Mail: American Intelligence in the Interwar Era," *Intelligence and National Security* 7, no. 2 (April 1992), 9.

52. Bruce W. Bidwell, *History of the Military Intelligence Division, Department of the Army General Staff, 1775–1941* (Frederick, Md.: University Publications of America, 1986), 380.

53. Col. Stanley H. Ford, "The Military Intelligence Division, War Department General Staff," lecture, G-2 course no. 3, November 29, 1929, #362A-3, USAMHI, 4.

54. McCabe, "The Military Intelligence Division," 3.

55. France had 50, Great Britain 38, the United States 34, Italy 30, and Germany and the Soviet Union each 24. See Alfred Vagts, *The Military Attaché* (Princeton: Princeton University Press, 1967), 68.

56. Angevine, "Gentlemen Do Read Each Other's Mail," 10.

57. Director, MID, *A Guide for Military Attaches* (1921), 6, 7.

58. Votaw, "United States Military Attaches," contains an excellent description of the military attaché system.

In identifying prospective attachés, MID sought officers fluent in the local language. While this was easy for the major European languages, finding officers who spoke Japanese and Chinese was difficult. In 1922 the Army began to remedy this shortfall by assigning two officers each to Japan and China to study as "special assistant military attachés." Duty as a language student was both exotic and challenging: exotic because it offered a young officer the opportunity to spend four years in Asia under little to no supervision, challenging because he was asked to master a twelve-year language curriculum in one-third that time. Students in Japan, for example, were required to spend their first year in Tokyo, after which they were "encouraged to travel extensively in order to gain an intimate knowledge of the country, its people, and their customs," reporting to the military attaché twice a year for examination and instruction.[59] Upon completing their studies, language officers were attached to a Japanese army regiment for a six-month tour. They also assisted the military attaché by translating press reports, training pamphlets, and technical manuals and reporting on conditions in the Japanese army. The program yielded substantial benefits, and two years later the Army quadrupled the number of officers studying Asian languages to sixteen: eight each in Japan and China. The program was cut to twelve in the mid-1930s, however, because of lack of funds.[60]

The Army took a keen interest in the development of foreign air forces during the interwar period. As a result, MID—like ONI—began appointing aviators as assistant military attachés for air matters to selected countries. These officers collected information on military and commercial aviation by reading the press and inspecting aircraft factories and air bases, often with their naval counterparts. By October 1, 1919, MID had assistant military attachés for air matters in England, France, and Italy.[61] By 1935, it had added Air Corps officers in Germany, Greece, and Spain.

The collection and analysis of technical intelligence was a notable weakness of the interwar attaché system. Only a small number of ordnance officers had the experience, language ability, and income necessary to allow them to become attachés. While nine served between 1920 and 1940, only two—Major Philip R. Faymonville in Tokyo and Moscow and Captain Rene R. Studler in London—served between No-

---

59. Lt. Warren J. Clear, "Oriental Language Detail," *Infantry Journal* 23, no. 2 (August 1923): 166.

60. Bidwell, *History of the MID*, 384.

61. E-9-a 12022, "Conference at The Hague of U.S. Military Attaches Stationed in Europe," *Naval Attaché Reports, 1921–1939*, Box 814, RG 38, NA.

vember 1930 and May 1940.[62] Studler, an expert in small arms and ammunition, held a roving accreditation that allowed him to report on weapon developments throughout Europe.[63] In May 1940, the Army sent two additional ordnance officers abroad: Colonel H. H. Zornig to Berlin and Captain Gervais W. Trichtel to Paris.[64]

Mobilization for war led to a wholesale expansion of MID. The office had begun to grow slowly in the late 1930s, but it was not until the summer of 1940 that Congress authorized it to increase its strength from 69 to 80 personnel. The next year saw tremendous growth: by December of that year, MID included 848 personnel, including two hundred officers and 648 civilians. The war also led to expansion of the office's missions. In particular, its censorship and counterintelligence functions grew considerably, as did planning and training. MID began to increase its espionage activities as well. Thus, by the time the United States entered World War II, MID contained branches responsible for administration, intelligence, counterintelligence, plans and training, and censorship.[65]

INTELLIGENCE SOURCES AND METHODS

The military attaché was at the heart of intelligence collection and assessment. The mission of the attaché was "to obtain military information of every nature for his government."[66] Army officers regarded Germany and France as the most prestigious posts because their reputation as world leaders in weapons, tactics, and training.[67] Naval officers favored duty in Britain for the same reason. As a rule, Army officers had more opportunities to observe their foreign counterparts than Naval officers did. Indeed, in a number of instances U.S. Army officers routinely got the opportunity to serve in foreign army units.

Attachés acquired most of their information openly in the course of their routine duties. As Raymond A. Spruance told a class at the Marine

---

62. Green, Thomson, and Roots, *The Ordnance Department*, 208.

63. "Proposed Travel Abroad of Captain Rene R. Studler," February 1, 1935, The René Studler Papers, USAMHI.

64. Green, Thomson, and Roots, *The Ordnance Department*, 260.

65. Roberta Wohlstetter, *Pearl Harbor: Warning and Decision* (Stanford, Calif.: University of Stanford Press, 1962): 281.

66. Director, MID, *A Guide for Military Attaches* (1921), 13.

67. Colonel T. Bentley Mott, *Twenty Years as Military Attaché* (New York: Oxford University Press, 1937): 103.

Corps School in Quantico, Virginia, "A man with good powers of observation, an analytical mind, and a willingness to work can send in a great deal of very valuable intelligence and still act at all times in a perfectly open and aboveboard manner."[68] Inspections of army garrisons, schools, air bases, ships, and dockyards yielded information on order of battle and materiel. The degree of access granted to attachés varied from country to country, and some facilities were inevitably off-limits. The Royal Navy, for example, prohibited foreign attachés from visiting ships under construction and put strict limits on the few visits to its naval vessels it did permit. Even if the host nation allowed an attaché to inspect an installation, it could conceal some details from him during the visit.[69]

Attachés generally conducted inspections on the principle of reciprocity. ONI advised officers requesting permission to observe "confidential and important experiments" to obtain permission from the Director of Naval Intelligence first, since "in many cases reciprocal privileges will be expected."[70] At times, U.S. attachés were constrained from visiting facilities overseas because the Navy was unwilling to give foreign governments access to its installations. For example, when the Navy forbade foreign attachés from visiting U.S. carriers to conceal the extent of U.S. progress in carrier construction, the British and Japanese navies restricted U.S. attachés in return.

Tours of factories were another source of information. Like visits to military installations, they were usually scheduled and supervised by the host government. On the other hand, most foreign arms manufacturers were open about their activities. Moreover, they were frequently willing to supply attachés with information in the hope of selling arms to the U.S. government. As ONI's *Instructions for Attachés* counseled, "Prospects of even a small contract often open the way to obtaining valuable information."[71]

The assistant military and naval attachés for air matters toured foreign aircraft factories. In some cases, they were accompanied by representatives of U.S. aircraft manufacturers. Some of the leading figures of the American aircraft industry visited Germany during the 1930s, including J. H. Kindelberger of the North American Aviation Company,

68. Spruance lecture, 9.

69. For a discussion of what a trained observer could learn from such visits, see Raymond L. Garthoff, "Intelligence Aspects of Cold War Scientific Exchanges: U.S.-USSR Atomic Energy Exchange Visits in 1959," *Intelligence and National Security* 15, no. 1 (spring 2000): 1–13.

70. ONI, "Instructions for Attaches," 8.

71. Ibid., 9.

Glenn Martin of the Glenn Martin Company, Laurence Bell of Bell Aircraft, and Igor Sikorsky of United Aircraft. Many toured British factories as well. Similarly, Charles A. Lindbergh visited Germany three times between July 1936 and October 1938, during which he passed a wealth of information to the U.S. military attaché in Berlin, Major Truman Smith.[72] Lindbergh inspected aeronautical facilities in Poland, Romania, Czechoslovakia, and the Soviet Union as well.[73]

Military exercises gave the intelligence officer an opportunity to observe armies under simulated combat conditions. MID was especially interested in the insights drawn from firsthand observation of maneuvers. As the 1931 edition of its *Standing Instructions for Military Attachés* put it, "While translations of general maneuver problems and orders and newspaper accounts of the exercises are of some use, what is really wanted is a good eye-witness type of description telling what has actually happened." MID also instructed the attaché that it was his duty to report accurately and critically his observations, not to pass judgment: "It is desired that the reasons be given for everything that was done, be it right or wrong."[74]

Although observing field maneuvers yielded insight into military tactics, drawing inferences regarding the army's overall effectiveness was at times exceedingly difficult. Foreign armies used exercises for different purposes. While the Germans used maneuvers to practice tactics under reasonably realistic conditions, the Japanese used them to rehearse staff work and planning. Thus, conclusions about Japanese military tactics drawn from exercises were misleading.[75] The British, more than the Germans and Japanese, used exercises as occasions to experiment with new concepts and organizations rather than to rehearse accepted doctrine. Inferences drawn from their maneuvers could be misleading as well.

American vessels had the opportunity to observe and to photograph foreign warships at sea as well. Intelligence officers aboard U.S. warships filed informative reports on the construction, handling, and seaworthiness of foreign combatants. At times the intelligence officers were able to observe naval operations firsthand. In March 1939, for example, the crew of the USS *Pecos* witnessed the British aircraft carrier

72. Robert Hessen, ed., *Berlin Alert: The Memoirs and Reports of Truman Smith* (Stanford: Hoover Institution Press, 1984), *passim*.

73. Walter S. Ross, *The Last Hero: Charles A. Lindbergh* (New York: Harper and Row, 1964): 277.

74. 1931 *SIMA*, 25.

75. Philip A. Towle, "British Estimates of Japanese Military Power, 1900–1914" in *Estimating Foreign Military Power*, ed. Towle (New York: Holmes and Meier Publishers, Inc., 1982): 126.

Eagle conducting flight operations in the Singapore Straits.[76] On other occasions, U.S. naval personnel were invited aboard foreign ships. In October 1931, for example, J. H. Foskett of the submarine *S-30* received a tour of the British submarine *Phoenix* in Hong Kong that revealed details of the boat's construction and operational capabilities.[77]

Port calls provided additional opportunities to collect intelligence. ONI received much information on the construction and handling of the British battleship *Rodney* during its passage through the Panama Canal in March 1931.[78] U.S. ships and naval bases submitted a similarly impressive stream of reports and photographs during the 1932 voyage of the German cruiser *Karlsruhe*. ONI received reports from the destroyers *Whitney* and *Kane*, which lay at anchor during the German ship's port call in San Diego. The commanding officer of the cruiser *Memphis* and future Director of Naval Intelligence, Captain Joseph V. Ogan, submitted his own report, as did the commander of the USS *Pensacola*, which was anchored next to the *Karlsruhe* at Bahia, Brazil.[79] These reports contained details of the ship's construction, power plant, and armament that the Navy subsequently used to prepare a set of blueprints.[80]

Central to an attaché's success was his ability to develop contacts within the armed forces of the country to which he was accredited. ONI's attaché manual advised officers that "in ordinary conversation there is a great deal to be learned by comparison and deduction. In familiar conversation it has indeed proved difficult for an officer to avoid telling more than he realizes when indulging in professional discussion with friends of his own cloth."[81] Captain Edward Howe Watson, who served in Tokyo in the early 1920s, proved adept at eliciting information from his Japanese counterparts. Watson and his assistants cultivated Captain (later Admiral and Ambassador) Nomura Kichisaburo, the director of Japanese naval intelligence; Captain (later Admiral and Chief of the Naval Staff) Nagano Osami; and Commander (later Admi-

76. "Aircraft Carriers," March 17, 1939, O–6-c 53551, "Aircraft Carriers, British (HMS Eagle)," *Naval Attaché Reports, 1921–1939*, Box 1225, RG 38, NA.

77. "Submarines," October 30, 1931, P-10-h 19847, "'P' and 'R' Classes of British Submarines," *Naval Attaché Reports, 1921–1939*, Box 1293, RG 38, NA.

78. O–6-a 15810C, "HMS *Nelson*," *Naval Attaché Reports, 1921–1939*, Box 1216, RG 38, NA.

79. O–10-a 17998, "German Cruisers 'B,' 'C,' and 'D,'" *Naval Attaché Reports, 1921–1939*, Box 1248, RG 38, NA.

80. O–10-a 17998-A, "German Cruisers Konigsberg, Karlsruhe, and Koln," *Naval Attaché Reports, 1921–1939*, Box 1248, RG 38, NA.

81. E-9-a 20313 "The Duties of Naval Attaches," May 1930 *Naval Attache Reports, 1921–1939*, Box 820, RG 38, 30.

ral, Premier, and Navy Minister) Yonai Mitsumasa as sources of information on Japanese naval policy. Watson regularly hosted parties for these and other Japanese naval officials at some of Tokyo's best *geisha* houses, probing them for information on Japanese naval policy. His methods proved effective; in 1921, for example, he learned from Nomura and Nagano that the Japanese position toward the United States at the upcoming Washington Naval Conference would be conciliatory, information confirmed independently by communications intercepted by Herbert O. Yardley's "Black Chamber."[82]

Educational exchanges offered an additional avenue for developing contacts with foreign armed forces. During the interwar period, the Army sent officers to study in French, Italian, Polish, and German military schools.[83] The most successful program was that which allowed one American officer per year to study in the *Kriegsakademie*'s two-year course, beginning in 1935. These students were carefully selected, spoke and read German well, and acquired a broad set of contacts among the *Wehrmacht* officers attending the school. They included Captain (later General) Albert C. Wedemeyer, Major (later Major General) Herman F. Kramer, Major (later Major General) Harlan N. Hartness, and Major (later Major General) Richard C. Partridge. Their instruction included all aspects of German tactics and operations and two to six weeks of service in a German unit. Kramer served in an infantry regiment and Wedemeyer in an antitank battalion; Major Percy Black served in an artillery regiment; and Lieutenant Paul Thompson spent two tours in a pioneer battalion. From June to September, while the school was on vacation, these students assisted the military attaché by documenting their experiences and writing reports on German military organizations. Wedemeyer's account of German tactical decision making, for example, stands out as one of the most insightful works on the subject.[84] Moreover, U.S. officers built bonds of friendship with their foreign counterparts that led to additional opportunities to gather information.

The U.S. Army also established a series of programs that allowed its officers to be seconded to foreign army units. In December 1925, the United States and Japan reached one such agreement. Over the next fifteen years, more than twenty American officers served in Japanese

82. Ladislas Farago, *The Broken Seal: The Story of "Operation Magic" and the Pearl Harbor Disaster* (New York: Random House, 1967): 28–29.

83. Bidwell, *History of the MID*, 384.

84. MID 2277-B-48, "German General Staff School," July 11, 1938, *Military Intelligence Division Correspondence, 1917–1941*, RG 165, NA.

army units; several later returned to Japan as assistant military attachés. Two—William C. Crane and Harry I. T. Creswell—became military attachés.

Because American officers assigned to Japanese units were junior—often lieutenants or captains—their most extensive contact was with junior Japanese officers. As a result, their reports were most informative on such issues as the quality of Japanese soldiers, their training, and tactics; the American officers were much less insightful about Japanese operational art and strategy. Their reports were nonetheless a rich source of information. For example, in August 1937 Captain Merritt B. Booth spent ten days with the Japanese 38th Infantry Regiment at Nara. He later spent three and one-half months with the 27th Infantry Regiment at Asahigawa on Hokkaido, where he participated in battalion and regiment exercises as well as the 7th Division's annual fall maneuvers. Despite what he termed a "mania for secrecy," Booth managed to compile an extensive report on Japanese tactics and training.[85]

U.S. attachés also traded information with their foreign counterparts. Especially in countries with tight security restrictions, collaboration within the attaché corps allowed intelligence officers to share insights. In some countries, the trading of information among attachés evolved into an art. For example, during his tenure as assistant naval attaché for air matters in Tokyo between 1939 and 1941, Lieutenant Stephen Jurika collaborated not only with his counterparts from Britain and France, but also with officers from the Soviet Union and Germany.[86]

Newspapers and magazines yielded considerable information. ONI recommended that every attaché monitor the press, "for newspaper and periodicals furnish most of the information that is accumulated by the Office of Naval Intelligence during peace."[87] The attaché's office clipped stories from newspapers, translated them, and sent them to the United States.[88] It also monitored foreign military publications for articles discussing tactics and doctrine, maneuvers, and war lessons. Some journals were valuable for what they said not only about their own armed forces, but others as well. The Estonian journal *Sodur* and the Swedish military publication *Ny Militär Tidskrift*, for example,

---

85. MID 2023–948/37 "27th Infantry Regiment," January 27, 1938, *Correspondence of the Military Intelligence Division Relating to General, Political, Economic, and Military Conditions in Japan, 1918–1941*, Roll 24, RG 165, NA.
86. Reminiscences of Capt. Stephen Jurika Jr., USN (retired), USNI, 393–403.
87. ONI, "Instructions for Attaches," 16.
88. Jurika Reminiscences, 407–408.

reprinted articles from Soviet military journals and published their own analyses of Soviet military exercises.

The Army and Navy discouraged their officers from recruiting foreign agents in peacetime for fear of repercussions should such operations be discovered. ONI's *Instructions for Naval Attachés* stated that in peacetime:

> it has been the policy of the Navy Department that our attachés should never resort to methods of obtaining information that might result in causing them a loss of prestige in the eyes of the foreign government. . . . By employing agents that resort to dubious methods, an attaché assumes responsibility for their actions and in so doing risks the loss of confidence of the officials upon whom he depends in carrying out his work.[89]

In time of war, by contrast, ONI acknowledged that agents would be necessary.

Despite the Navy's official injunction against espionage, it nonetheless occasionally employed clandestine sources. During the 1930s, ONI established a network of spies in China under the control of Major William A. Worton.[90] Attachés cultivated intelligence sources as well. Kinkaid developed contacts within the Italian armed forces who gave him detailed information on the damage inflicted on the Italian battleship *Littorio* by the British at Taranto.[91] In addition, reporting from a Japanese agent provided important technical information regarding the Type 93 *Long Lance* torpedo and modifications to the cruiser *Mogami*'s armament.[92]

The Army used liaison with foreign intelligence services extensively. In 1926, for example, the U.S. and Canadian governments reached an agreement to exchange military information.[93] The Army developed informal relationships with other military intelligence services as well. France, Latvia, and Poland supplied MID with information on covert military cooperation between Weimar Germany and the Soviet Union in the late 1920s and early 1930s.[94] Similarly, U.S. attachés in Riga and

---

89. Office of Naval Intelligence, "Instructions for Attaches," 1933, *Naval Attaché Reports, 1921–1939*, Box 10, RG 38, NA, 43.

90. Dennis L. Noble, "A U.S. Naval Intelligence Mission to China in the 1930s," *Studies in Intelligence* 43, no. 2 (1999): 73–78.

91. Wheeler, *Kinkaid of the Seventh Fleet*, 119.

92. Smith-Hutton Reminiscences, USNI, 299–302.

93. Bidwell, *History of the MID*, 266.

94. MID 2037–1823/4, "Germany Assisting Soviet Russia," March 12, 1927, *Correspondence of the Military Intelligence Division Relating to General, Political, Economic, and Military Conditions in Russia and the Soviet Union, 1918–1941*, Roll 15, RG 165, NA; MID

Warsaw acted as a conduit between MID and the military intelligence services of Estonia, Finland, Latvia, and Poland regarding military developments in the Soviet Union. Information received in this manner included order of battle estimates for the Soviet army, as well as analyses of Soviet armor and airborne exercises.[95] This web of contacts partially compensated for the limited number of U.S. military attaché officers and the lack of clandestine reporting.

The Navy used peacetime liaison with foreign intelligence services much less than did the Army. One notable exception was a set of detailed reports French intelligence provided ONI through the U.S. military attaché in Riga describing the Soviet navy's operations in the Baltic in the late 1920s and early 1930s.[96]

After the outbreak of World War II, ONI and the British intelligence services began cooperating closely.[97] As part of this relationship, the British provided ONI with a large volume of technical intelligence on German aircraft. The U.S. naval attaché in London at the time, Captain Alan Kirk, and his assistant for air matters, Commander N. R. Hitchcock, submitted a stream of reports on German aircraft that had been downed over the British Isles. On August 7, 1940, for example, they inspected a Bf-110 fighter the Royal Air Force had shot down. The following month they forwarded a British Air Ministry report describing the airframe, engine, armament, and radio equipment of a downed Ju-87B2 dive bomber and another regarding a Ju-88A1 bomber the British had salvaged from Druridge Bay in Northumberland.[98]

Kirk scored his greatest coup in early October 1940 when, at his request, the British Ministry of Aircraft Production agreed to send the U.S. Navy a Bf-110 that the RAF had shot down over Southern England but remained in reasonably good condition. De Havilland Aircraft disassembled the airframe and packed it for shipment, and the Woolrich Arsenal did the same for the aircraft's cannon and machine gun ammunition. The British Air Ministry also agreed to supply the U.S. Navy

---

2016–1109/10, "German-Soviet Cooperation," February 19, 1931, *Military Intelligence Division Correspondence, 1917–1941*, Box 624, RG 165, NA.

95. David M. Glantz, "Observing the Soviets: U.S. Army Attachés in Eastern Europe During the 1930s," *The Journal of Military History* 55, no. 2 (April 1991).

96. P-2-b 16144, "Russian Baltic Fleet," *Naval Attaché Reports, 1921–1939*, Box 1272, RG 38, NA.

97. Donald McLachlan, *Room 39: Naval Intelligence in Action, 1939–1945* (London: Weidenfeld and Nicolson, 1968), chap. 10.

98. A-1-i 17474-C, "Junkers Airplanes—Junkers Factory," September 10, 1940, *Intelligence Division, Secret Reports of Naval Attaches, 1940–1946*, Box 6, RG 38, NA.

with missing parts for the aircraft. The British moved the disassembled German fighter to a warehouse in southwest London for crating. Although a German bombing raid damaged the building the following night, the aircraft was unscathed. The crates containing the aircraft were shipped to the American consul at Halifax, Nova Scotia, and then on to the United States.[99]

Observing foreign armies and air forces in combat allowed attachés to evaluate their military effectiveness. The U.S. Army sought opportunities to observe the Sino-Japanese War, the Italian-Ethiopian War, and the Spanish Civil War. The war in Spain in particular served as a proving ground of new weaponry and doctrine. Colonel Stephen O. Fuqua, the U.S. military attaché in Spain, believed that the war provided "a 'dress rehearsal' for the next war."[100] Moreover, the United States dispatched an impressive group of officers to observe the war. Of the ten observers who submitted the most reports on the conflict, nine were college graduates (in an era in which one-quarter to one-third of Army officers lacked a college degree), one had a graduate degree, nine were Command and General Staff School or Army War College graduates, and two had attended foreign military schools. Fuqua was the former Chief of Infantry, while two would retire as brigadier generals and two as major generals.[101]

U.S. intelligence collection during the war also illustrated the limitations of reliance on attachés during hostilities. Because attachés are attached to embassies, they must travel wherever the embassy does. During the Spanish Civil War this turned out to be a significant constraint, as successive Nationalist offensives forced the Republican government to evacuate Madrid in December 1936 for Valencia and then Barcelona. Moreover, the identification of an attaché with an embassy and a host government also constrains his ability to collect information on opposition movements. During the war, the military attaché in Spain and his assistant for air matters provided much better information on Republican forces and operations than on those of the Nationalists.

Although U.S. military observers got several opportunities to observe Soviet aircraft such as the Polikarpov I-15 and I-16 flown by Republican pilots, the observers had substantially less information regarding German and Italian air units aiding the fascists. MID

99. A-1-i 22529, "Messerschmitt Airplanes," October 8, 1940, *Intelligence Division, Confidential Reports of Naval Attaches, 1940–1946*, Box 21, RG 38, NA.

100. Odom, *After the Trenches*, 217.

101. Ibid., 217.

nonetheless received some useful reports on Nationalist air operations. Attachés in Valencia and Paris described the employment of the Bf-109 during the 1937 Nationalist Bilbao offensive.[102] Lieutenant Colonel H. H. Fuller, the military attaché in Paris, learned from his German counterpart of the difficulty the *Luftwaffe* was having with level bombing and close air support during operations in Spain.[103]

ONI and MID thus cultivated a range of sources and methods for collecting information on foreign military developments. The precursors of World War II—and the war itself—led to increased security measures that foreclosed or restricted some traditionally fruitful methods, such as inspections, visits, and educational exchanges. Increasing censorship reduced the utility of open sources of information, such as newspapers and professional journals. At the same time, combat operations opened up new opportunities to collect intelligence. Attachés were able to observe the battlefield effectiveness of foreign forces and to discuss operations with the combatants. America's neutrality prior to December 1941 gave Army and Navy officers privileged access to the belligerents.

U.S. INTELLIGENCE IN PEACE AND WAR

While ONI and MID clearly faced limitations on their human and material resources during the 1920s and 1930s, historians often overstate the impact of these constraints on U.S. intelligence operations. Throughout the period, the Army and Navy were able to attract highly capable officers to intelligence duty. Moreover, they developed a wide variety of intelligence sources and methods. At the heart of this system was a corps of attachés trained to gather information on foreign armed forces. As the following chapters demonstrate, ONI and MID did a creditable job of uncovering military innovation in Japan, Germany, and Great Britain.

102. MID 2093–213/15, "Armament and Equipment—Nationalist Pursuit," *Correspondence of the Military Intelligence Division Relating to General, Political, Economic, and Military Conditions in Spain, 1918–1941*, Roll 12, RG 165, NA.

103. MID 2657-S-144/71, "Military Information on Civil War in Spain," *Correspondence of the Military Intelligence Division Relating to General, Political, Economic, and Military Conditions in Spain, 1918–1941*, Roll 7, RG 165, NA; "Notes on Spanish Aviation (July 1937)," Office of Naval Intelligence, West Europe Section, Foreign Intelligence Branch, *Records re. Spanish Civil War, 1936–1939*, Box 4, RG 38, NA; MID 2657-S-144/243, "War Operations in Spain," *Correspondence of the Military Intelligence Division Relating to General, Political, Economic, and Military Conditions in Spain, 1918–1941*, Roll 7, RG 165, NA.

The Army and Navy collected information on Japan, Germany, and Great Britain for markedly different reasons. Japan was a priority of U.S. intelligence because it represented the most likely threat to U.S. interests in Asia. By contrast, the possibility of war between the United States and Germany was remote throughout much of the period. U.S. intelligence—particularly MID—nonetheless devoted considerable attention to the German military because of Berlin's reputation for producing innovative weapons and doctrine. The U.S. Army monitored Germany not because it expected to face the German army in a reprise of World War I, but because it hoped to identify tactics and technology that it could copy. U.S. intelligence observed the British armed forces for similar reasons.

The three countries represented unique challenges as well. Japan possessed a society considerably different from that of the United States. Moreover, the size and sophistication of the Japanese armed forces grew substantially during the interwar period. Germany's covert arms development in the 1920s and its rapid remilitarization under Hitler presented Washington with a much different challenge. Britain, while culturally similar to the United States, nonetheless took great pains to conceal details of many of its military developments from the United States.

In all three countries, ONI and MID identified new ways of war most easily in areas of interest to the U.S. armed forces, particularly after the value of those areas was demonstrated on the battlefield or in realistic maneuvers. U.S. intelligence operations had considerably less success when confronted with technology and doctrine that differed substantially from that of the U.S. armed forces.

[3]

Japan
Assessing a Rising Regional Power

Japan scored a series of lopsided battlefield victories against the United States, Great Britain, and the Netherlands in the opening months of World War II. In just four months, eleven Japanese army divisions and barely two thousand combat aircraft managed to subjugate the Philippines, Malaya, Burma, and the Dutch East Indies, giving Tokyo three-quarters of the world's rubber, two-thirds of its tin, and self-sufficiency in oil.

Japan's ability to seize so much with so little was in part due to the precarious position of Asia's colonial masters. By the time Japan struck in December 1941, the *Wehrmacht* occupied the Netherlands and the *Luftwaffe* threatened the British Isles. Modest forces remained to defend their Asian colonies. The British garrisoned Malaya and Singapore with three divisions, while a division of local troops and a few Indian army units protected Burma. The United States, in the midst of mobilization, was unprepared to meet a Japanese attack.

The speed and decisiveness of Japan's early victories were also the result of its adoption of new ways of war. The Japanese navy's mastery of carrier aviation allowed it to strike a crushing blow against the U.S. fleet at Pearl Harbor. Japan's emphasis on night combat and long-range gunfire allowed it to cripple the American, British, Dutch, and Australian fleets at the Battle of the Java Sea and to batter the U.S. Navy during the Guadalcanal campaign. The Japanese army and navy's development of amphibious warfare allowed Japan to seize American, British, and Dutch possessions throughout Southeast Asia and the Pacific.

In the four decades that preceded World War II, Japan grew from dependence on foreign technology and expertise to the ability to produce first-rate weapons and develop innovative doctrine. The growth of Japan's competence as a military power, and its mastery of new ways of war, posed a significant challenge to U.S. intelligence. Throughout the period, the effectiveness of Japan's armed forces was largely unknown. Their last significant combat experience had been the 1904–1905 Russo-Japanese War. The emergence of new ways of war forced U.S. officers to evaluate the merit of concepts that had yet to be proven in combat. Cultural and linguistic barriers complicated the task considerably. To succeed, U.S. intelligence officers had to look beyond Japan's history of dependence on outside assistance to perceive its growth as a regional power. That U.S. intelligence organizations were only partially successful illustrates many of the barriers that stand in the way of recognizing foreign military innovation.

U.S. MILITARY INTELLIGENCE AND JAPAN

Japan was the primary focus of U.S. Army and Navy intelligence during the interwar period. While Washington and Tokyo enjoyed largely cordial relations in the years immediately after World War I, the growth of Japanese power in Asia set Tokyo on a collision course with Washington. U.S. leaders grew increasingly wary of Japan's escalating demands, such as the proposed inclusion of a racial equality clause in the Covenant of the League of Nations, as well as Tokyo's repeated demands for naval parity with Britain and the United States. Wariness yielded to suspicion during the 1930s after a series of Japanese provocations, including the annexation of Manchuria, withdrawal from the League, abrogation of naval arms control commitments, the Anti-Comintern Pact with Germany and Italy, and the invasion of China and then French Indochina.

A war with Japan was the U.S. Navy's top planning contingency throughout the interwar period. Only the Japanese fleet was strong enough to threaten U.S. interests in Asia. Beginning in 1897, the Army and Navy developed a series of plans for a war with Japan, known as War Plan ORANGE.[1] In 1923, the Joint Army-Navy Board, composed of the Army Chief of Staff, the Chief of Naval Operations, their deputies, and their chief planners, identified a war with Japan as the most pressing contingency facing the United States, a judgment reaffirmed five years later.[2]

1. On the origins and development of War Plan ORANGE see George W. Baer, *One Hundred Years of Sea Power: The U.S. Navy, 1890–1990* (Stanford, Calif.: Stanford University Press, 1994): 124–28; Edward S. Miller, *War Plan ORANGE: The U.S. Strategy to Defeat Japan, 1897–1945* (Annapolis, Md.: Naval Institute Press, 1991); Louis Morton, "War Plan ORANGE: Evolution of a Strategy," *World Politics* 11, no. 2 (January 1959).

2. Joint Board to Secretary of War, "Coordination of Army and Navy War Plans," June 7, 1923, JB 325, Ser. 210, *Records of the Joint Board,* Roll 9, Record Group (hereafter referred to as RG) 225, National Archives (hereafter referred to as NA), 1. This was reiterated in

Although Japan during the 1920s and 1930s was not closed to the United States, it was nonetheless a private and alien society. American intelligence officers seeking to monitor Japanese military developments had to contend with formidable cultural and linguistic obstacles. The Japanese military police, the *kempaitai*, monitored American attachés closely, repeatedly attempting to entrap them with the lure of secret information.[3] Despite such obstacles, the naval attaché in Tokyo believed that about ninety-five percent of the information he sought was available in open sources.[4]

The Army and the Navy each developed a cadre of intelligence specialists who possessed the language skills and practical experience needed to observe the Japanese military. An intelligence officer assigned to Japan could expect to spend several tours in the country during his career, first as a language student and then as an attaché. Some augmented this experience with a tour of duty in the Far East sections of MID or ONI or in the Army or Navy's communication intelligence organizations.

The Military Attaché's Office

In the years immediately following World War I, the United States and six other countries had military attachés in Tokyo.[5] Of these, the British were the best-informed, largely because of extensive Anglo-Japanese military cooperation.[6] Between 1922 and 1926, for example, British officers served with fifteen of Japan's seventeen army divisions and attended six military schools.[7] The Japanese also regularly invited British officers to observe maneuvers that were off-limits to other foreigners. Aviators from the Royal Air Force helped train the Japanese navy's air wing, and British dockyards built ships for the Japanese navy.

1928. See Joint Planning Committee to Joint Board, "Order of Priority in Preparation of War Plans," April 21, 1928, *Records of the Joint Board*, Roll 9, RG 225, NA, 1.

3. Capt. Wyman H. Packard, USN (retired), *A Century of U.S. Naval Intelligence* (Washington, D.C.: Department of the Navy, 1996): 66; John Prados, *Combined Fleet Decoded: The Secret History of American Intelligence and the Japanese Navy in World War II* (New York: Random House, 1995): 27.

4. Packard, *A Century of Naval Intelligence,* 68.

5. These were the United States, China, France, Great Britain, Italy, Poland, and the Soviet Union. Maj. Gen. F. S.G. Piggott, *Broken Thread: An Autobiography* (Aldershot, England: Gale & Polden, 1950): 278.

6. See, for example, Arthur J. Marder, *Old Friends, New Enemies: The Royal Navy and the Imperial Japanese Navy 1, Strategic Illusions, 1936–1941* (Oxford: Clarendon Press, 1981): chap. 1.

7. Piggott, *Broken Thread,* 68, 166.

Table 1   U.S. Military Attachés in Tokyo, 1917–1941

Military Attaché	Tour of Duty
Lt. Col. Karl F. Baldwin	March 1917–September 1919
Lt. Col. Charles Burnett	September 1919–February 1924
Maj. Philip R. Faymonville	February 1924–January 1926
Lt. Col. Charles Burnett	January 1926–August 1929
Lt. Col. James G. McIlroy	August 1929–October 1933
Lt. Col. William C. Crane	October 1933–December 1937
Lt. Col. Harry I. T. Creswell	December 1937–December 1941

Source: Correspondence of the Military Intelligence Division Relating to General, Political, Economic, and Military Conditions in Japan, 1918–1941, finding aid (Washington, D.C.: National Archives and Records Service, 1984), 10.

The United States was generally represented in Tokyo by a lieutenant colonel who had served at least one tour in Japan (see Table 1). Several devoted their careers to studying the Japanese army. Karl Baldwin, who served successively as military attaché in Tokyo and as head of MID's Far East Section, wrote a history of the Japanese army.[8] Charles Burnett spent more than seven years in Japan between 1919 and 1929 and was regarded by his foreign counterparts as one of the best-informed and most highly respected attachés in Tokyo. He later served as an advisor to the U.S. delegation to the 1930 London Naval Conference and as the head of MID's Military Attaché Section.

Not all attachés were as effective as Baldwin and Burnett, however. The military attaché at the time of Japan's attack on Pearl Harbor, Lieutenant Colonel Harry Creswell, lacked the curiosity and ingenuity required of a good intelligence officer. In fact, he rarely left his office. As one of his contemporaries complained, "[H]e wasn't out on trips or looking, or over in China, where the operations were, or asking to go up and see, watch, the operations in Manchuria at Nomonhon, on the Soviet border. He just seemed to be there in his office at eight o'clock every morning and leave at four-thirty in the afternoon."[9] Colonel Rufus S. Bratton, head of MID's Far East Section at the time, judged that Creswell sent him "practically no information" of value.[10]

8. MID 2023–411, "A Historical Sketch of the Japanese Army," 1926, *Military Intelligence Division Correspondence, 1918–1941*, Roll 17, RG 165, NA.

9. Reminiscences of Capt. Stephen Jurika Jr., USN (retired), U.S. Naval Institute Archives (hereafter referred to as USNI), 386.

10. Ladislas Farago, *The Broken Seal: The Story of "Operation Magic" and the Pearl Harbor Disaster* (New York: Random House, 1967): 209.

One or more assistants aided the military attaché. In addition, he had the services of some of the forty-two Army officers who served four-year tours as language students in Japan between 1920 and 1941. Several of these later became assistant military attachés, and two—William Crane and Harry Creswell—became attachés.[11]

While MID assigned aviators to a number of countries as assistant military attachés for air matters, it never sent one to Japan, apparently because the Army did not believe that the Japanese army's air force warranted special attention. As a result, the Army lost a valuable opportunity to gather information on Japanese aeronautical developments. Instead, it was the assistant military attaché, often an infantry or artillery officer, who monitored the Japanese air forces, preparing "Aviation Statistics" reports in cooperation with his naval counterpart, producing monthly surveys of Japanese aeronautic developments, and reporting on the organization of Japanese military aviation and Japanese aircraft manufacturers.

The Naval Attaché's Office

More than half of the eleven U.S. naval attachés who served in Tokyo during the interwar period were captains, which reflected the importance the Navy attached to relations with its Japanese counterpart. Identifying senior officers who possessed the requisite language skills and were willing to accept a tour of duty in Japan often proved difficult, however. Although the U.S. Navy created a substantial cadre of junior officers who spoke Japanese, the pool of senior officers with Japanese language skills was much smaller. Moreover, Tokyo—hot and humid in the summer and devoid of many of the amenities of Western life—was hardly a desirable post.

ONI included a number of officers who had lived and studied in Japan. Arthur H. McCollum, the head of ONI's Far East Section at the time of the Pearl Harbor attack, was born and raised in Japan. Stephen Jurika, who served as assistant naval attaché for air matters in the late 1930s, grew up in the Philippines and attended high school in Kobe, Japan. In addition, the attaché drew upon the talents of sixty-five Navy officers who served as language officers in Japan between the two world wars.[12]

11. Alvin Coox states incorrectly that only one language officer ever became an attaché. See Coox, "The Effectiveness of the Japanese Military Establishment in the Second World War" in *Military Effectiveness* III, *The Second World War*, eds. Allan R. Millett and Williamson Murray (Boston: Unwin Hyman, 1988): 1.

12. Prados, *Combined Fleet Decoded*, 8–10.

Table 2 U.S. Naval Attachés in Tokyo, 1914–1941

Naval Attaché	Tour of Duty
Comdr. Frederick J. Horne	December 1914–January 1919
Capt. Edward H. Watson	January 1919–January 1922
Capt. Lyman A. Cotten	January 1922–December 1923
Lt. Comdr. Garnet Hulings (acting)	December 1923–July 1924
Lt. Comdr. Franz B. Melendy	July 1924–July 1926
Comdr. George McC. Courts	July 1926–November 1928
Capt. Joseph V. Ogan	November 1928–September 1930
Capt. Isaac C. Johnson Jr.	September 1930–August 1933
Capt. Fred F. Rogers	August 1933–June 1936
Capt. Harold M. Bemis	July 1936–April 1939
Lt. Comdr. Henri H. Smith-Hutton	April 1939–December 1941

Source: *Register of the Commissioned and Warrant Officers of the United States Navy and Marine Corps* (Washington, D.C.: Government Printing Office, various years).

In 1927, the Asiatic Fleet began assigning pilots to Japan on temporary duty to report on Japanese naval aviation.[13] In 1935, the Navy formalized the arrangement by assigning an aviator as the assistant naval attaché for air matters. The four officers who served in this capacity, Lieutenant Commanders Ofstie and Bridget and Lieutenants Jurika and Phares, inspected Japanese naval air facilities and factories, drafted estimates of Japanese air strength, and analyzed new aircraft models.

U.S. intelligence officers stationed in Tokyo not only monitored the Japanese army and navy's order of battle, but also studied their concepts and doctrine. Throughout the interwar period, the Japanese armed forces explored a range of new approaches to combat, including amphibious operations, surface warfare, and carrier aviation. In 1941–1942, Japan's mastery of these innovative ways of war gave it a marked advantage over the United States, Britain, Australia, and the Netherlands. U.S. Army and Navy intelligence services enjoyed mixed success in detecting and characterizing Japanese innovation. Although they succeeded in tracking Japanese military technology, identifying innovative weapons proved difficult, even with accurate information. Determining how Japan would use that technology proved even more challenging.

13. The first such aviator, John J. Ballentine, went on to command a carrier and carrier division in the Pacific and to serve as the chief of staff of the Navy's Pacific air command. Ibid., 32.

In the opening months of World War II, the Japanese army and navy launched a series of amphibious landings against the Philippines, Hong Kong, Malaya, Guam, Wake, the Solomons, New Britain, and the Netherlands East Indies. In each case, the Japanese struck with a speed and vigor that demoralized their adversaries. The Japanese conquered the Philippines in six months, Malaya and Singapore in three months, the Netherlands East Indies in two months, Wake in two weeks, and Guam in two days. Tokyo's success was born of decades of experience: the army and navy had conducted landings against the Chinese during the Sino-Japanese War in 1894–1895, the Russians during the Russo-Japanese War in 1904–1905, and the Germans during World War I. It was also the result of innovation and experimentation in the years immediately following World War I.

The Japanese army's interest in amphibious warfare grew out of the geographic reality that future wars, whether fought on the Asian mainland against the Soviet Union or China or in the Pacific against the United States, would require landings on hostile shores. In 1918 the Japanese government adopted a national defense policy naming the United States as the primary threat to Japan and giving the army responsibility for seizing the Philippines and Guam, increasing interest in amphibious landings.[14]

The United States devoted considerable attention to monitoring the Imperial Japanese Army (IJA) in the interwar period. One of the most common methods of doing so was to observe its field training exercises. The military attaché in Tokyo began to report on Japanese maneuvers in 1917 and continued to attend them regularly throughout the period. Although Britain, France, and China invariably sent the largest contingents, the United States was generally well represented. The information that an officer could infer from maneuvers was limited, however: because the army generally scripted and rehearsed exercises, they did not necessarily offer an accurate measure of the army's effectiveness under fire.[15]

The U.S. Army also received information from American officers seconded to Japanese army units. Between 1925 and 1940, twenty-three

14. Edward J. Drea, "The Development of Imperial Japanese Army Amphibious Warfare Doctrine," in *idem, In the Service of the Emperor: Essays on the Imperial Japanese Army* (Lincoln: University of Nebraska Press, 1998): 16.

15. John Ferris, "Worthy of Some Better Enemy?: The British Estimate of the Imperial Japanese Army, 1919–1941, and the Fall of Singapore," *Canadian Journal of History* 28, no. 2 (August 1993): 229.

Army officers—mainly lieutenants and captains—served in Japanese regiments for several months each. Nearly half were seconded to infantry regiments; others joined artillery and cavalry regiments or attended military schools. The officers had to contend with pervasive security measures, and some complained that the tours were a waste of time. Still, many of their reports contained useful information on Japanese tactics, organization, and equipment.

In the years immediately following World War I, there were plenty of reasons to doubt the effectiveness of amphibious warfare. Indeed, the Allied landing at Gallipoli seemed to prove that assaults from the sea were doomed to failure. Early reports on the development of Japanese amphibious doctrine reflected such skepticism. In 1922, the United States got its first glimpse of Japan's amphibious capabilities when the Japanese permitted the U.S. military attaché, Lieutenant Colonel Charles Burnett, to attend a landing exercise at Takuma Bay. Although his hosts did not permit him to watch the initial landing, he and other attachés observed the debarkation of follow-on forces later that day. Burnett was critical of the operation, noting that "a few mines in the harbor, a certain amount of barb wire along the shore, with a few machine guns and field guns hidden in the sandy dunes, would have made this landing very difficult, if not impossible."[16] The observation, while accurate, was based on the false assumption that the Japanese, like the Allied forces at Gallipoli, planned to make an amphibious assault in the face of a strong opposition. In fact, the Japanese army anticipated landing troops at undefended points along an adversary's coast at night to achieve surprise and avoid a replay of the slaughter of Gallipoli. Failure to recognize this distinction led the United States to underestimate the army's progress in developing amphibious warfare doctrine.

The Japanese army refined its approach to amphibious warfare throughout the 1920s, designating the 5th, 11th, and 12th divisions for amphibious training.[17] It also acquired two classes of self-propelled landing craft: the Type A (*daihatsu*), a 49-foot vessel with a bow ramp designed to carry 100 troops, and the Type B (*shohatsu*), a 30-foot craft built to carry 30 men.[18] In 1925 the army began using these craft in exercises. It conducted additional landings at Niijima in the Izu Islands in

---

16. MID 2023–441/4, "The Grand Maneuvers of 1922," December 1, 1922, *Military Intelligence Division Correspondence, 1918–1941*, Roll 17, RG 165, NA, 4.

17. Drea, "Development of Amphibious Warfare," 17–18.

18. Millett, "Assault from the Sea: The Development of Amphibious Warfare Between the Wars—the American, British, and Japanese Experiences" in *Military Innovation in*

1926 and along the Wakayama coast in 1929. These maneuvers allowed the army to develop concepts for naval gunfire support and ship-to-shore command and control, and to test various types of landing craft.[19] Because it was successful at concealing its activities, sizable gaps resulted in the U.S. military's understanding of Japan's development of amphibious doctrine, organizations, and equipment.

American observers had valid reasons to discount the Japanese army's capabilities. It had not fought a major engagement since the Russo-Japanese War and lagged significantly behind Western nations in equipment and tactics. Moreover, Japan's army planned and trained to fight the Soviet Union, not the United States. U.S. assessments nonetheless warned against underestimating the Japanese. MID's 1927 monograph on Japan, for example, concluded that: "It is safe . . . to rate the fighting value of the Japanese troops very high, expecting that they can and will be the equal of the best troops (including Occidental) which could be brought against them in eastern Asia."[20]

In general, the greater an officer's exposure to the Japanese army, the higher his regard for it was. Although reports from officers who had observed the Japanese firsthand were often insightful, those penned by officers with less experience in Asia often reflected ethnocentric assumptions. Rather than measuring the Japanese army against the yardstick of a war in Asia, some judged it by the standards of Western armies trained to fight in much different circumstances. One 1933 MID assessment of Japanese combat methods, for example, explicitly viewed the Japanese doctrine through the lens of Western tactics and—not surprisingly—found it wanting. The report criticized the Japanese army for deriving lessons from combat in China rather than modeling its development on that of Western armies, concluding that:

> It appears probable that many of our so-called immutable principles of war will continue to be disregarded in the Japanese tactical doctrine which will adhere to the exaggerated and faulty methods which were so successful in the Russo-Japanese War and in the modem operations in

the Interwar Period, eds. Murray and Millett (Cambridge: Cambridge University Press, 1996): 81

19. David C. Evans and Mark R. Peattie, *Kaigun: Strategy, Tactics, and Technology in the Imperial Japanese Navy, 1887–1941* (Annapolis, Md.: Naval Institute Press, 1997): 442.

20. Military Intelligence Division, *Situation Monograph Orange*, January 1, 1927 AG no. 166, *Army AGO, Administrative Services Division, Operations Branch, Special Projects, War Plans "Color," 1920–1948*, Box 63, RG 1407, NA, 82.

China and Manchuria. Too easy success has made many Japanese leaders
intolerant of western military ideas.[21]

The author appears not to have questioned how the Japanese could
have achieved so much success while employing "faulty" methods.

The 1932 Shanghai Incident gave U.S. intelligence its first glimpse of
Japan's ability to launch amphibious operations under combat conditions. In February, the Japanese 9th Division, together with units of the
5th and 12th divisions, landed near Shanghai to relieve naval troops
under siege from Nationalist Chinese forces. Two weeks later, the 11th
Division conducted a dawn landing north of the city in an attempt to
outflank the Chinese. Although the landing itself went well, the division suffered heavy casualties at the hands of the crack Chinese 19th
Route Army.[22]

The U.S. Marine Corps was understandably keen to observe amphibious warfare methods firsthand, given its own interest in landings.
Indeed, the officers and men of the 4th Marine Regiment, stationed in
Shanghai, had a front-row seat for the fighting. Despite the army's poor
showing, the performance of Japanese soldiers impressed Marine observers According to one estimate prepared by the intelligence staff of
the Fleet Marine Force, "Throughout the operation they exhibited a
bull dog aggressiveness that would test the fighting ability of any opponent."[23] While noting their deficiency in firepower, the assessment
concluded that the Japanese formations were well tailored to fight in
Asia.[24]

The Shanghai Incident also sparked interest in amphibious warfare
within the Japanese navy. Most Japanese ships had a portion of their
crew designated as landing parties, or *rikusentai*. The mediocre performance of naval troops in Shanghai convinced the service's leaders of
the need for dedicated amphibious units. In the years that followed,
the navy formed Special Naval Landing Forces (SNLF) at Shanghai and

---

21. MID 2023–898/7 "Combat Methods of the Japanese," April 14, 1933, *Military Intelligence Division Correspondence, 1918–1941*, Roll 23, RG 165, NA, 2.

22. Drea, "Development of Amphibious Warfare," 18; Evans and Peattie, *Kaigun*, 443;
Meirion and Susie Harries, *Soldiers of the Sun: The Rise and Fall of the Imperial Japanese
Army* (New York: Random House, 1991): 160–61.

23. Lt. Col. Robert L. Denig, assistant chief of staff, F-2, 1st Lt. Stuart W. King, assistant
F-2, *Monograph of Japanese Mandate Islands*, prepared by the Intelligence Section of the
Fleet Marine Force (1934), Strategic Plans Division Files, Series 111, Box 57, Naval Histor-
ical Center (hereafter referred to as NH), 331.

24. Ibid., 343.

at Japan's four principal naval bases.[25] Each was a battalion-sized unit equipped with small arms and mortars, trained extensively in amphibious operations and configured to conduct surprise night landings against lightly defended positions, such as America's Central Pacific territories. Because the Japanese government denied U.S. observers access to naval landing force exercises, the United States lacked reliable information on their operational capabilities.

Japan's escalating war in China and the revival of the Soviet threat tempered the army's interest in amphibious landings during the 1930s. Between 1932 and 1940, the army conducted only two landing exercises.[26] Moreover, the three divisions it had designated for amphibious operations were assigned to support the war in Manchuria. Interest in amphibious operations continued nonetheless. In 1935 the army took delivery of *Shinshu-maru*, the world's first ship designed specifically for amphibious operations. Built in great secrecy, the vessel could carry twenty fully laden landing craft in a well deck that could be flooded and was capable of discharging vehicles directly onto a pier. It could also launch seaplanes from catapults on its deck.[27]

The July 7, 1937, attack on a detachment of the Japanese North China Garrison Army, known as the Marco Polo Bridge Incident, served as a pretext for Japan to extend its control across China. The war that ensued created new opportunities for, and constraints on, intelligence collection. In the months after the incident, the Japanese government clamped down on U.S. military officers in Japan and enacted strict censorship laws. As a result, the bulk of U.S. intelligence collection shifted to China, where American officers could observe Japanese combat operations firsthand. Although Japanese and Chinese military authorities tried their best to keep foreign observers from the war zone, U.S. Army and Marine Corps officers occasionally got an opportunity to observe Japanese forces in combat.

U.S. attachés in China played an important role in collecting and analyzing intelligence on Japanese military performance. The best known of these was Colonel Joseph W. Stilwell, who served from July 1935 to May 1939. He and his assistants, Captain Frank Dorn and Major David D. Barrett, confronted obstacles repeatedly in trying to cover the war. The Japanese in particular went to great lengths to restrict the movements of American officers to Peking and China's ports. The Chi-

25. Evans and Peattie, *Kaigun*, 443.

26. Drea, "Development of Amphibious Warfare," 18–19.

27. Hansgeorg Jentschura, Dieter Jung, and Peter Mickel, *Warships of the Imperial Japanese Navy, 1869–1945*, trans. Antony Preston and J. D. Brown (Annapolis: Naval Institute Press, 1992): 231; Evans and Peattie, *Kaigun*, 443.

nese also tried to keep observers away from the front, but the Americans routinely ignored their admonitions. The Chinese jailed Dorn twice during the nearly sixteen months he spent observing the war.[28]

The U.S. government received information from the U.S. naval attaché in Peking and his assistants as well. As Japan's war in China escalated, ONI attempted to move the attaché's office to Shanghai, site of the Japanese naval headquarters in China. The State Department rejected the idea, with Assistant Secretary of State Breckenridge Long explaining that ONI could dispatch attachés only to foreign capitals. Instead ONI assigned one of its most able and experienced operatives, Major Gregon A. Williams, to Shanghai. Williams, a veteran of intelligence operations in Latin America and the Caribbean, proved to be a valuable resource, working eighteen-hour days and developing a network of sources along the China coast.[29]

U.S. officers, particularly those attached to the 4th Marines in Shanghai, repeatedly risked imprisonment, injury, or death to report on the war. During the attack on Shanghai, for example, the regiment's intelligence officers—Majors James Monahan and Howard Stent and Captain R. A. Boone—and their assistants—Lieutenants Donn Hart and Victor Krulak—filed daily reports on ground, sea, and air operations. They also sent ONI and the Asiatic Fleet detailed maps of Chinese and Japanese positions, photographs of Japanese equipment, and weekly intelligence summaries.[30] They gathered information not only from firsthand observation, but also from Chinese agents, Americans working in China, and the attaché community.

The Japanese army conducted its first amphibious landing of the war on August 22–23, 1937, when troops from the 11th Division landed at Liuho and Woosung near the mouth of the Yangtze River in order to outflank Chinese forces and relieve their beleaguered garrison in Shanghai. The landing gave the United States its first opportunity in five years to observe Japanese amphibious operations. Krulak, the 4th Marines' assistant intelligence officer, filed the most comprehensive account of the landing. As Krulak later recalled, he and a Navy photographer's mate:

watched troops debarking into boats from transports. We watched destroyers deliver naval gunfire on the beach prior to the landing and in

28. John N. Hart, *The Making of an Army "Old China Hand": A Memoir of Colonel David D. Barrett,* Institute of East Asian Studies, University of California, Berkeley China Research Monograph 27 (1985): 22.

29. Jeffery M. Dorwart, *Conflict of Duty: The U.S. Navy's Intelligence Dilemma, 1919–1945* (Annapolis: Naval Institute Press, 1983): 134.

30. Ibid., 134; Reminiscences of Capt. Henri Smith-Hutton, USN (retired), USNI, 238.

support of the advancing troops afterwards. Most important, we got near enough to take close-up photographs of the assault landing craft.[31]

Krulak's detailed report described his observations of the landing.[32] He was particularly interested in the Japanese *daihatsu* landing craft, for it was precisely what the U.S. Marines had been looking for to implement the service's amphibious doctrine: a sturdy landing craft with a ramp bow that allowed it to drive up onto a beach. In Krulak's words, "What we saw was that the Japanese were light years ahead of us in landing craft design."[33] Marine intelligence reports emphasized the importance the landing, concluding that the "technique of landing from flat bottomed motor-scows which were carried 'nested' in the transports" represented "the only real surprise" of the conflict."[34]

Upon returning to Washington, D.C., in July 1939, Krulak took the report and a foot-long model of the landing craft to the commander of the 1st Marine Brigade at Quantico, Virginia, Brigadier General Holland M. Smith. The design intrigued Smith, who took Krulak to see the Commandant of the Marine Corps, General Thomas Holcomb, who eventually showed the model to the Secretary of the Navy.[35] Andrew Higgins, the Louisiana boat builder who designed the first Marine Corps landing craft, subsequently used pictures of the *daihatsu* to modify his boat's design to include a bow ramp.[36]

Japan conducted three other division-sized landings over the next few months: at Hangchow Bay near Shanghai in November 1937, Bias Bay near Hong Kong in October 1937, and Boca Tigris near Canton the same month.[37] While the 4th Marines witnessed the Japanese assault on Shanghai, they learned about these other operations secondhand. Nonetheless, in March 1939 ONI published a thirty-two-page classified assessment of Japanese landing operations in China. The report noted

31. Lt. Gen. Victor H. Krulak, USMC (retired), *First to Fight: An Inside View of the U.S. Marine Corps* (Annapolis: U.S. Naval Institute Press, 1984): 90.

32. First Lt. Victor H. Krulak, Asst R-2, Fourth Marines, "Report on Japanese Assault Landing Operations, Shanghai Area 1937," n.d. (received by ONI March 18, 1938), Box 77, *ONI Monograph Files*, RG 38, NA. See also "Japanese Landing Operations in the Present China Japanese Hostilities", n.d., in the same file.

33. Krulak, *First to Fight*, 91.

34. "Resume of Present China Incident," July 17, 1939, *Intelligence Reports from Headquarters, U.S. 4th. Marines, Shanghai, China*, Box 2, RG 38, NA, 3.

35. Krulak, *First to Fight*, 91.

36. Lt. Col. Kenneth J. Clifford, USMCR, *Progress and Purpose: A Developmental History of the United States Marine Corps, 1900–1970* (Washington, D.C.: U.S. Marine Corps, 1973): 51; Millett, "Assault from the Sea," 84.

37. Evans and Peattie, *Kaigun*, 444.

that "military students seeking answers to the multitudinous and infinitely detailed questions of modern landing force techniques soon realize that these operations are the first major landings conducted since the ill fated Gallipoli Expedition and that the tactics employed should be both an exposition and a test of the Japanese idea of modern landing operations."[38] The report described in great detail the techniques the Japanese used to reconnoiter a landing zone, the organization and command of amphibious forces, and naval gunfire support. It also contained a tactical reconstruction of the landings at Liuho-Woosung, Hangchow Bay, and Bias Bay, as well as the occupation of Hainan Island.

ONI paid particular attention to the *Shinshu-maru*, which it characterized as a "landing force tender." Although the Navy was able to photograph the ship and to estimate its dimensions, it remained an enigma. What little information the Navy obtained on its mission came secondhand. ONI reported that "no creditable foreign observer has seen boats launched in this manner or seen boats inside the hull."[39] Indeed, the office dismissed the *Shinshu-maru's* use as a landing craft transport. Instead, the Navy concluded that the Japanese used the vessel as a protected floating base and supply depot for landing forces, drawing an analogy to Britain's use of the merchant vessel SS *River Clyde* for the same purpose at Gallipoli. ONI failed to understand the unique mission of the *Shinshu-maru*, characterizing it as "an improvement" on the British prototype, nothing more.[40]

As the prospect of war increased, the Japanese began to strengthen and enlarge their amphibious forces. The Special Naval Landing Forces doubled in size and acquired heavy weapons, including 3-inch naval guns and howitzers. In late 1940, under the cover designation "Experiment 1001," the navy began secret paratroop training for select landing force members, a capability it put to use during the invasion of the Netherlands East Indies in 1941.[41] In October 1940 the Japanese army's 5th Division began to train for amphibious operations against a yet-unnamed adversary. Two months later, the 18th and Guards divisions also began amphibious training. The following year, these three divisions formed the core of Lieutenant General Tomoyuki Yamashita's 25th Army in the invasion of Malaya. In 1941, the newly raised 48th, 55th, and 56th divisions also acquired an amphibious mission. These units

38. "Japanese Landing Operations in the Present Sino-Japanese Conflict," *Monthly Information Bulletin* 18, no. 1 (March 1939): 79.
39. Ibid., 107.
40. Ibid., 110.
41. Evans and Peattie, *Kaigun*, 445.

subsequently participated in the invasion of the Philippines and Netherlands East Indies. This training, which occurred far from U.S. military observers in China, went largely unnoticed by the Army and Navy.

U.S. Intelligence and Japanese Amphibious Warfare

Washington had mixed success in monitoring the Japanese armed forces' development of amphibious landing techniques in the years leading up to World War II. By the time the United States entered the war, the U.S. armed forces had acquired an accurate understanding of Japanese amphibious tactics. Japanese landings in China were a valuable source of information on the doctrine and equipment necessary to carry out landings from the sea. In particular, information regarding Japanese landing craft designs influenced the acquisition of similar craft by the Marine Corps. ONI disseminated information regarding Japanese amphibious techniques throughout the armed forces in official publications.[42]

This understanding was, however, the product of at least two fortuitous events. First, the U.S. Marine Corps' experimentation with amphibious warfare made the Marines all the more interested in Japan's landing-force doctrine. Whereas early Army reports displayed considerable skepticism toward amphibious operations—based in part on the "lessons" of Gallipoli—the Marine Corps' exploration of similar concepts made it more open-minded. Second, despite Japanese attempts at concealment, the Marines were fortunate enough to witness a convincing demonstration of the effectiveness of amphibious techniques during the Shanghai Incident and the war in China. It is doubtful whether U.S. intelligence would have been nearly as effective were it not for such vivid evidence.

The utility of prewar intelligence had limits, however. Although U.S. observers gained insight into Japanese combat operations in China, such information could only provide the Army and Marine Corps clues to how the Japanese army would perform in the jungles of the Western Pacific and Southeast Asia. This was, however, hardly a failure of intelligence, for such information simply did not exist at the time. Not until January 1941 did the Japanese army form the Taiwan Army Research Department to study the requirements of jungle warfare. In June the army's special units on Formosa and in south China and French In-

---

42. See the reprint of ONI manual 225-J, "Japanese Landing Operations" in *Japanese Naval Vessels of World War Two as Seen by U.S. Naval Intelligence* (Annapolis: U.S. Naval Institute Press, 1987).

dochina began training for jungle warfare and developing countermeasures against American and British tactics; in September the army began to assemble troops for the operation.[43] Acquiring information on such preparations was simply beyond the capabilities of U.S. intelligence.

NAVAL SURFACE WARFARE

Japanese naval doctrine posed a different intelligence challenge. While the Japanese fleet superficially resembled that of Western navies, the prospect of fighting the larger, more technologically advanced U.S. Navy drove Tokyo to explore innovative approaches to war at sea. The Japanese navy developed a unique tactical system built on long-range guns and torpedoes and night combat. The navy also fielded innovative naval weapons, including the heavy destroyer, torpedo cruiser, midget submarine, and oxygen-propelled torpedo. Although U.S. naval intelligence uncovered the broad outlines of Japanese naval strategy, it failed to grasp crucial details of Japanese tactics and technology. These failures had deadly consequences when the two fleets met in the night battles off Guadalcanal between August 1942 and February 1943.

The Japanese navy's strategy of "interception-attrition operations" (*yogeki zengen sakusen*) sought to whittle down the American battle fleet before annihilating it in a decisive battle. At the outset of hostilities, the Japanese navy planned to destroy the U.S. Asiatic Fleet and occupy the Philippines and Guam. It would then sortie submarines into the Eastern Pacific to monitor the relief force and to harry it on its voyage west. Naval aircraft based in the Marshall, Mariana, and Caroline Islands would join the battle as soon as U.S. forces steamed into range. After the Japanese fleet reduced the American force to parity or less, it would conduct a decisive fleet action in seas near Japan. An advance body of cruisers and destroyers supported by fast battleships would engage the American fleet in a night attack using salvos of long-range torpedoes to weaken and confuse the Americans. At daybreak, the Japanese commander would throw the full weight of his battle line against the American fleet in a bid to annihilate it.[44]

---

43. Colonel Masanobu Tsuji, *Japan's Greatest Victory, Britain's Worst Defeat*, ed. H. V. Howe, trans. Margaret E. Lake (New York: Sarpedon Books, 1993): 1–18.; "History of Imperial General Headquarters, Army Section (1941–1945)" in *War in Asia and the Pacific, 1937–1949* 3, *Command, Administration, and Special Operations*, eds. Donald S. Detwiler and Charles B. Burdick (New York: Garland, 1980): 23, 43.

44. Evans and Peattie, *Kaigun*, 202–204; Rear Adm. Yoichi Hirama, Japan Maritime Self-Defense Force (JMSDF) (retired), "Japanese Naval Preparations for World War II," *Naval War College Review* 44, no. 2 (spring 1991): 64.

Not surprisingly, the Japanese navy was the primary target of U.S. naval intelligence during the interwar period. U.S. communications intelligence efforts in particular focused upon the Japanese navy. In 1938–1939, for example, Japanese naval codes and ciphers consumed all of the Navy's cryptanalysis and ninety percent of its translation activities.[45] Despite the concentration of resources, the Navy was able to read only about ten percent of the Japanese navy's coded traffic, mostly material encrypted in eight to ten minor cipher systems dealing with personnel, engineering, administration, weather, and fleet exercises. Because of both the difficulty of the task and a dearth of encoded material, the Navy read the main Japanese naval code, known as JN-25, only intermittently and was unable to read the flag officer's code.[46]

Despite these limitations, the U.S. Navy learned a lot about Japanese naval strategy from communications intercepted during fleet exercises. Radio transmissions confirmed that Japan's plans for a war with the United States centered on the seizure of Guam and the Philippines and the destruction of the American fleet as it steamed west.[47] U.S. intelligence estimates predicted that the Japanese navy would project its submarines as far east as possible, establish observation posts in the Marshall, Mariana, and Caroline Islands covering the most likely routes of U.S. advance, and dispatch fast surface combatants to reduce the U.S. fleet. U.S. intelligence also envisioned the use of aircraft based on carriers and flying from airfields in Japan's Micronesian island mandates to attack U.S. forces.[48] In other words, U.S. naval intelligence understood the main elements of Japanese naval strategy. The Navy incorporated this intelligence into both the U.S. plan for a war with Japan and war games at the Naval War College in Newport, Rhode Island.[49]

Although the Navy uncovered Japan's strategy for a war with the United States, ONI only partially understood Japanese naval tactics. The combination of U.S. preconceptions regarding war at sea and

45. Laurance F. Safford, "A Brief History of Communications Intelligence in the United States," SRH-149, *Records of the National Security Agency*, RG 457, NA.

46. David Kahn, *The Codebreakers: The Story of Secret Writing* (New York: Macmillan, 1967): 7. See also Richard J. Aldrich, *Intelligence and the War Against Japan: Britain, America, and the Politics of Secret Service* (Cambridge: Cambridge University Press, 2000): chap. 5.

47. "Op-20 Report on Japanese Grand Fleet Maneuvers (May-June 1930)" SRH-222, *Records of the National Security Agency*, RG 457, NA.

48. Joint Board to Secretary of the Navy, *Blue-Orange Joint Estimate of the Situation*, January 11, 1929, JB 325, Ser. 280, *Joint Board Records*, RG 225, NA, 43.

49. Michael Vlahos, *The BLUE Sword: The Naval War College and the American Mission, 1919–1941* (Newport, R.I.: Naval War College Press, 1980).

Japanese secrecy blinded naval intelligence to the unique features of Japan's approach.

Leaders of the Japanese navy believed that it needed to defeat the U.S. fleet in a decisive battle to win a war at sea. The quantitative superiority of the American battle fleet forced Japan to seek ways to offset the U.S. advantage. The Japanese naval staff believed that its ability to defeat the United States rested on ships that could outrange their American counterparts. Striking U.S. ships beyond their capability to return fire would allow the Japanese to inflict damage without sustaining losses. The Japanese navy therefore expended considerable effort to increase the range and accuracy of its gunfire, culminating in the *Yamato*-class battleships.[50] It also developed the Type 93 oxygen-propelled torpedo, also known as the *Long Lance*, a weapon with a larger warhead, greater speed, and longer range than American and British models.[51]

The Japanese navy also developed a tactical system for night combat.[52] In contrast to American tactics, which called for ships to deploy in a single column, Japanese ships deployed in short, multiple columns, often with destroyers positioned ahead of the main force to prevent ambush. On detecting an enemy force, the Japanese would close, pivot, fire torpedoes, then turn away. To exploit the characteristics of the Type 93, the Japanese developed the tactic of long-distance concealed firing (*enkyori ommitsu hassha*), which called for cruisers to fire between 120 and two hundred of the torpedoes at a distance of at least twenty thousand meters from the enemy battle line. Even if only ten percent of the weapons found their mark, the Japanese would be able to inflict considerable damage on their adversary.[53] To hone their skills, they conducted training exercises that were arduous and sometimes fatal. As a result, during World War II Japanese ships were often able to sight their targets before they themselves were spotted. Japanese warships would open engagements with salvos of torpedoes launched while still outside the range of U.S. gunfire. Only after the Japanese crews launched torpedoes would they resort to gunfire, and when they did they minimized use of searchlights to prevent U.S. ships

---

50. Evans and Peattie, *Kaigun*, chap. 8.

51. On the development of the *Long Lance*, see John Bullen, "The Japanese 'Long Lance' Torpedo and Its Place in History," *Imperial War Museum Review* no. 3 (1988): 69–79; Jiro Itani, Hans Lengerer, and Tomoko Rehm-Takahara, "Japanese Oxygen Torpedoes and Fire Control Systems" in *Warship 1991*, ed. Robert Gardiner (Annapolis, Md.: Naval Institute Press, 1991): 121–33; Evans and Peattie, *Kaigun*, 266–70.

52. Evans and Peattie, *Kaigun*, 273–81.

53. Ibid., 270–71.

from spotting them.[54] Such tactics could be extremely effective. During the Guadalcanal campaign, for example, Japanese torpedo barrages hit their targets up to twenty percent of the time.[55]

Night combat influenced the tactical organization of the Japanese navy as well. In 1924 the navy began to form night combat groups (*yasengun*) composed of destroyer squadrons led by light cruisers. In 1929 the Combined Fleet created a dedicated night battle force led by a heavy cruiser squadron.[56] Beginning in the mid-1930s, the navy equipped all eighteen of its heavy cruisers, some light cruisers, and most destroyers with launchers for the Type 93. The ultimate expression of this design philosophy was the reconstruction of the light cruisers *Oi* and *Kitakami* beginning in 1938 as "torpedo cruisers" carrying forty and thirty-two torpedo launchers, respectively.[57]

ONI noted the Japanese navy's emphasis on night action. The office's monograph on Japan observed that:

> The Japanese Navy places great emphasis on training for night operations. The Japanese are of the opinion that, at night, many of the disadvantages of having inferior materiel disappear and that spirit and morale—in which they believe they excel—combined with training and the ability to cooperate and coordinate will give them a decided advantage over an enemy fleet.[58]

U.S. naval doctrine reflected such a concern as well: the Navy's 1934 *War Instructions* warned that "at night the superior or equal force risks forfeiture of the superiority or equality of its most valuable asset, its coordinated hitting power."[59] A 1933 war game at the Naval War College vividly demonstrated the devastating impact of night attacks. During the game, held nine years before Vice Admiral Mikawa Gunichi battered Rear Admiral Richmond Kelly Turner's task force during the Battle of Savo Island, two ORANGE (Japanese) night attacks resulted

---

54. Paul S. Dull, *A Battle History of the Imperial Japanese Navy (1941–1945)* (Annapolis: Naval Institute Press, 1978): 60.

55. Wayne P. Hughes, *Fleet Tactics: Theory, and Practice* (Annapolis, Md.: Naval Institute Press, 1986), 120.

56. Hirama, "Japanese Naval Preparations for World War II," 67; Evans and Peattie, *Kaigun*, 275–76.

57. Jentschura, Jung, and Mickel, *Warships of the Imperial Japanese Navy*, 106.

58. ONI Report no. 261, "Night Training and Operations," October 18, 1934, 907–3000, Box 77, *ONI Monograph Files*, RG 38, NA.

59. *War Instructions, United States Navy*, FTP 143 (1934), World War II Command File, Chief of Naval Operations, Box 108, OA/NHC, 37.

in the loss of a BLUE (American) battleship and aircraft carrier, damage to two more battleships, and loss of or damage to twelve heavy cruisers, three light cruisers, thirty-one destroyers, and several auxiliaries.[60]

ONI nonetheless failed to recognize the full implications of the Japanese navy's emphasis upon night-fighting methods. Rather, too often American officers projected their own naval concepts on Japan. In 1941, for example, former Director of Naval Intelligence W. D. Puleston wrote that a "naval campaign in the western Pacific would be a clash of two well-prepared navies, with ships of the same types, organized in similar formations, trained along similar lines, imbued with similar tactical ideas."[61] War games at the Naval War College assumed that Japanese naval tactics were identical to those of the U.S. Navy and that Japanese torpedoes had a maximum range of six thousand yards at forty-six knots—less than one-quarter the range of the Type 93.[62]

Naval arms-control agreements influenced the size and composition of the Japanese navy. The 1922 Washington Naval Treaty between the United States, Great Britain, Japan, France, and Italy limited Japanese capital ships to 315,000 tons, sixty percent of the American and British allowance. The treaty forbade the construction of capital ships displacing more than 35,000 tons or guns in excess of sixteen inches. It permitted Japan to retain carriers totaling 81,000 tons and to convert two ships displacing 33,000 tons or less to carriers.[63] Although the treaty did not constrain total cruiser tonnage, it limited their displacement to 10,000 tons and main armament to eight inches.[64] The 1930 London Naval Agreement completed the arms limitation framework established in Washington eight years earlier by setting cruiser tonnage limits that allowed Japan to build seventy percent of the cruiser and destroyer tonnage of the United States and accorded it parity in submarines.[65]

---

60. Tactical Problem V-1933-SR (Operations Problem IV-1933-SR), critique by Capt. R. B. Coffey, January 16, 1934, RG 4, Naval Historical Collection, U.S. Naval War College, 25.

61. W. D. Puleston, *The Armed Forces of the Pacific* (New Haven, Conn.: Yale University Press, 1941): 232.

62. David Alan Rosenberg, "Being 'Red': The Challenge of Taking the Soviet Side in War Games at the Naval War College," *Naval War College Review* 41, no. 1 (winter 1988): 83; Ronald H. Spector, *Eagle against the Sun: The American War with Japan* (New York: The Free Press, 1984): 19.

63. Japan chose to convert the battle cruisers *Kaga* and *Akagi* to aircraft carriers rather than scrapping them under the terms of the treaty.

64. Harold and Margaret Sprout, *Toward a New Order of Sea Power: American Naval Power and the World Scene, 1918–1922* (New York: Greenwood Press, 1969): 302–11.

65. Stephen E. Pelz, *Race to Pearl Harbor: The Failure of the Second London Naval Conference and the Onset of World War II* (Cambridge: Harvard University Press, 1974): 2–3.

Although Japan was hardly an open society, the U.S. Navy obtained considerable information regarding Japanese naval construction—including accurate figures on the dimensions, tonnage, speed, and armament of Japanese warships—from public sources. U.S. naval attachés in Tokyo, for example, gleaned information on the Japanese naval order of battle from appropriations debates in the Diet.[66] The Navy also studied articles by naval commentators such as British journalist Hector Bywater.[67]

The Japanese navy's reliance on foreign expertise and technology offered yet another avenue for intelligence collection. The naval attaché in Tokyo monitored the arrival and movements of German and British specialists hired to help ameliorate shortfalls in Japan's aeronautics and shipbuilding industries, as well as the training of Japanese technicians in France.[68] A former German naval attaché and *Kriegsmarine* captain supplied ONI with rosters of German nationals employed by Japan.[69] The office also monitored Japanese purchases of machinery, steel, optics, radio equipment, and aircraft engines and parts from Germany, as well as diesel and steam turbine engines from Germany, Switzerland, and Italy.[70]

Periodic visits to shipyards and naval bases allowed attachés to gather information on Japanese naval construction. From the mid-1920s to the mid-1930s, the naval attaché or one of his assistants visited most Japanese naval bases, air stations, and aircraft factories at least once a year. During his tenure as assistant naval attaché between October 1928 and June 1930, for example, Arthur McCollum made regular trips to Kure, Sasebo, and Yokosuka, albeit under close Japanese scrutiny.[71] Because U.S. ships at sea faced no such restrictions, intelligence officers stationed aboard U.S. combatants were able to provide

66. Smith-Hutton Reminiscences, 151.

67. Bywater, an astute observer of the Japanese navy with an extensive network of contacts, was on a number of occasions able to uncover the construction of new Japanese ships and submarines before the Navy. See William H. Honan, *Visions of Infamy* (New York: St. Martin's Press, 1991); Robert B. Davies, "Hector C. Bywater and American Naval Journalism During the 1920s" in *New Aspects of Naval History: Selected Papers from the 5th Naval History Symposium*, ed. U.S. Naval Academy (Baltimore, Md.: The Nautical and Aviation Publishing Co. of America, 1981).

68. "Japanese Aeroplane and Submarine Mechanics to Go Abroad," *Monthly Information Bulletin* no. 8 (August 1920): 112.

69. C-10-j 12164, "Employment of ex-German Officers by Japan," *Naval Attaché Reports, 1921–1939*, Box 584, RG 38, NA.

70. William R. Braisted, *The United States Navy in the Pacific, 1909–1922* (Austin: University of Texas Press, 1971): 544.

71. Reminiscences of Rear Adm. Arthur H. McCollum, USN (retired), USNI, 111.

valuable information on the design and seaworthiness of Japanese vessels.

Before 1915, British shipyards built most of the Japanese navy's ships. Although Japanese construction programs paralleled those of the Royal Navy in the years that followed, by the late 1920s Japan had begun to develop a series of innovative naval designs, including fast, heavily armed cruisers and large, powerful destroyers.

The battleship was the centerpiece of both the American and Japanese navies during the interwar period. Thus, ONI devoted considerable attention to tracking Japanese battleship programs. Between January 1919 and June 1929, for example, the *Monthly Information Bulletin* contained thirty-five articles on Japanese battleships. Moreover, U.S. naval attachés toured half of Japan's ten battleships: the *Haruna, Fuso, Yamashiro, Nagato,* and *Mutsu*. Like other visits, they were brief and closely supervised. Nevertheless, just walking the decks of a Japanese battleship often yielded clues to their wartime effectiveness. Lieutenant Commander Franz Melendy, for example, noted details of the *Fuso's* fire control systems during his visit to the ship in 1925. [72] Information collected during such tours could also reveal vulnerabilities of Japanese ship designs. As Captain Lyman A. Cotton noted after visiting the *Mutsu,*

> The most striking feature of the entire ship is the appalling size of the one and only engine room. There isn't the semblance of a bulkhead anywhere in this enormous space and consequently the ship is pitifully vulnerable.[73]

Japanese cruiser designs featured high speed, wide radius of action, and heavy armament. The *Myoko* class was the first to exploit the Washington Naval Treaty's 10,000-ton displacement limit.[74] U.S. naval officers had several opportunities to observe the ships under construction. In March 1928, for example, Commander George Courts saw the *Ashigara* at the Kawasaki shipyard at Kobe and the *Haguro* at the Mitsubishi shipyard at Nagasaki.[75] The destroyer tender USS *Black Hawk* got a better view of the *Haguro's* hull under construction as the auxiliary lay at anchor in Nagasaki harbor. The ship's intelligence officer

72. "Visit to the Battleship *Fuso*," November 12, 1925, O–12-c 1977, "Japanese Battleship *Fuso*," *Naval Attaché Reports, 1921–1939,* Box 1262, RG 38, NA.

73. "Data Regarding *Mutsu* (BB)," February 17, 1922, O–12-c 2971, "Japanese Battleships of 1913 Program," *Naval Attaché Reports, 1921–1939,* box 1262, RG 38, NA, 9.

74. Designed to meet treaty limits, its final standard tonnage grew to 10,940 as a result of requirements levied by the Navy General Staff.

75. O-12-c 16068 "Japanese Cruisers (Myoko Class—10,000 Tons)," *Naval Attaché Reports, 1889-1939,* Box 1267, RG 38, NA.

sent Washington a detailed report on the vessel, including accurate figures for its dimensions and displacement.[76]

The Japanese navy envisioned using its torpedo-equipped light cruisers as destroyer group leaders. Such a mission required that the ships combine heavy armament with high speed in a hull of modest size. The *Yubari* class was a prototype of such a design, followed by the ships of the *Furutaka* and *Kako* classes. The *Furutaka* class in particular drew international scrutiny. Smaller and less expensive than a heavy cruiser, the ship nonetheless packed a considerable punch. As Bywater noted in a May 1925 column, "No other country but Japan is building cruisers which combine moderate size and cost with a battery of heavy guns, for the foreign ships which approximate to the *Furutaka* in tonnage do not approach her in fighting power." The British naval attaché, for his part, noted that Britain had "not been able to design a ship of the tonnage of the *Furutaka* with a battery of that size and give her the required speed, cruising radius, and structural strength." Naval attaché reports provided accurate figures for the cruiser, including its maximum speed of thirty-three knots and its armament of six eight-inch guns and twelve twenty-one-inch torpedo tubes.[77]

While ONI generally succeeded in determining the characteristics of Japanese warships, the combination of Japanese secrecy and U.S. ethnocentrism often distorted perceptions of Japanese capabilities in subtle but important ways. In several cases U.S. naval intelligence officers managed to gather what turned out to be accurate information on new weapon systems, only to have the Navy disregard it because it contradicted an ingrained belief of U.S. technological superiority. In the words of a former head of ONI's Far East Section, "The tendency was to judge technical developments on the basis of our own technology and on the assumption that our technology was superior to any other. So if something was reported that the Japanese did have and we didn't then, obviously, it was wrong."[78] The failure to understand novel technological developments would have dire consequences when the American and Japanese navies met in combat.

Japan's development of long-range naval gunfire is a case in point. In 1931, the Japanese navy adopted the Type 91 armor-piercing shell, which had a tapered base and streamlined nose that allowed it to travel

76. O-12-c 16068A "Japanese Cruisers (Myoko Class—10,000 Tons)," *Naval Attaché Reports, 1889–1939,* Box 1269, RG 38, NA.

77. O-12-c, 14524, "Japanese Light Cruisers (7100 tons) of *FURUTAKA* Class," *Naval Attaché Reports, 1889–1939,* Box 1268, RG 38, NA.

78. McCollum Reminiscences, 146.

much farther than similar American shells.[79] The ordnance first saw action during the Shanghai Incident the following year. During the Japanese navy's bombardment of the city, the Asiatic Fleet's intelligence officer observed that the eight-inch guns on Japanese cruisers appeared to outrange their American counterparts. The Navy's Bureau of Ordnance (BuOrd), asked to evaluate the report, responded that such a capability was impossible. The reason for the discrepancy became apparent when the Asiatic Fleet recovered some of the rounds and sent them to Washington for analysis. BuOrd had assumed that the Japanese were using projectiles identical to those used by U.S. cruisers, rather than the long-range Type 91 shell. Indeed, the United States lacked a comparable capability until several years later, when the Navy modified the *Portland*-class heavy cruisers to fire similar projectiles.[80]

The war in China had a considerable impact on U.S. intelligence collection. As tension between Tokyo and Washington mounted, the Japanese government tightened restrictions on U.S. naval attachés. In 1939 Japan enacted a law classifying a broad range of information secret and providing stiff penalties for disclosure.[81] The government censored newspapers and magazines and ordered its officers to avoid contact with Americans. The Japanese navy also began to deny all requests to visit its facilities. As a result, between 1939 and 1941 the naval attaché and his assistants were unable to make a single official visit to a Japanese naval installation.[82] The combination of increasing security and expansion of the Japanese fleet after Tokyo's abrogation of its naval arms limitation commitments decreased markedly the accuracy of U.S. assessments in the five years prior to World War II.

Under such restrictions, attachés resorted to clandestine methods of intelligence collection. Between 1939 and 1941, the U.S. naval attaché repeatedly dispatched Lieutenant Stephen Jurika to gather information regarding Japanese ship launchings, based on notices in the press. Jurika would observe activity at the Mitsubishi shipyard in Kobe from a room in the Tor or Orient hotels, snapping photographs of ships lying on the slipways below using his office's Leica camera. He used a similar arrangement in Sasebo. Observing the Mitsubishi yard at Yokohama was easier, as a number of Americans employed by the U.S. consulate and by Standard Oil Company had houses on the bluffs above the shipyard.[83]

79. Evans and Peattie, *Kaigun,* 260.
80. McCollum Reminiscences, 151.
81. Prados, *Combined Fleet Decoded,* 31.
82. Jurika Reminiscences, 353.
83. Ibid., 334, 345, 350.

[65]

Naval reserve officers working for American shipping lines helped Jurika gather information on Japanese building programs as well. The Navy required him to log a certain number of flight hours in the Philippines each year to maintain his qualifications as an aviator. His voyages to and from the islands provided ideal opportunities to gather intelligence on Japanese naval construction. By arrangement with the captain, his ship would sail close to vessels under construction in the harbor. Meanwhile, he would set up a camera inside the porthole of his stateroom so that he could snap several pictures as the ship passed the docks. As he later recalled:

> We got some information that way, usually just enough to say, yes, there's a big ship or there's a medium-sized ship or there's something that's going to be launched in the next ninety days or they've just laid a keel. You could tell by the bulk and the scaffolding around the particular thing, but not really too much information that way [*sic*].[84]

During the 1930s, the Japanese navy modernized its older battleships to increase their speed and protection; this included installing new boilers, larger masts, high-elevation guns for long-range firing, thicker deck armor and torpedo bulges, and catapults for sea planes.[85] The *Kongo* class twice got new boilers and more efficient machinery, a process that boosted the power of their engines from 64,000 to 136,000 horsepower and increased their speed from twenty-six to thirty knots. Other battleships received similar treatment.[86] Japanese security measures prevented the U.S. Navy from learning the impact of these changes, however. Although attaché reports described the reconstruction of Japanese capital ships in detail, ONI did not incorporate this information in its performance estimates of the Japanese battle fleet. The office continued to list the battleships at their pre-modernization displacement, even though the addition of deck armor and torpedo bulges had added substantial weight to the ships, pushing some over the 35,000-ton limit established by the Washington Naval Treaty (see Table 3). Nor did ONI reports reflect that the reconstruction of Japanese battleships had substantially increased their speed. In fact, the reports underestimated the post-modernization speed of the vessels by as much as four knots in the case of *Kongo* and her sister ships. It was not until the Guadalcanal

84. Ibid., 346.
85. O-12-c 20839 "Modernization of Japanese Capital Ships," *Naval Attaché Reports, 1921–1939*, Box 1269, RG 38, NA.
86. Evans and Peattie, *Kaigun*, 276.

Table 3   ONI Estimate of Japanese Battleship Tonnage and Speed, December 1941

Battleship	Std. Displacement (tons)		Max. Speed (kts)	
	Estimate	Actual	Estimate	Actual
Kongo *Hiei* *Kirishima* *Haruna*	29,300	32,156	26	30
Fuso *Yamashiro*	29,300	34,700	23	24.7
Ise *Hyuga*	29,990	35,800	23	25.3
Nagato *Mutsu*	32,720	39,130	26	26

Actual. Hansgeorg Jentschura, Dieter Jung, and Peter Mickel, *Warships of the Imperial Japanese Navy, 1869–1945,* trans. by Antony Preston and J.D. Brown (Annapolis: Naval Institute Press, 1992).

Estimate. "Japan Navy Ships," December 18, 1941, O-12-c 7314, "Lists of Vessels, Japanese Navy," *Confidential Reports of Naval Attaches, 1940–1946,* RG 38, NA.

campaign in October 1942 that U.S. forces began to realize that older Japanese battleships were much faster than expected.[87]

Radio intelligence provided the only solid evidence that the reconstruction of Japanese battleships had significantly increased their speed. Intercepts collected during the *Nagato*'s post-modernization trials in 1936 indicated that the ship's maximum speed was twenty-six knots, two-and-a-half knots higher than had been previously believed. From these intercepts, the Navy inferred that the *Mutsu* and vessels then under construction would also have such speed.[88] As a result of this information, the Navy increased the maximum speed of the *North Carolina* class to twenty-seven knots and that of the *South Dakota* class to thirty.[89]

87. Malcolm Muir Jr., "Rearming in a Vacuum: United States Naval Intelligence and the Japanese Capital Ship Threat, 1936–1945," *The Journal of Military History* 54, no. 4 (October 1990): 474.

88. CAPT L. F. Safford, USN, "'The Undeclared War', History of R.I.," SRH-305, *Records of the National Security Agency,* RG 457, NA.

89. Baer, *One Hundred Years of Sea Power,* 137; Norman Friedman, *U.S. Battleships: An Illustrated Design History* (London: Arms and Armour Press, 1985): 285; Safford, "'The Undeclared War'," 243.

Japanese secrecy also undermined the ability of the United States to determine the characteristics of the *Yamato*-class battleships. When launched, the leviathans had a standard displacement of 64,000 tons and a speed of twenty-seven knots; each ship also had nine eighteen-inch guns that could fire 3,220-pound shells more than twenty-five miles. The ships possessed armor belts more than sixteen inches thick, while the faceplates on the main battery turrets were more than twenty-five inches thick, the heaviest armor ever installed on a warship.[90]

The Japanese navy went to extraordinary lengths to conceal the construction of the massive ships. Workers at the Kure Naval Arsenal erected a large fence around the dry dock, which had been deepened to accommodate the massive hull of the *Yamato*. The task of hiding the construction of the *Musashi* at Mitsubishi's Nagasaki shipyard was more difficult, since the city's streets (and the U.S. consulate) over-looked the docks, and mountains surrounded the harbor on three sides. To screen construction from prying eyes, dock workers wove huge hemp curtains to enclose the slipway on which the *Musashi* was being built and erected a long two-story warehouse to block the con-sulate's view of the harbor.[91]

ONI managed to gather only fragmentary data on construction of the battleships. Some nine months after the keel of the *Musashi* had been laid, a British assistant naval attaché informed his American counterpart that the Japanese navy was building a battleship on the ways of the Mitsubishi dockyard at Nagasaki. Moreover, the lengthen-ing and reinforcement of the slipway indicated that the vessel was "extra large and heavy."[92] Japanese security measures nonetheless de-nied the United States accurate information on both the total number of ships under construction as well as their technical characteristics. ONI believed that the Japanese navy was building eight battleships displac-ing between 40,000 and 45,000 tons instead of the four 64,000-ton ships that were actually under construction. Moreover, the office believed the ships would have twelve sixteen-inch guns instead of the nine eighteen-inch guns they in fact carried.[93] The British, French, German, and Italian attachés shared the view.[94] It was not until after the out-

90. Janusz Skulski, *The Battleship Yamato* (Annapolis: Naval Institute Press, 1988).

91. Akira Yoshimura, *Build the Musashi!: The Birth and Death of the World's Greatest Battleship* (Tokyo: Kodansha International, 1991); Muir, "Rearming in a Vacuum," 476.

92. O–12-e 7206-S, "Capital Ship Construction," January 16, 1939, *Selected Naval At-taché Reports Relating to the World Crisis, 1937–1943*, RG 38, NA, 1.

93. "The Japanese Naval Building Program," April 1, 1940, O–12-c 7206, *Confidential Reports of Naval Attachés, 1940–1946*, RG 38, NA.

94. Prados, *Combined Fleet Decoded*, 22.

Table 4 ONI Estimate of Japanese Cruiser Tonnage and Speed, December 1941

Cruiser	Std. Displacement (tons)		Max. Speed (kts)	
	Estimate	Actual	Estimate	Actual
Furutaka Kako	7,100	8,700	33	32.9
Aoba Kinugasa	7,100	9,000	33	33.4
Nachi Haguro Myoko Ashigara	10,000	13,000	33	33.8
Takao Atago Chokai Maya	9,850	13,400	33	34.2
Mogami Mikuma Suzuya Kumano	8,500	11,200	33	35
Tone Chikuma	8,500	11,215	33	35.2

Actual. Hansgeorg Jentschura, Dieter Jung, and Peter Mickel. *Warships of the Imperial Japanese Navy, 1869–1945,* trans. Antony Preston and J. D. Brown. (Annapolis: U.S. Naval Institute Press, 1992).

Estimate. "Japan Navy Ships," December 18, 1941, O–12-c 7314, "Lists of Vessels, Japanese Navy," *Confidential Reports of Naval Attaches, 1940–1946,* RG 38, NA.

break of World War II that communications intelligence, captured documents, and prisoner interrogation began to give the Navy a more accurate understanding of the ships' characteristics.[95]

After the Japanese government abrogated its naval arms control commitments, the navy embarked on an extensive program to modernize its cruisers, equipping them with tubes for the Type 93 torpedo and new anti-aircraft armament. Such modifications substantially increased the tonnage of the ships, pushing all classes of heavy cruisers over the 10,000-ton limit. However, ONI failed to comprehend the impact of the modernization program on the ships' performance.

Indeed, the Navy dismissed whatever accurate information naval attachés were able to gather regarding Japanese cruiser modernization. Between 1939 and 1940, the navy replaced the fifteen six-inch mounts

95. Muir, "Rearming in a Vacuum," 483.

on the *Mogami*-class cruisers with ten eight-inch guns. The U.S. naval attaché in Tokyo, Lieutenant Commander Smith-Hutton, learned of the reconstruction of the cruisers in early April 1940 from a source who had been aboard the ship and dutifully reported the information to ONI in Washington. The Bureau of Ordnance dismissed the report, arguing that the ship's design could not tolerate the weight of the new turrets.[96]

The Japanese navy also fielded new types of weapons, such as the Type 93 torpedo. The weapon was large, with a weight of 2,700 kilograms (nearly three tons), a diameter of sixty-one centimeters (approximately twenty-four inches), a length of some nine meters, and nearly 500 kilograms (over 1,000 pounds) of explosive in its warhead. The torpedo was capable of speeds of up to forty-eight knots and of ranges up to 40,000 meters. Fueled by high-pressure oxygen, it left virtually no wake. The Japanese navy went to considerable lengths to keep the weapon secret, conducting closely guarded tests and recovering practice torpedoes to minimize the chance they would fall into foreign hands. The Type 93 was first launched successfully in 1933, and within six years most cruisers and destroyers had been equipped to carry the weapon.[97]

The development of the Type 93 offers yet another example of how preconceptions can skew analysis. Contrary to popular belief, U.S. naval intelligence did obtain evidence of the development of the weapon. The first clue to its existence appeared in a May 1934 ONI translation of a Japanese article claiming that "our latest torpedoes ran with practically no track." Although one of the officers who read the report highlighted the passage, there is no evidence that ONI pursued the issue.[98]

Indeed, the matter might have rested there had the naval attaché in Tokyo, Smith-Hutton, not been approached one day in late 1939 or early 1940 at the Tokyo Tennis Club by a Japanese medical student. The man, Chinese by birth and heritage, turned to the American out of anger over the atrocities committed by the Japanese army in China. Moreover, as a Japanese citizen he could provide Smith-Hutton with

96. Smith-Hutton Reminiscences, 302. See also "Re-Gunning of *Mogami* Class Cruisers with 8-Inch Guns," April 8, 1940, "Japanese 8500-T 6in Gun Cruisers," O-12-b 21303, *Confidential Reports of Naval Attaches, 1940–1946*, Box 1216, RG 38, NA.

97. A subsurface version of the weapon, the Type 95, was adopted in 1935. An aerial version of the weapon, the Type 94, was also developed. In 1940, an improved version began to be installed on Japanese destroyers. Evans and Peattie, *Kaigun*, 266–70. See also Carl Boyd, "Japanese Military Effectiveness: The Interwar Period," in Allan R. Millett and Williamson Murray, eds., *Military Effectiveness*, Volume II, *The Interwar Years* (Boston: Unwyn Hyman, 1988), 159.

98. P-10–1 6452-s, "Submarines, Japan," *Naval Attaché Reports, 1921–1939*, Box 1297, RG 38, NA.

information that would have otherwise been beyond the American's reach. Although U.S. officers faced mounting restrictions on their activities, the Japanese navy regularly gave students tours of its vessels to foment nationalism and to boost recruitment. Smith-Hutton asked the student to ascertain whether Japanese destroyers had been equipped to carry torpedoes larger than standard twenty-one-inch models. The man subsequently toured a destroyer and reported that its torpedo tubes had a diameter of approximately twenty-five inches. More important, he informed the attaché that the Japanese had developed an oxygen-propelled torpedo with a warhead of 1,200 pounds capable of traveling 10,000 yards at a speed of forty-five knots.[99] Although the report understated the range of the torpedo, it nonetheless gave ONI a hint of the weapon's capabilities.

Smith-Hutton sent a report describing the torpedo's characteristics to ONI's Far East Section on April 20, 1940. Lieutenant Commander McCollum, director of the section, was struck by the "phenomenal" speed, range, and payload of the weapon, and forwarded the report to the Bureau of Ordnance for evaluation. The Navy's technical experts declared such a weapon to be impossible. In so doing, they apparently dismissed the possibility that in using oxygen the Japanese would have mastered a propellant that was both light and energetic, allowing them to produce a torpedo that was fast and capable of carrying a large warhead over a long distance.[100] Rather, BuOrd appears to have assumed that the new torpedo continued to use air/steam propulsion. Why BuOrd officials would have made this assumption is unclear, especially considering Smith-Hutton's report from Tokyo. Such an assumption could have been based on misperceptions about U.S. technical superiority; after all, neither the United States nor Britain had mastered oxygen propulsion, so how could Japan have done so?[101] Or it may have been that BuOrd's analysts were unable to estimate the weapon's characteristics accurately because the U.S. Navy lacked experience in oxygen-propelled torpedoes. Regardless of the reason, the effect was the same: analytical constructs based on the orthodox view of naval technology blinded the U.S. Navy to the development of an innovative weapon by the Japanese. Allied forces would pay the price of this

99. When Smith-Hutton asked ONI for funds to pay the source, ONI told him to discontinue contact with him. The Japanese attacked Pearl Harbor shortly thereafter, and the source was never heard from again. Smith-Hutton Reminiscences, 299–301.

100. McCollum Reminiscences, 147.

101. Ironically, the Japanese navy decided to pursue oxygen propulsion because they mistakenly believed that the British already possessed a similar capability. See Itani, Lengerer, and Rehm-Takahara, "Japanese Oxygen Torpedoes," 123–24; Marder, *Old Friends, New Enemies*, 309.

failure when the Japanese used the Type 93 to deadly effect during the battles of Java Sea, Savo Island, and Tassafaronga. It was not until April 1943, three years after Smith-Hutton had informed ONI of the existence of the Type 93, that ONI finally concluded, based on interrogations of Japanese prisoners, that enemy cruisers and destroyers were armed with twenty-four-inch torpedoes.[102]

U.S. Naval Intelligence and the Japanese Fleet

The U.S. Navy did a reasonably good job of monitoring Japanese naval technology throughout the 1920s and early 1930s. Still, preconceptions influenced U.S. assessments of the Japanese navy in subtle ways. The Navy's experts repeatedly dismissed accurate information indicating that the Japanese had mastered technologies that the United States lacked. The Navy's willingness to discount indicators of Japanese innovation was in part a reflection of the widespread assumption that Japan was inferior to the United States in naval technology. It was also, however, the result of the Navy's inability to empirically verify the claims made by the intelligence reports.

The combination of secrecy and rapid development of technology degraded considerably the Navy's ability to track Japanese naval technology in the years preceding World War II. Naval attachés who were used to collecting intelligence in a relatively overt manner were handicapped when Tokyo took away these avenues. In the years that followed, the Japanese government effectively denied the United States clandestine avenues of gathering information.

Deeply held beliefs about war at sea also influenced the Navy's perception of Japanese tactics. Although ONI noted the Japanese navy's interest in night combat, for example, it failed to appreciate fully the features of Japanese naval doctrine and the leverage it would offer in a future war.

CARRIER AVIATION

Mastery of carrier air power gave Tokyo its most decisive battlefield success of World War II. On December 7, 1941, torpedoes and dive-bombers from all six of Japan's aircraft carriers struck the U.S. Pacific Fleet at anchor at Pearl Harbor. The attack dealt the U.S. Navy the greatest defeat in its history, killing or wounding more than 3,500

102. Prados, *Combined Fleet Decoded*, 31–32.

Americans and destroying or damaging nine battleships and nearly 350 aircraft.

The Imperial Japanese Navy laid the groundwork for the attack on Pearl Harbor with experimentation throughout the 1920s and 1930s. Although U.S. intelligence did a good job of tracking the development of Japanese technology, particularly prior to the outbreak of the war in China, it experienced much greater difficulty determining how the Japanese navy would employ aircraft carriers. The secrecy that shrouded Japanese carrier programs, the rapid evolution of aircraft technology, and the navy's own uncertainty over carrier doctrine compounded the problem. Because Japanese naval air power matured only in the late 1930s, the United States had little time to accumulate evidence of Tokyo's advances.

From the perspective of the 1920s and early 1930s, there was little reason to believe that the aircraft carrier would supplant the battleship as the centerpiece of war at sea. Early carriers suffered from difficulties with propulsion, hull structure, and seaworthiness. Ship designers had yet to figure out how best to configure a carrier to accommodate aircraft. The first naval aircraft were small and fragile, with short range and low payload. Not until the mid-1930s did high-performance aircraft constructed of metal and equipped with powerful radial engines and retractable landing gear begin to appear. These aircraft, in turn, transformed the carrier from a defensive to an offensive weapon.

It was similarly easy for Western powers to underestimate Japanese naval air power. During the 1920s, Japan employed mainly obsolete aircraft licensed from European manufacturers and had a shortage of pilots. The British aviators who trained the Imperial Japanese Navy Air Force (IJNAF) considered their students mediocre.[103] Japan nonetheless began to build a substantial domestic aviation industry, first through licensed production of foreign engines and airframes, and then through the manufacture of increasingly capable indigenous designs.[104] By the late 1930s, Japan had become a force to be reckoned with in the air. The central challenge facing Western intelligence was to look beyond Japan's traditional dependence on foreign technology and expertise and to detect its development of a mature air force.

Japanese carrier aviation took its first steps under British tutelage. Britain supplied Japan with its first naval aircraft, and British naval architects helped design its first carrier, the *Hosho*. Displacing less than

---

103. Marder, *Old Friends, New Enemies*, 345. See also "British Instructor's Statement Regarding Japanese Aviators," *Monthly Information Bulletin* no. 10 (October 1922): 87.

104. See Robert C. Mikesh and Shorzoe Abe, *Japanese Aircraft: 1910–1941* (Annapolis: U.S. Naval Institute Press, 1990).

8,000 tons and capable of embarking only twenty or so aircraft, the *Hosho* was essentially an experimental vessel. Though handicapped by small size, the carrier served as a valuable laboratory for carrier design, construction, and flight operations.[105]

The Washington Naval Agreement permitted Japan to convert two capital ships to aircraft carriers. The navy elected to exercise this option with the battleship *Kaga* and battle cruiser *Akagi*.[106] As completed in 1926, the carrier *Kaga* displaced 26,000 tons, had a speed of over twenty-eight knots, and carried sixty aircraft. Her sister ship, completed the following year, embarked a similar complement of aircraft but was both heavier and faster.[107] The two carriers featured three flight decks stacked one atop the other, an arrangement the Japanese believed would accelerate flight operations by making it possible simultaneously to launch and to recover aircraft.[108] Each had ten eight-inch guns in armored casemates.

In contrast to the access U.S. naval attachés enjoyed to Japanese battleships, gathering intelligence on aircraft carriers proved to be a challenge, and reports on their characteristics were few and far between. Indeed, the Japanese navy treated carrier operations with utmost secrecy, hiding films of the first flight operations on the *Hosho* from even the pilot hired to perform the landings.[109]

Most intelligence reports describing Japanese carriers were based on glimpses of the ships during dockyard visits or on fortuitous sightings at sea. U.S. naval attachés nonetheless managed to gather accurate information by observing the *Kaga* under construction at Yokosuka and the *Akagi* at Kure. They also attended fleet reviews in which the carriers participated. ONI was also able to identify modifications implemented when the carriers were modernized in the mid- 1930s.[110]

Communications intelligence proved to be the most lucrative source of information regarding Japanese carrier operations. The U.S. Navy, for example, went to great lengths to collect intelligence during the Japanese navy's 1927 Grand Fleet Maneuvers, which included op-

---

105. Evans and Peattie, *Kaigun,* 314–15.

106. The Japanese navy originally planned to convert the battle cruiser *Amagi,* but she was badly damaged during the earthquake that struck the Tokyo area on September 1, 1923, and was subsequently scrapped. The *Kaga* was converted in her place.

107. Jentschura, Jung, and Mickel, *Warships of the Imperial Japanese Navy,* 42–44.

108. Between 1934 and 1938 the two carriers were reconstructed to give them a full-length flight deck. The *Kaga* received a starboard-side island; *Akagi* received a port-side island.

109. "Airplane Landings on Hosho," *Monthly Information Bulletin* no. 5 (May 1923): 7.

110. O-12-c 12484, "Vessels Fitted for Carrying Aircraft, Japan," *Naval Attaché Reports, 1921–1939,* Box 1265, RG 38, NA.

erations from the *Akagi*. The Navy took advantage of the fact that the light cruiser USS *Marblehead* had previously been scheduled to pay a courtesy call on Kobe and Nagasaki. Naval intelligence smuggled monitoring equipment and radio operators aboard the cruiser as she lay at anchor in Shanghai's harbor.[111] At sea, a destroyer squadron from the Philippines that had been sent to observe the exercise visually joined her.

Some one hundred seventy Japanese ships took part in the maneuvers. When U.S. destroyers steamed across the path of the Japanese force, the *Akagi*'s escorts interposed themselves, laying a smoke screen to conceal flight operations. All the while, the *Marblehead* lurked over the horizon, plucking radio signals out of the ether. The equipment on board the cruiser gave U.S. naval intelligence its first opportunity to pierce the veil of secrecy that had surrounded Japanese naval operations and to locate and identify Japanese naval combatants participating in the maneuvers. The surveillance also indicated that the Japanese had yet to perfect techniques for landing on the carrier's narrow deck.[112]

Monitoring Japanese aircraft development required less ingenuity. From the early 1920s until the outbreak of the war in China in 1937, U.S. attachés and their assistants visited Japanese aircraft factories frequently. From time to time, they escorted representatives of U.S. aircraft manufacturers on tours of Japanese aircraft plants. ONI solicited the views of representatives of U.S. and British aviation companies regarding Japanese aeronautical developments.[113] MID, by contrast, was reticent to exploit U.S. businessmen as a source of intelligence. As one officer put it, "In order not to embarrass or handicap representatives of American aviation firms in Japan, the Military Attaché pursues the policy of having practically no contact with these American business men. As a consequence, the information obtained by these qualified observers is not available to this office."[114]

The U.S. Navy also dispatched aviators to inspect Japanese naval air bases. In the spring of 1927, Commander George Courts arranged for

---

111. Ellis M. Zacharias, *Secret Missions: The Story of an Intelligence Officer* (New York: G. P. Putnam's Sons, 1946), 104; "The Orange Maneuvers and Analysis of Information Obtained," SRH-206, in *Listening to the Enemy: Documents on Communications Intelligence in the War with Japan*, ed. Spector (Wilmington, Del.: Scholarly Resources, 1988): 14.

112. Zacharias, *Secret Missions*, 105.

113. A-1-a 21684, "Efficiency of Japanese Aviation, Material and Personnel," *Naval Attaché Reports, 1889–1939*, Box 10, RG 38, NA.

114. MID 2085–895/1, "Air Information," April 28, 1934, *Military Intelligence Division Correspondence, 1918–1941*, Roll 30, RG 165, NA.

the Commander-in-Chief of the U.S. Asiatic Fleet to assign a naval aviator to Japan for a two-month tour to inspect Japan's naval air stations. The first such aviator, Lieutenant J. J. Ballentine, toured all of Japan's naval air stations.[115] Others followed.

The belief that the Japanese were poor pilots dominated the popular press. The naval author Fletcher Pratt advanced a number of theories to explain the inability of Japanese pilots to fly, including the claim that a fluid imbalance in their inner ears prevented them from flying straight.[116] Former Director of Naval Intelligence William D. Puleston described Japanese naval aviation in more measured terms. He said that although Japan had made considerable efforts to catch up to the West, Japanese naval aviation was "usually a phase behind" its foreign counterparts.[117]

Ethnic stereotypes aside, Japanese naval aviation in the early years did experience a host of problems. Japanese aircraft lagged behind those of Great Britain and the United States throughout much of the interwar period. The Japanese navy, unlike its American and British counterparts, relied overwhelmingly on enlisted men for aviators. At the time of Pearl Harbor, ninety percent of Japanese naval aviators were enlisted.[118] As a result, aviation enjoyed low prestige within the navy.[119]

Uncovering Japanese naval air doctrine proved to be a challenge. In part this was because during the early 1920s the Japanese navy had no formal doctrine for employing aircraft carriers. Rather, the navy viewed carriers as experimental platforms. Not until the navy combined the *Hosho, Kaga,* and *Akagi* into the First Carrier Division in 1928 did naval officers begin to think seriously about carrier aviation.[120] In the years that followed, the navy viewed the carrier as a defensive asset. In fleet maneuvers between 1928 and 1935, commanders employed carrier-based fighters almost exclusively to repel enemy spotter aircraft and to protect friendly observation planes.[121]

115. Smith-Hutton Reminiscences, 74.

116. Fletcher Pratt, *Sea Power and Today's War* (New York: Harrison-Hilton Books, 1939): 177–79.

117. W. D. Puleston, *The Armed Forces of the Pacific: A Comparison of the Military and Naval Power of the United States and Japan* (New Haven: Yale University Press, 1941): 226.

118. Evans and Peattie, *Kaigun,* 325.

119. Marder, *Old Friends, New Enemies,* 304–305; Evans and Peattie, *Kaigun,* 324–25.

120. Evans and Peattie, *Kaigun,* 332.

121. Boyd, "Japanese Military Effectiveness," 134; Thomas C. Hone and Mark D. Mandeles, "Interwar Innovation in Three Navies: U.S. Navy, Royal Navy, Imperial Japanese Navy," *Naval War College Review* 40, no. 2 (spring 1987): 71; Marder, *Old Friends, New Enemies,* 312.

Japanese naval aviation played an important role in the opening phases of the war in China. Aircraft operating from carriers and from the island of Formosa secured air superiority over Shanghai and cooperated with the Shanghai Expeditionary Army in its attack on the city.[122] The war also offered new opportunities to observe the performance of the IJNAF. During the attack, for example, the Japanese established an air base near the Shanghai Electric Company, an American-owned plant on the outskirts of the city. The Asiatic Fleet's commander in chief, Rear Admiral Harry Yarnell, assigned a naval aviator to command the landing force sent to protect the plant. Lieutenant J. P. Walker got to observe Japanese air operations for three weeks and reported favorably on Japanese naval aviation.[123]

In August 1937 the naval attaché in Tokyo, Captain Harold Bemis, asked Yarnell for permission to send his assistant, Lieutenant Commander Ralph Ofstie, to China to observe the Japanese firsthand. As Bemis wrote to Yarnell:

> At the present time, I think it is more important for him to be in China than here as regards aviation intelligence. While undoubtedly your aviators are obtaining most valuable information, I believe that Ofstie . . . may have leads to follow in connection with [Japanese] war operations that might possibly escape your aviators.[124]

Ofstie reached Shanghai on September 16, spent a week talking with other aviators and observers, then headed for the front lines to witness the air war firsthand. He was unimpressed by what he saw and concluded that the Japanese had won air superiority largely because of the weakness of the Chinese air force. The assistant naval attaché in Shanghai, Marine Major Edward G. Hagen, was similarly unimpressed, judging Japanese tactics to be ineffective. Yarnell concurred, concluding that "a few of our well-trained squadrons would drive their planes out of the air."[125]

Such views soon began to change. Over the course of the conflict, U.S. officers noted improvement in both the skill of Japanese pilots and the quality of their aircraft. Major Ronald A. Boone, the 4th Marines' intelligence officer, reported that Japanese pilots were "aggressive, very

122. "Air Operations in the China Area (July 1937–August 1945)" in *War in Asia and the Pacific, 1937–1945*, volume 9, *China, Manchuria, and Korea (Part II)*, eds. Donald S. Detwiler and Charles B. Burdick (New York: Garland, 1980): 15, 17, 27–28.

123. Smith-Hutton Reminiscences, 78.

124. Quoted in William M. Leary, "Assessing the Japanese Threat: Air Intelligence Prior to Pearl Harbor," *Aerospace Historian* 34, no. 4 (winter 1987): 273.

125. Ibid., 273.

courageous and learn by experience."[126] By 1939, Japan's combat performance had convinced ONI that "the Japanese have gained more practical experience in air operations in war and on a bigger scale than any nation has enjoyed in the past 20 years." The office concluded that "the impetus such experience may be expected to give to further aeronautical development in Japan is a factor of considerable importance."[127]

The war in China also gave the United States its first glimpse of a new generation of Japanese aircraft, models with capabilities that rivaled or surpassed those of the United States, Great Britain, and the Soviet Union. Japan's air forces entered the war armed with such reliable but unremarkable fighters as the Type 90 (Nakajima A1N) and Type 95 (Nakajima A4N) fighters and Type 94 (Aichi D1A) dive-bomber. Within months, however, Tokyo began to replace these cloth biplanes with more sophisticated, all-metal monoplanes such as the Type 96 (Mitsubishi A5M "Claude") naval fighter and the Type 97 (Nakajima Ki-27 "Nate") army fighter.

U.S. intelligence received a wealth of information on Japanese aircraft from attachés, the Chinese government, and Claire L. Chennault, the leader of the American Volunteer Group in China. Although information from Japanese newspapers and magazines provided some clues, security restrictions reduced the utility of such sources. As the military attaché in Tokyo complained in one report, "With the enforcement of the Military Secrets Law it has become impracticable to obtain good photographs of materiel, and such reproductions as are published are freely retouched to conceal details of construction and equipment."[128] The first official photo of the Ki-27 "Nate" did not appear in the Japanese press until May 1939, two years after the aircraft entered service.

The war gave the United States an opportunity to gather technical intelligence on Japanese aircraft. The assistant naval attaché in China, James H. McHugh, supplied ONI with a variety of equipment, including radios, aircraft parts, and bomb fragments.[129] Getting Japanese materiel out of the war zone, however, proved hazardous. In the days before the fall of Nanking in December 1937, Chennault brought McHugh a collection of equipment culled from the wreckage of Japanese aircraft

126. Ibid., 276.

127. "Notes on the Present Conflict in China," *Monthly Information Bulletin* 18, no. 1 (March 1939): 77.

128. MID 2085–821/41 "Photographs of Aircraft," May 31, 1939, *Military Intelligence Division Correspondence, 1918–1941*, Roll 29, RG 165, NA, 3.

129. Leary, "Assessing the Japanese Threat," 274.

with the understanding that it would be passed on to the Air Corps after the Navy had examined it. The material was crated and taken to what was thought to be the safest place nearby—the U.S. Navy gunboat *Panay*. Two days later, on December 12, aircraft from the carrier *Kaga* sank the boat, sending its cargo to the muddy bottom of the Yangtze River.[130]

The Type 0 (Mitsubishi A6M "Zeke") was the best fighter in existence at the outbreak of the war in the Pacific. It could turn tighter and climb faster than any other production aircraft. It had high speed and a range double that of contemporary American and British fighters. In June 1940 it received its first operational assignment with the 12th Naval Air Group at Wuhan. The aircraft made its debut in the skies over Chungking on September 13, 1940, destroying twenty-six Chinese fighters without a loss. By early October, it had swept the Chinese air force from the skies over Chungking and Chengdu.[131]

It is often said that the United States did not learn of the existence of the Zero until Pearl Harbor.[132] In fact, U.S. intelligence received and distributed accurate though incomplete information on the fighter's performance before the outbreak of the war. ONI received its first report on the Zero two and a half months after the fighter first entered combat in China. The report, based on the interrogation of a captured Japanese bomber pilot, accurately described the maximum speed of the aircraft, its armament, and its fast rate of climb. On May 20, 1941, Chinese anti-aircraft guns shot down a Zero over Chengdu. The Chinese recovered the wreckage of the aircraft, and the ensuing report—forwarded to ONI by McHugh—confirmed the fighter's characteristics.[133]

In the fall of 1940, Chennault delivered a similar message to Washington, possibly based on the same source. In his memoirs, Chennault claims that the Army ignored his warnings.[134] In fact, the day after meeting with Chennault, Army Chief of Staff General George C. Marshall informed officials at a high-level conference that a fast new Japanese fighter had grounded the Chinese air force. In February 1941, Marshall characterized the Zero in letters to Lieutenant General Walter C. Short, Commanding General of the Hawaii Department, and Major

130. Claire Lee Chennault, *Way of a Fighter: The Memoirs of Claire Lee Chennault*, ed. Robert Hotz (New York: G. P. Putnam's Sons, 1949), 93. Chennault does not specifically name McHugh as the officer to whom he gave the equipment. It seems likely, however, given his activities at the time.

131. Leary, "Assessing the Japanese Threat," 275.

132. Martin Caidin, *Zero Fighter* (New York: Ballentine Books, 1969): 24–25, 133.

133. Leary, "Assessing the Japanese Threat," 276.

134. Chennault, *Way of a Fighter*, 94.

General George Grunert, Commanding General of the Philippine Department. Although Marshall incorrectly described the Zero as possessing leakproof tanks and an armored fuselage, his description of the aircraft's speed (322 mph) and armament (two 20mm and two thirty-caliber guns) was accurate. He promised to send P-40B *Warhawk* fighters to both Hawaii and the Philippines to offset the new Japanese fighter.[135]

Although the Japanese attempted to conceal the characteristics of the Zero from the United States, their security was at times lax. Indeed, in January 1941, the Japanese actually allowed Lieutenant Jurika, the assistant naval attaché for air matters in Tokyo, to sit in the cockpit of a Zero during an aviation exhibit at Tokyo's Haneda airport. Jurika gathered figures for the aircraft's weight and engine power. He examined the alloy used in the aircraft's wings and fuselage, the design of its landing gear, and other features. All of this he included in a report to ONI. Unfortunately, Jurika's report received no better reception than Smith-Hutton's description of the Type 93 torpedo. The bureau doubted the accuracy of Jurika's figures, accusing him of both underestimating the fighter's weight and overestimating its speed.[136] The Navy's technicians apparently could not understand why Japan would want to build a fast but light fighter, a design philosophy at variance with that of American manufacturers. The key issue appears to have been the inability of the Navy to recognize the merit of practices markedly different from their own.

Army and Navy publications on Japanese air forces reflected intelligence from China. The 1941 edition of the Army's standard reference on Japanese aircraft contained accurate figures for the Zero's flight characteristics, speed, and service ceiling.[137] Information also reached U.S. naval aviators before Pearl Harbor, but many refused to take it seriously. One who did was Lieutenant Commander John S. Thach, commanding officer of Fighter Squadron Three in San Diego. As Thach later recalled, he received one of the reports from China in the spring of 1941. He used the information to develop the "Thach Weave" as a tactic to counter the Zero's superior speed, climb, and turn radius. As he later wrote, "Without that intelligence report that was said to have

135. Larry I. Bland, ed., *The Papers of George Catlett Marshall*, volume 2, *"We Cannot Delay", July 1, 1939—December 6, 1941* (Baltimore: The Johns Hopkins University Press, 1986): 412, 414.

136. Jurika Reminiscences, 348. For the date of the incident, see Prados, *Combined Fleet Decoded*, 38n.

137. War Department, Field Manual 30–38, *Military Intelligence: Identification of Japa-*

come out of China, I think we would have gone right along, fat, dumb, and happy, and eventually run into the Zero and not had nearly the success we did have."[138]

Extrapolating from the technical characteristics of Japanese carriers to the features of Japanese naval doctrine proved challenging. In the years before the outbreak of the Pacific War, the Japanese navy was divided over the proper role of the aircraft carrier. Although the navy's battleship gunnery staffs believed that carriers should have enemy battleships as their priority targets, aviators thought the enemy's carriers should be the main target of carrier air strikes. By the mid-1930s a preemptive strike on the enemy carrier force had become the focus of Japanese naval aviation.[139] However, because debates over carrier doctrine took place within a small circle of naval officers, the Japanese were able to conceal these discussions from the United States. As a result, Washington remained ignorant of Japanese carrier doctrine.

The Japanese navy also attempted to conceal its carrier operations from the United States. In April 1940, however, Jurika got a rare opportunity to view a carrier as it conducted flight operations off the southeast coast of Kyushu from the deck of an American passenger liner.[140] Jurika, who had served aboard the USS *Saratoga*, noted that the tempo of Japanese flight operations was slower than that of American carriers.[141] During one observation, for example, it took six and one-half minutes to land three aircraft.[142]

In April 1941 the Japanese navy formed the 1st Air Fleet to separate carrier aviation from land-based naval air forces and to centralize control of the carrier force. The fleet, composed of seven carriers and 474 aircraft, represented the single most powerful concentration of naval air power in the world. It included some of the best naval aircraft and the most highly trained aviators in the world.[143] Japanese secrecy nonetheless prevented U.S. naval attachés from collecting information on changes in the doctrine and organization of the carrier forces. That

138. Adm. John S. Thach, "The Thach Weave Is Born" in *The Pacific War Remembered: An Oral History Collection*, ed. John T. Mason Jr. (Annapolis: U.S. Naval Institute Press, 1986): 97.

139. Evans and Peattie, *Kaigun*, 332–33.

140. Jurika Reminiscences, 346–47.

141. The U.S. Navy was able to achieve shorter aircraft cycle times by rearming and refueling its aircraft on deck, using crash barriers to isolate them from landing aircraft.

142. Jurika provided such information not only to ONI but also to the deputy chief of naval operations for aviation. See "Landing Intervals on Japanese Aircraft Carriers," April 6, 1940, "Aircraft Carriers, Japan," O-12-c 12484, *Confidential Reports of Naval Attachés, 1940–1946*, Box 1217, RG 38, NA.

143. Evans and Peattie, *Kaigun*, 349.

many key developments, including formation of the 1st Air Fleet, occurred only months before the beginning of the Pacific War further limited collection opportunities.

U.S. Naval Intelligence and Japanese Carrier Aviation

Gathering information regarding Japan's development of carrier aviation presented the United States with a greater challenge than observing the navy's surface forces. Although the United States generally did a good job of monitoring Japanese aircraft and carrier technology, the Navy tended to overlook or dismiss evidence of innovation. Naval attachés collected accurate intelligence regarding the Zero, only to have the Navy's experts disregard it. The Bureau of Aeronautics proved no more inclined to accept reports that Japan had developed a superior fighter aircraft than the Bureau of Ordnance had been willing to believe that Japan had developed an oxygen-propelled torpedo.

Extrapolating from technology to doctrine proved to be a considerable challenge as well. During much of the 1920s, the Japanese navy treated aircraft carriers as experimental assets. In the years that followed, it was divided over the proper employment of the aircraft carrier in war at sea. Quite simply, U.S. intelligence could not gather information that did not yet exist.

The war in China shook stereotypes of Japanese weakness and offered the United States new opportunities to collect information. Navy and Marine Corps officers observed Japanese air operations firsthand. Moreover, both the Army and Navy obtained considerable technical intelligence on the performance of Japanese aircraft such as the Zero. Although some ignored the information, others, such as Thach, put it to good use before Pearl Harbor.

DETECTING JAPANESE INNOVATION

Japan's emergence as a major military power during the first half of the twentieth century represented a formidable challenge to U.S. intelligence. The Japanese troops that fought the Russians at Mukden and the Tsushima Strait were trained by European military instructors and dependent on foreign arms. Four decades later, the United States faced a battle-hardened adversary armed with sophisticated weapons and employing innovative doctrine. U.S. Army and Navy intelligence failed to grasp the full ramifications of this transformation. As late as the mid-1930s, U.S. intelligence assessed that Japan had only a limited understanding of modem military technology and a rudimentary ability to produce advanced arms. Although such reports accurately portrayed the current state of the Japanese military, they overlooked its efforts to exploit new ways of war.

Certainly much of the difficulty U.S. intelligence encountered can be attributed to Japanese security. The Japanese were able to conceal the development of new weapons and to deny U.S. attachés the ability to observe training exercises. The cultural distance that separated the United States and Japan further complicated the task. Although experts on Japan within ONI and MID often wrote insightful reports, those without firsthand experience often fell back on increasingly obsolete stereotypes of Japanese competence. The absence of credible and authoritative information on the Japanese navy further obscured unique aspects of its tactical system and abetted the temptation to see it as a mirror image of its American counterpart. Thus, many American officers assumed that Japan would fight a future war with tactics similar to those employed by the U.S. Navy.

Japanese security measures had a pervasive effect on U.S. intelligence in the five years prior to the outbreak of World War II in the Pacific. The sources and methods of intelligence that had yielded the lion's share of data on Japanese military developments in the relatively open environment of the 1920s and early 1930s proved inadequate in the face of mounting restrictions on U.S. attachés. Limits on the activities of U.S. personnel in Japan obscured the expansion and reorganization of amphibious forces, the construction and modification of battleships and cruisers, and the growth of naval aviation. The restrictions also masked Japan's preparations for attacks on American, British, and Dutch possessions in Asia. As a result, information on the Japanese naval and amphibious forces on the eve of World War II was often ambiguous, incomplete, or contradictory.

Although Japan's war in China led to a crackdown on American officers in Japan, it gave their counterparts in China a rare opportunity to observe the Japanese armed forces in action. Information gathered in China partially remedied the shortfall of intelligence coming out of Japan.

Even though secrecy undoubtedly contributed to U.S. analytical errors, much of the difficulty ONI and MID experienced was the result of the rapid pace of change during the interwar period. Predicting the shape of wars to come is always risky, especially in an era marked by the emergence of new military technology, concepts, and organizations. Japan's development of new approaches to warfare presented U.S. intelligence with a conundrum. On the one hand, it was difficult to recognize technological and doctrinal innovation without reference to some type of preconceived notion of how a future war could be fought.

[83]

On the other hand, measuring foreign concepts with preconceptions derived from American concepts ran the risk of mirror-imaging.

Monitoring Japan's development of innovative technology represented a considerable challenge. In some cases, the Japanese managed to conceal the development of new weapons from American observers. In others, U.S. intelligence gathered what turned out to be accurate information, only to see American technical experts dismiss it. Indeed, the Army and Navy repeatedly discounted credible reports that Japan had achieved a capability that the United States lacked, whether it was the Type 91 long-range armor-piercing naval shell, the Type 93 oxygen-propelled torpedo, or the Type 0 fighter.

Attributing these failures to ethnocentrism or even to racism would be simplistic. Although such an explanation coexists comfortably with the notion that Washington failed to appreciate fully Japan's rise to power, it obscures the difficulty inherent in assessing new and unproven technology. Determining the veracity of attaché reports describing the Type 91 shell and Type 93 torpedo proved exceedingly difficult, because the United States lacked analogous weapons. U.S. intelligence quite simply did not have the ability to prove—or disprove—such claims. Its greatest failure was not its inability to verify attaché reports, but rather its willingness to dismiss even the possibility that Japan had developed innovative technology.

The combination of secrecy and ingrained assumptions about the character and conduct of war limited the U.S. armed forces' ability to detect Japan's development of innovative doctrine as well. Prior to the war in China, for example, the Japanese military prevented the United States from gaining an appreciation of Japan's development of amphibious warfare doctrine. Similarly, Japanese secrecy and U.S. preconceptions about war at sea conspired to mask the unique features of Japanese naval doctrine.

Extrapolating from technology to doctrine proved challenging as well. Even when U.S. intelligence had a good grasp of Japanese technology, U.S. experts often had difficulty determining the doctrine that governed use of the technology. Although the United States gained insight into Japanese ship design, for example, it lacked a comparable understanding of Japanese surface warfare doctrine. And even though the United States understood the development of Japanese aircraft and aircraft carriers, it lacked an appreciation of Japanese naval air effectiveness and doctrine.

This case also illustrates difficulties that arise when intelligence organizations attempt to understand innovative approaches to war. In some cases, the lessons of past wars may skew assessments of future performance. The poor performance of Allied forces at Gallipoli during

World War I, for example, caused many U.S. observers to be skeptical of amphibious warfare in general and of Japanese amphibious operations in particular. In other cases, intelligence organizations may be unable to identify foreign doctrine because no such doctrine exists. The Japanese navy acquired aircraft carriers long before it began to think in a systematic way about the doctrine that should govern carrier air operations.

[4]

Germany
Understanding a Resurgent Power

While Japan's efforts to master new ways of war were incremental, Germany's reemergence as a military power was both swift and dramatic. After fifteen years of nominal disarmament under the Versailles Treaty, Berlin managed to field in five years a powerful army and air force armed with modern weapons and employing innovative doctrine.

The opening campaigns of World War II showcased Germany's new armed forces. As French President Paul Reynaud wrote on May 21, 1940:

> The truth is that our classic conception of the conduct of war has come up against a new conception. At the basis of this . . . there is not only the massive use of heavy armoured divisions or cooperation between them and airplanes, but the creation of disorder in the enemy's rear by means of parachute raids. . . . We must think of the novel type of warfare which we are facing and take immediate decisions.[1]

The combination of combined-arms armored warfare, tactical aviation, and airborne operations allowed Germany to conquer Poland in four weeks, Norway in two months, Belgium in seventeen days, the Netherlands in five days, and—most dramatically—France in seven weeks. Both participants and observers viewed these campaigns as inaugurating a new era in warfare.

Germany's military innovations did not spring forth overnight. Rather, they were the result of experimentation that spanned several decades. During the early period, the vast majority of this activity was covert. It was not until Hitler's rise to power in 1933 that the armed forces underwent a rapid public expansion. Each period challenged

---

1. Quoted in Matthew Cooper, *The German Army, 1933–1945: Its Political and Military Failure* (New York: Stein and Day, 1978): 113–14.

U.S. intelligence. In the years immediately following World War I, American attachés confronted the difficult task of penetrating German attempts at concealment and deception to uncover covert weapons development programs. When Germany's rearmament became overt, the attachés faced the challenge of understanding ways of war that had yet to be tested on the battlefield. Although the attachés initially had difficulty comprehending the scope and pace of Germany's military resurgence, their assessments improved over time. Indeed, they did a remarkably good job of understanding German armored warfare concepts before the campaigns in Poland and France demonstrated their effectiveness. By contrast, incomplete information and mirror-imaging hampered their ability to understand German air doctrine.

U.S. MILITARY INTELLIGENCE AND GERMANY

In the years immediately following World War I, most Americans, military and civilian alike, would have found it inconceivable that the United States would ever again fight Germany. In reaction to Wilsonian idealism, America freed itself from entanglement in European affairs and returned to a conception of national interest that stressed freedom of action and unilateralism. Even after Hitler gained power and accelerated German rearmament, public sentiment favored remaining aloof from European affairs.[2] It was not until late 1938 that the Army and Navy's leaders began to view Germany as a threat. Even then, planning focused not on a war in Europe, but on an incursion into the Western Hemisphere in violation of the Monroe Doctrine.[3]

The Versailles Treaty imposed a harsh settlement on Germany, ceding territory to France, Belgium, and Poland and placing the Saar and Memel regions and the city of Danzig under the supervision of the League of Nations. The treaty also obliged the German government to demilitarize the right bank of the Rhine, to internationalize the Kiel Canal and several other waterways, to forfeit overseas colonies, and to pay some $33 billion in war reparations. The treaty was intended to emasculate the German military by abolishing conscription and limiting the size of the army to 100,000. It prohibited Berlin from possessing

2. Selig Adler, *The Isolationist Impulse: Its Twentieth-Century Reaction* (New York: The Free Press, 1957): 226–49; Manfred Jonas, *Isolationism in America, 1935–1941* (Ithaca: Cornell University Press, 1966): chap. 6.

3. "Joint Planning Committee Exploratory Studies in Accordance with J.B. 325 (Serial 634)," *Records of the Joint Board*, Roll 10, RG 225, National Archives (hereafter referred to as NA).

tanks, heavy artillery, and chemical weapons and sharply limited its stockpile of light artillery pieces, mortars, and machine guns. It abolished the General Staff and staff colleges and closed military academies. It limited the German navy to a strength of 15,000, restricted it to obsolete warships, and banned the construction of submarines, naval aircraft, and ships displacing more than 10,000 tons. It also prohibited Germany from possessing a flying corps and military aircraft.

The first U.S. intelligence officers to be stationed in Germany after the war were the military and naval observers attached to the American Mission to Germany headed by Ellis Dresel.[4] The Army in particular assigned capable, experienced officers to the mission. The U.S. military observer, Lieutenant Colonel Edward O. Davis, had been seconded to Field Marshal Edmund Allenby's forces in Palestine. His assistant for air matters, Benjamin Foulois, had been one of the Army's first aviators.[5] From their office on Berlin's Viktoriastrasse, Davis and his naval counterpart, Commander Weyman P. Beehler, witnessed the political chaos that descended on Germany in the aftermath of the war, monitored the implementation of disarmament, and attempted to glean the lessons of the war for future conflicts.[6]

The United States and Germany enjoyed good relations throughout the Weimar era. Indeed, no less of an authority than Gerhard L. Weinberg has concluded that "no two major powers were on better terms with each other than Germany and the United States before 1933."[7] Links to the United States gave Germany access to weapons developments and training methods that would have been otherwise unavailable. The Germans were particularly interested in the organization of the U.S. war industry as well as U.S. progress in aviation, artillery, armor, and chemical weapons.[8] German officers visited artillery installations, air fields, Reserve Officer Training Corps units, National Guard camps, the U.S. Military Academy, Massachusetts In-

4. In addition, in January and February 1919, Captain Walter R. Gherardi headed an American delegation to gather information on the German armed forces. See Captain Wyman H. Packard, USN (retired), *A Century of U.S. Naval Intelligence* (Washington, D.C.: Department of the Navy, 1996): 41, 136.

5. DeWitt S. Copp, *A Few Great Captains: The Men and Events That Shaped the Development of U.S. Air Power* (Garden City, N.Y.: Doubleday and Co., 1980): 87.

6. Col. Edward Davis, U.S. Army, "Military Attache," The Edward Davis Papers, U.S. Army Military History Institute (hereafter referred to as USAMHI): chap. 10.

7. Gerhard L. Weinberg, *The Foreign Policy of Hitler's Germany: Diplomatic Revolution in Europe, 1933–36* (Chicago: University of Chicago Press, 1970): 133.

8. Manfred Kehrig, *Die Wiedereinrichtung des Deutschen Militärischen Attachédienstes nach dem Ersten Weltkrieg (1919–1933)* (Boppard am Rhein: Harald Boldt Verlag, 1966): 86–87.

stitute of Technology, Army War College, and the Tank School at Fort Meade, Maryland.[9]

In 1925 the War Department began admitting two German officers per year to U.S. military schools.[10] These students included Captain (later Lieutenant General) Walter Warlimont, who became Deputy Chief of the German Armed Forces Operations Staff; Captain (later Lieutenant General) Wilhelm Speidel of the *Luftwaffe;* Captain (later Major General) Adolf von Schell, who became Inspector General of Armor and Army Mobilization; Captain (later Major General) Gerd von Massow, head of the *Luftwaffe*'s training program; Captain (later Lieutenant General) Hans von Greiffenberg, Chief of the Operations Division of the German General Staff; Captain (later Brigadier General) Fritz Thiele, Chief of the Signal Command Section of the German Armed Forces; and Lieutenant General (later Field Marshal) Werner von Blomberg, the Reich Minister of Defense.[11] Many of these officers provided U.S. attachés with valuable information during the Weimar and Nazi eras.

American officers were periodically seconded to the German army as well. Major P. W. Evans, the assistant military attaché in London, was attached to the *Reichswehr*'s 5th Division during its 1930 maneuvers.[12] From July to September 1932, Second Lieutenant Irvin R. Schimmelpfennig served as an artillery observer with the 3rd Battalion, 2nd Prussian artillery regiment.[13] Both subsequently filed reports detailing their experiences and offering insights into German tactics and technology.

The German army continued to treat U.S. officers favorably during the Nazi era.[14] Wilhelm Deist has concluded that American attachés

9. W. Karin Hall, "Truman Smith: United States Military Attaché, an Examination of His Career" (master's thesis, San Jose State University, 1992): 73.

10. From 1925 to 1929 they were admitted as civilians; between 1929 and 1934 they were admitted as military officers. See Wilhelm Deist, "Die Deutsche Aufrüstung in Amerikanischer Sicht: Berichte des US-Militärattachés in Berlin aus den Jahren 1933–1939" in *Russland–Deutschland–Amerika: Festschrift für Fritz T. Epstein zum 80. Geburtstag,* eds. Alexander Fischer, Günter Moltmann, and Klaus Schwabe (Wiesbaden: Franz Steiner Verlag, 1978): 280.

11. Col. Bruce W. Bidwell, U.S. Army (retired), *History of the Military Intelligence Division, Department of the Army General Staff: 1775–1941* (Frederick, Md.: University Publications of America, 1986): 383.

12. MID 2016–1095/3, "German Army Maneuvers 1930," October 3, 1930, *Military Intelligence Division Correspondence, 1917–1941,* Box 624, RG 165, NA.

13. MID 2016–1156/1, "Duty with 3rd Battalion, 2nd Pr. Art. Regiment," October 6, 1932, *Military Intelligence Division Correspondence, 1917–1941,* Box 625, RG 165, NA.

14. The German army ranked foreign attachés in terms of diplomatic considerations, tact, and the treatment of German attachés in their country. U.S. military attachés ranked

were "the best-informed foreign military observers in Berlin."[15] Major General Sir Kenneth Strong, the British military attaché in Berlin from 1937 to 1939, echoed the sentiment.[16] Because the German government saw the United States as neutral in European affairs, it granted American observers privileges extended to few other nations. Indeed, U.S. attachés were able to use their acquaintance with German military leaders to gain access to units that were off-limits to representatives of other governments.

The Military Attaché's Office

The U.S. Army was generally represented in Berlin by a colonel or senior lieutenant colonel who served a four-year tour. The military attaché in Berlin was accredited not only to the German government, but also to those of the Netherlands, Norway, Sweden, and Denmark. Monitoring developments in Germany took precedence, however; Truman Smith, for example, made four trips to the Netherlands, two to Denmark, and one to Sweden in his four years as military attaché.[17]

The attaché's office produced a large volume of reports on the German army and air force. Between 1935 and 1939, for example, it sent MID an average of six hundred dispatches per year.[18] U.S. intelligence activity in Germany focused on identifying innovative tactics and technology that the U.S. armed forces could borrow or buy. Indeed, because Germany was an acknowledged leader in military matters, U.S. attachés regarded Berlin as one of the most interesting posts.[19]

The Army assigned some of its best officers to Berlin. Of the thirteen who served as military attachés and assistant military attachés between

---

highest, together with those from Bulgaria, Hungary, Italy, Japan, Nationalist Spain, Sweden, and Yugoslavia. Those of the Soviet Union were ranked lowest. See Robert S. Cameron, "Comprehending the Tank: U.S. Military Intelligence and Foreign Armored Development in the 1930s" (paper presented at the 63rd Annual Meeting of the Society for Military History, Arlington, Va., April 21, 1996): 14.

15. Deist, "Die Deutsche Aufrüstung," 280.

16. Strong thought the British and Swedes were well-informed as well. Major General Sir Kenneth Strong, KBE, CB, *Intelligence at the Top: The Recollections of an Intelligence Officer* (London: Cassel and Company, 1968): 48.

17. Truman Smith, Speeches and Writings, "Activities of the Office of the Military Attaché, America Embassy, Berlin, Germany—August 1935 to March 1939," Truman Smith Papers, Box 1, Hoover Institution Archives (hereafter referred to as HIA), 5.

18. Hall, "Truman Smith: United States Military Attaché," 91.

19. Colonel T. Bentley Mott, *Twenty Years as Military Attaché* (New York: Oxford University Press, 1937): 103.

Table 5 U.S. Military Attachés in Berlin, 1920–1941

Military Attaché	Tour of Duty
Col. Edward Davis	January 1920–October 1921
Lt. Col. Creed F. Cox	October 1921–November 1924
Col. Arthur L. Conger	November 1924–July 1928
Col. Edward Carpenter	July 1928–March 1932
Lt. Col. Jacob W. S. Wuest	March 1932–April 1935
Capt. James C. Crockett (acting)	April 1935–August 1935
Maj./Lt. Col. Truman Smith	August 1935–March 1939
Maj. Percy G. Black (acting)	March 1939–September 1939
Col. Bernard R. Peyton	September 1939–September 1941

Source: Registers of Communications Received from Military Attachés and Other Intelligence Officers ("Dispatch Lists"), 1889–1941, Roll 3, RG 165, NA; Scott Alan Koch, "Watching the Rhine: U.S. Army Military Attache Reports and the Resurgence of the German Army, 1933–1941" (Ph.D. dissertation, Duke University, 1990): 292.

1933 and 1941, nine were graduates of the Command and General Staff School or its predecessor, the School of the Line, including three distinguished graduates. Six attended the Army War College, and five were graduates of both.[20] Three—Truman Smith, Percy Black, and Harvey Smith—went on to form MID's German Section during World War II.[21]

Many attachés also had combat experience that gave them insight into the potential effectiveness of new ways of war. Arthur Conger, for example, was a veteran of the Spanish-American War, the Moro insurrection in the Philippines, and the Boxer Rebellion. He also served as an intelligence officer in General John Pershing's headquarters staff in France during World War I. His most notable achievement was developing a scheme to conceal the start of the August 1918 St. Mihiel offensive.[22]

Unlike their counterparts in Tokyo, attachés in Germany as a rule spent a single tour in Berlin. The exception was Truman Smith, who served in Germany three times. Indeed, by the time he assumed the

20. Scott Alan Koch, "Watching the Rhine: U.S. Army Military Attaché Reports and the Resurgence of the German Army, 1933–1941" (Ph.D. dissertation, Duke University, 1990), 154.

21. Author's conversation with Mrs. R. Townsend Heard, December 1, 1995.

22. "Col. Conger Hero of Secret Battle," *Akron Beacon Journal*, July 22, 1927; Rod Paschall, "Deception for St. Mihiel, 1918," *Intelligence and National Security* 5, no. 3 (July 1990): 160.

post of military attaché in 1935, he had already spent five years—one-quarter of his military career—in Germany.

The military attaché in Berlin had two assistants: a captain or major who served as assistant military attaché and an Air Corps officer who acted as assistant military attaché for air matters. In all, ten officers served as assistant attachés in Berlin between 1933 and 1941: Captain John H. Hinemon, Captain Hugh W. Rowan, Captain James C. Crockett, Captain Theodore J. Koenig, Major Percy G. Black, Major Arthur W. Vanaman, Lieutenant Colonel William D. Hohenthal, Major John R. Lovell, Lieutenant Colonel Harvey H. Smith, and Major Willard R. Wolfinbarger.[23] Other officers were assigned to temporary duty in Berlin, including First Lieutenant Paul W. Thompson of the Army Corps of Engineers, Major Edgar Hume of the Medical Corps, and Major E. M. Powers of the Air Corps.[24]

The War Department showed a keen interest in Germany's development of military technology and doctrine. Because of this, the Army periodically augmented the attaché office with experts in technical intelligence. Between July 1936 and October 1940, the Ordnance Department sent Captain Rene R. Studler to Europe to cover foreign military technology developments. Although based in London, he visited Berlin repeatedly.[25] Temporary postings had limited utility, however; German authorities proved to be highly suspicious of foreign officers on short "observation" tours in their country, and this wariness grew as war approached. By the time the Chief of Ordnance formally requested that one of his officers be sent to Berlin, restrictions on foreign attachés had mounted. Colonel H. H. Zornig finally arrived in Berlin in May 1940 to provide a firsthand view of German armaments; he left three months later, frustrated by his inability to collect information because of German restrictions.[26]

American officers needed to appear impartial regarding European affairs to maintain access to sources of information on German military developments. U.S. military attachés in Berlin therefore collaborated with their foreign counterparts far less than those in Japan did. Still, American attachés periodically worked with their British, French, Polish, and Swedish counterparts to verify and exchange information.[27]

23. Koch, "Watching the Rhine," 153.
24. Smith, "Activities of the Office of the Military Attaché," 3.
25. Ibid., 4.
26. Constance McLaughlin Green, Harry C. Thomson, and Peter C. Roots, *The Ordnance Department: Planning Munitions for War* (Washington, D.C.: Office of the Chief of Military History, Department of the Army, 1955): 260.
27. Strong, *Intelligence at the Top*, 48.

ARMORED WARFARE

The armored divisions that formed the spearhead of Germany's attack on France were the result of experimentation that spanned two decades. To some extent, German concepts of armored warfare grew out of the Prussian military tradition of mobile warfare and the storm-troop tactics developed during World War I. The novelty consisted of the development of a combined-arms organization—the *Panzer* division—equipped with the doctrine needed to translate a tactical breakthrough into an operational penetration of enemy positions. To appreciate the radical break with past practice that German combined-arms warfare represented, U.S. observers had to look beyond the employment of tanks in World War I and their envisioned use by other European armies and to recognize Germany's development of a fundamentally different approach to warfare.

In the interwar years, German army leaders attempted to perceive the shape of future wars through the fog of peace. Some, such as General Walther Reinhardt, advocated a static defensive strategy such as the French adopted. Others, such as Lieutenant Colonel Joachim von Stülpnagel, believed Germany should adopt a "people's war" strategy. Hans von Seeckt and Werner von Blomberg, by contrast, argued that Germany needed a small, mobile, and professional army.[28] It was their philosophy that guided the development of the *Reichswehr* during the Weimar era.

During the early 1920s, von Seeckt began to rebuild the shattered *Reichswehr* according to a blueprint that combined traditional German military theory, lessons learned from World War I, and new technologies such as the airplane and motorized vehicles. Under von Seeckt, the *Truppenamt*, the covert General Staff, formed fifty-seven secret committees manned by four hundred officers—ten percent of the German officer corps—to study the lessons of World War I. The result was Army Regulation 487, *Leadership and Battle with Combined Arms*, issued in two parts between September 1921 and June 1923. The document, which described in detail an offensive war of maneuver, was refined throughout the interwar period.[29]

28. Larry H. Addington, *The Blitzkrieg Era and the German General Staff, 1865–1941* (New Brunswick, N.J.: Rutgers University Press, 1971): 30–31; James S. Corum, *The Roots of Blitzkrieg: Hans von Seeckt and German Military Reform* (Lawrence: University of Kansas Press, 1992): chap. 2; Deist, Manfred Messerschmidt, Hans-Erich Volkmann, and Wolfram Wette, *Germany and the Second World War*, volume I, *The Build-up of German Aggression*, ed. Militärgeschichtliches Forschungsamt, trans. P. S. Falla, Dean S. McMurry, and Ewald Osers (Oxford: Clarendon Press, 1990): 377–82.

29. Corum, *Roots of Blitzkrieg*, 39–43.

British armor developments exerted considerable influence on the German army. During the early postwar period, the British possessed the world's largest and most capable and experienced tank force. Moreover, British theorists such as J. F. C. Fuller and Basil Liddell Hart were the world's foremost exponents of armored warfare. The German army weekly *Militär-Wochenblatt* regularly translated their writings and printed accounts and analyses of British tank exercises. In 1927, for example, it described in detail the maneuvers of the British Experimental Mechanized Force in four consecutive issues. The intelligence arm of the *Truppenamt* also accorded high priority to British armored maneuvers.[30]

Because the Versailles Treaty prohibited Germany from possessing tanks, the *Reichswehr* was forced to develop its concept of armored warfare in secret. The hub of German armor activity was the army's Inspectorate of Motorized Transport Troops (*Inspektion der Kraftfahrtruppen*), which developed doctrine and tactics for armored warfare and trained a cadre of armor officers.[31] From 1927 to 1930, Heinz Guderian, the most prominent German armor advocate, studied and lectured on tank tactics with the Motor Transport Instructional Staff. By 1929, he had developed the general formula that characterized German armored operations in the years to come. The key was the concept of the armored division as a combined-arms formation. Each unit was to be a complete armored and motorized team composed of elements of all branches, designed to allow tanks to fight with full effect. As Guderian explained, "Within the tank regiments, every detachment is furnished with the machine-guns and the varieties of artillery it needs to wage fire-fights at short, medium, and long range, and to answer the urgent call to meet an enemy tank attack with a sufficient number of armour-piercing weapons."[32] The armored division would have the means not only to breach enemy lines but also to convert the breakthrough into an operational penetration.

Although German army publications devoted considerable attention to foreign armor developments, the covert nature of its tank research limited the ability of foreign intelligence services to detect Berlin's interest in armored warfare. Neither MID nor its French and British counterparts identified the Inspectorate of Motorized Transport Troops

30. Azar Gat, "British Influence and the Evolution of the Panzer Arm: Myth or Reality? Part I," *War in History* 4, no. 2 (April 1997): 160 and *passim*.

31. Major General Heinz Guderian, *Achtung—Panzer! The Development of Armoured Forces, Their Tactics, and Operational Potential*, trans. Christopher Duffy (London: Arms and Armour Press, 1992): 160–62.

32. Ibid., 171.

as the hub of thinking on armored warfare. Nor did they detect attempts to translate the lessons of World War I into armored-warfare doctrine. Even if they had, any such interest would have been theoretical, since the *Reichswehr* was prohibited from possessing tanks. It is thus hardly surprising that neither the United States nor the former Allied powers yet understood the extent of German interest in armored warfare.

In 1926 the *Reichswehr* began experimenting with armored units, inaugurating an annual program of two sets of large force-on-force maneuvers and a war game for army commanders and their staffs. U.S. military attachés collected considerable information on German doctrine by attending field maneuvers. Indeed, because of the close ties between the U.S. and German armies, the U.S. observers were in several cases the only foreigners invited to exercises.

The first *Reichswehr* maneuver that U.S. military attachés attended was held on September 10–11, 1923, near the German-Polish border by elements of the 1st Infantry Division. Modeled on the Battle of Tannenberg, the maneuver resembled World War I in its tactical execution and culminated in an infantry assault supported by machine guns. Colonel Conger, observing the exercise, praised the quality of German officers, soldiers, and equipment and noted the premium they placed on mobility.[33] Conger also attended the division's 1925 maneuvers, which examined the *Reichswehr*'s ability to counter a Polish invasion. The exercise marked the German army's first attempt to simulate tanks on the battlefield, something the attaché described in detail.[34]

In 1926 the German army invited Conger to attend its first postwar multidivisional exercise.[35] The maneuver's scenario envisioned a defensive German force blocking an invading French army from crossing the Rhine and cutting Bavaria off from northern Germany. While the army invited a number of foreign representatives to observe the maneuvers of the Second Corps, it excluded British, French, and Polish attachés. Only U.S. military representatives were allowed to accompany both corps.

Conger's ninety-two-page report on the exercise is testament to his understanding of German tactical concepts. It highlighted the prominence of combined-arms operations during the maneuvers and noted

33. Robert M. Citino cites U.S. military attaché reports on German exercises heavily throughout his book. See his *The Evolution of Blitzkrieg Tactics: Germany Defends Itself against Poland 1918–1933* (Westport, Conn.: Greenwood Press, 1987): 79–80.

34. Ibid., 84–85.

35. Citino, *The Path to Blitzkrieg: Doctrine and Training in the German Army, 1920–1939* (Boulder, Colo.: Lynne Rienner, 1999): 130–1.

the *Reichswehr*'s simulation of equipment prohibited by Versailles, such as heavy artillery, tanks, and combat aircraft. To Conger, the maneuver marked a notable break with past tactics. He noted that rather than advancing on a broad front, "battalions and companies within the battalion pushed forward and continued to push forward, regardless of whether there were troops on their right or left, until stopped by the enemy." Conger was struck by the difference between the tactics employed in World War I and those in the exercise. As he reported to MID:

> At first the impression was given that these irregularities in the advance came from the fact that the troops were unaccustomed in maneuvers on a big scale and were due to errors in carrying out the intentions and orders of superiors. But later it was proved to be done by intent. The German regulations call for troops to push on their own battle sectors and get a grip on all points of vantage, irrespective of what troops on their flanks are successful in accomplishing. At the same time, there was always observed complete cooperation between adjacent units in all situations in which one unit found itself in a position to facilitate the advance of a neighboring unit.[36]

The *Reichswehr* continued to experiment with tank operations in the years that followed. In 1928, the 3rd (Spandau) Battalion of the 9th Infantry Regiment conducted maneuvers using tank surrogates. The next summer's exercises included a simulated tank division. These maneuvers gave the army a gradually clearer appreciation of armored warfare and convinced enthusiasts such as Guderian of the need for a combined-arms approach.[37]

By monitoring field exercises, U.S. officers gained a window on the German army's experimentation with new military organizations. In the fall of 1930, the assistant military attaché in Berlin, Major H. H. Zornig, witnessed an exercise that pitted defenders employing the standard *Reichswehr* organization and equipment against attackers possessing additional motorized vehicles and artillery pieces, more pioneer and signal troops, and robust logistical support. It was, in other words, a force optimized for mobile warfare, and it prefigured organizational changes the *Wehrmacht* implemented in the mid-1930s.[38]

36. Corum, *Roots of Blitzkrieg,* 185. See also Conger's report on the exercise, MID 2016–1007/ 37, "Fall Maneuvers, 1926, German Army," October 12, 1926, *Military Intelligence Division Correspondence, 1917–1941,* Box 620, RG 165, NA.

37. Guderian, *Panzer Leader,* trans. Constantine Fitzgibbon (New York: Da Capo, 1996): 23–24.

38. MID 2016–1095/9, "The 1930 Fall Maneuvers of the German Army," December 19, 1930, *Military Intelligence Division Correspondence, 1917–1941,* Box 624, RG 165, NA.

The German army was far from united over the proper employment of tanks, however. Armor enthusiasts such as Guderian and Oswald Lutz favored the establishment of independent armored divisions. Others, such as General Ludwig Beck, wanted tanks to perform cavalry and infantry support missions. By contrast, General Otto von Stülpnagel, the *Reichswehr*'s Inspector of Motorized Transport Troops, forbade the employment of tanks in greater than regiment strength. Some cavalry officers opposed the development of armored divisions altogether because the tank threatened to usurp the cavalry's traditional missions.[39]

In February 1931, Guderian took command of the 3rd (Prussian) Motorized Battalion, a supply unit. With Lutz's support, he converted it into a prototype combined-arms battalion by equipping its four companies with armored reconnaissance cars, motorcycles, dummy tanks, and simulated anti-tank guns. General von Stülpnagel, the Inspector of Motorized Transport Troops, nonetheless prohibited Guderian from conducting combined exercises with other units.[40]

This setback proved to be temporary. In April, Lutz replaced Stülpnagel as Inspector of Motorized Transport Troops and named Guderian his chief of staff. He subsequently organized two sets of exercises at the training centers at Grafenwöhr and Juterbog to test methods of coordinating the operations of a dummy tank detachment and a reinforced infantry regiment. The next fall four motorized reconnaissance detachments and a complete motorcycle battalion conducted combined exercises.[41] These maneuvers were, however, closed to foreigners.

Professional journals continued to devote considerable attention to armored warfare. In the early 1930s, for example, *Militär-Wochenblatt* published imaginary tactical problems describing the employment of independent armored brigades. It also printed various schemes for organizing armored formations.[42] Translating and analyzing open-source publications such as these gave the U.S. Army's intelligence arm insight into German thinking regarding tanks.

The Army also gleaned information regarding German tactical concepts from lectures by German officers in the United States. In 1932, for example, Captain Anton Freiherr von Bechtolsheim of the *Truppenamt* lectured on tactics at the U.S. Army's Field Artillery School at Fort Sill,

---

39. Deist et al., *Germany and the Second World War*, 432, 435.
40. Guderian, *Panzer Leader*, 24.
41. Guderian, *Achtung—Panzer!*, 162.
42. Gat, "British Influence," 166.

Oklahoma. He explained that, according to German doctrine, "Movement is the first element of war and only by mobile warfare can any decisive result be obtained." He emphasized that German tactics employed mobility and surprise to achieve and exploit a breakthrough in enemy lines. As he told his audience, "If I as leader of a rifle company, for example, notice that my right neighbor is advancing better than I am, I immediately leave my zone and fight alongside my neighbor in his zone, for there is the weak point in the enemy line."[43] His description of German tactical concepts echoed Conger's insights six years earlier.

The *Reichswehr* also began acquiring the weapons needed to implement its concept of mobile warfare. In May 1925 the German army issued specifications for its first postwar tank, known euphemistically as a "heavy tractor"; two years later it developed requirements for a light tank, known as a "light tractor." The programs progressed slowly, since the vehicles had to be built by small groups of engineers operating in secrecy to avoid detection by Allied arms inspectors.[44] The measures succeeded, however, in that neither French, British, nor American intelligence services learned of the programs. The British, for example, knew that the German army was interested in armored vehicles but were unable to identify which companies were conducting research.[45]

Germany pursued close military cooperation with the Soviet Union as a means of lessening diplomatic isolation. In 1920–1921, von Seeckt formed a special staff within the Intelligence Section of the *Truppenamt*, known as Special Group R (*Sondergruppe R*) to pursue contacts with the Soviet army. In the spring of 1927, Germany and Russia agreed to open an armor training and test center at Kazan. The "Heavy Vehicle Experimental and Test Station," as it was known, trained German armored officers, tested tank prototypes, and conducted comparative evaluations of foreign vehicles. By 1930, the Germans had shipped ten tanks and several armored car prototypes to Kazan; the Soviet army contributed an additional thirty vehicles. The *Reichswehr* conducted company- and battalion-level armored maneuvers at Kazan and observed the Soviet army's 1930 armored maneuvers. The following year, the two armies conducted joint exercises. By the time the center closed

---

43. Anton Freiherr von Bechtolsheim, captain, German Leaderstaff, "The German Army," lecture before the Field Artillery School, Fort Sill, 1932, in The Willis D. Crittenberger Papers, U.S. Army Military History Institute (USAMHI), 7.

44. Corum, *Roots of Blitzkrieg*, 112–19.

45. J. P. Harris, "British Military Intelligence and the Rise of German Mechanized Forces, 1929–1940," *Intelligence and National Security* 6, no. 2 (April 1991): 398.

in the summer of 1933, it had trained a cadre of more than fifty armored specialists.[46]

Despite attempts by Berlin and Moscow to conceal their cooperation, details of the program gradually leaked out. On December 3, 1926, the *Manchester Guardian* revealed the existence of military collaboration between Germany and the Soviet Union. Shortly thereafter, in a debate triggered by the exposé, a member of the German *Reichstag* disclosed the existence of *Sondergruppe R*.

Four months later, Lieutenant Colonel N. E. Margetts, head of MID's Military Attaché Section, asked the attachés in London, Paris, and Berlin to send him information on Russo-German cooperation, noting that:

> Reports have been received from various sources both by the State Department and G-2, to the effect that Germany is assisting Soviet Russia in many ways, among them the following: (a) commercial aviation, (b) furnishing airplanes, (c) German mechanics and specialists for various reasons; (d) furnishing munitions of various classes; (e) German firms operating in Soviet Russia for the manufacture of airplanes, chemical warfare material, etc.[47]

In response, the military attaché in Paris, Brigadier General William W. Harts, forwarded a report prepared by the *Deuxième Bureau* assessing the state of Russo-German cooperation. It accurately described German arms manufacturing in the Soviet Union, concluding that "Not only have there been exchanges of information, but there has been technical collaboration on questions of arms between the Russian government and the ministry of the Reichswehr." The report did not, however, mention the armored training center at Kazan. Moreover, Harts played down the French report, stating that "Our own reports give very little indication of German assistance [to Russia]."[48]

In 1932 British journalist Cecil Melville published a nearly complete account of Soviet-German military ties. The book made only a passing reference to the tank school at Kazan, referring to it as "a camp."[49] In

---

46. Corum, *Roots of Blitzkrieg*, 191–95; Manfred Zeidler, *Reichswehr und Rote Armee, 1920–1933: Wege und Stationen einer ungewöhnlichen Zusammenarbeit* (Munich: R. Oldenbourg Verlag, 1994), chap. 9.

47. MID 2037–1823, "Germany Assisting Soviet Russia," March 12, 1927, *Correspondence of the Military Intelligence Division Relating to General, Political, Economic, and Military Conditions in Russia and the Soviet Union, 1918–1941*, Roll 15, RG 165, NA.

48. *Ibid.*

49. Cecil F. Melville, *The Russian Face of Germany: An Account of the Secret Military Relations Between the German and Soviet-Russian Governments* (London: Wishart and Co., 1932): 121.

May, Major Emer Yeager, the military attaché in Warsaw, sent MID more detailed information on the facility from *Oddzial II*, the Polish military intelligence service. Although the Poles had enjoyed considerable success collecting intelligence against Germany, they had been unable to penetrate Kazan. According to Yeager, "The existence of a tank factory and training center in the region indicated above has been confirmed several times, but all efforts to secure more definite information as to the capacity of the factory, the number of troops at the training center, etc., have failed."[50]

U.S. military intelligence gathered a good deal of information on the German army's overt experimentation with new operational concepts and organizations. It also received indications of some of the *Reichswehr*'s covert activities. Yet it still lacked some important information, such as the fact that the Inspectorate of Motorized Transport Troops was the hub of the army's armor research. U.S. military attachés were also excluded from some of the German army's most interesting experiments with simulated armored units. As a result, the United States possessed at best a fragmentary picture of German experimentation with armor.

The rise to power of Adolf Hitler accelerated German rearmament. His initial public proposals appeared moderate. Although Hitler withdrew Germany from the League of Nations in October 1933, he also sought an alliance with Britain, negotiated the Anglo-German Naval Agreement, and called for revision of the Versailles Treaty to permit limited German rearmament. In early 1935, however, he openly broke with Versailles and embarked on a wholesale expansion of the German military. In March, he renounced the treaty and revealed the existence of the *Luftwaffe*. Two weeks later, he claimed that Germany had reached parity with Britain in the air and announced the expansion of the army to a force of thirty-six divisions and 500,000 men, taking foreign and domestic observers, including *Wehrmacht* leaders, by surprise.[51]

It was against this backdrop that in the summer of 1935 Major Truman Smith assumed the post of military attaché in Berlin. He was the lowest-ranking attaché to be assigned to Germany in twenty years. Moreover, his path to the Army had been circuitous. Despite coming from a military family (his father, Captain Edmund D. Smith, had been killed in the Philippines in February 1900), he chose to attend Yale rather than West Point. When he left graduate school at Columbia University to join the military, it was not as an officer in the Army, but as a

50. MID 2331-B-54/1, "Autonomous German Tank Factory in Russia," May 12, 1932, *Military Intelligence Division Correspondence, 1917–1941,* Box 905, RG 165, NA.

51. Deist et al., *Germany and the Second World War,* 422.

lieutenant in the New York National Guard. He was, however, superbly qualified for the job of military attaché in Berlin. After World War I, he was attached to the Army's Office of Civil Affairs in Coblenz; he then served as assistant military observer between June 1920 and April 1924 and then as assistant military attaché in Berlin. Between 1928 and 1932 Smith taught at the Army's Infantry School at Fort Benning, Georgia, under Colonel George C. Marshall. There he acted as an interpreter and escort for the half-dozen or so German officers detailed to duty with the U.S. Army, many of whom later rose to positions of influence within the *Wehrmacht* and *Luftwaffe*. In 1932–1933 Smith attended the Army War College, where he wrote and lectured on German history, politics, and military affairs. At the invitation of General von Blomberg, the German minister of war, Smith returned to Germany in 1932 to attend the 1st Division's fall maneuvers in East Prussia.[52]

In 1935 the German army began to require that foreign governments submit requests for information to the army's military attaché office. It also prohibited its officers from frequenting the homes of foreigners unless a prior friendship existed.[53] The rule was useless as far as Smith was concerned, however. He had accumulated a wealth of contacts within the German military as assistant military attaché in Berlin and at Fort Benning, including von Blomberg and Hans Speidel, the head of the General Staff's intelligence office responsible for France and later Field Marshal Erwin Rommel's chief of staff. Perhaps his best source of information on German armor developments was Adolf von Schell. Smith cultivated Schell as a source, writing that "I have made it my business to be in as intimate personal relationship with him as possible, continuing a friendship begun at Fort Benning."[54] Smith considered Schell to be a reliable source of information. Indeed, in a January 1936 letter to George C. Marshall, Smith described him as "a devoted friend of America."[55] Schell was well placed to provide information on the development of the German tank corps, serving successively as an instructor at the German General Staff School, the Chief of Staff of the War Ministry's Motor Inspectorate, and Inspector General of Armor and Army Mobilization.

52. Smith, "Activities of the Office of the Military Attaché," 6.

53. Friedrich-Carl Rabe von Pappenheim, *Erinnerungen des Soldaten und Diplomaten 1914–1955* (Osnabrück: Biblio Verlag, 1987): 56.

54. Robert S. Cameron, "Americanizing the Tank: U.S. Army Administration and Mechanized Development within the Army, 1917–1943" (Ph.D. dissertation, Temple University, 1994): 303.

55. Larry I. Bland, ed., *The Papers of George Catlett Marshall*, volume 1, *"The Soldierly Spirit," December 1880–June 1939* (Baltimore: The Johns Hopkins University Press, 1981): 484.

Smith's assistant military attaché for ground force matters, Captain James C. Crockett, had arranged to attend the *Kriegsakademie* in his spare time, making acquaintances within the German army and studying its tactics. Although Crockett's service as an intelligence officer was commendable, he became romantically involved with a German baroness who was allegedly on the German government's payroll. Upon learning of the affair, Smith asked MID to recall Crockett to the United States in early February 1937 to save his career and marriage.[56] He was replaced by Major Percy G. Black, who served in Germany through the fall of 1939.

MID acquired a valuable source of information on the German military in 1935, when the *Wehrmacht* and the U.S. Army agreed to permit one U.S. Army officer per year to attend the two-year course at the *Kriegsakademie*.[57] These students were carefully selected, spoke and read German, and acquired a broad set of contacts among the *Wehrmacht* officers attending the school. They included Captain Albert C. Wedemeyer, Major Herman F. Kramer, Major Harlan N. Hartness, and Major Richard C. Partridge. Their instruction included all aspects of German tactics and operations. Moreover, because *Kriegsakademie* students often studied experimental organizations and concepts, U.S. students frequently provided U.S. intelligence sources with the first indications of German organizational and tactical innovations. Between the first and second years at the academy, each student served in a command or staff position in a field unit and participated in maneuvers. Black served in an artillery regiment, Kramer an infantry regiment, and Wedemeyer an antitank battalion; Lieutenant Paul Thompson served two tours in a pioneer battalion. While on summer vacation, the students documented their experiences by writing reports on German military organizations. In addition, in 1937 Major R. Townsend Heard, a veteran intelligence officer, spent several weeks in a German field artillery regiment.[58]

56. Katherine Alling Hollister Smith, "My Life: Berlin, August 1935–April 1939", Truman Smith Papers, Box 4, HIA, 138–39.

57. Each class consisted of approximately 120 German officers. In addition, nine foreign students were admitted to the school each year: two each from China and Argentina and one each from Bulgaria, Italy, Japan, Turkey, and the United States. See General Albert C. Wedemeyer, *Wedemeyer Reports!* (New York: Henry Holt & Company, 1958): 50, 54.

58. Heard later served as the head of MID's Latin American Section and in intelligence assignments in Europe and the Pacific. Smith, "Activities of the Office of the Military Attaché," 4.

The *Wehrmacht* created its first tank unit, equipped with fifty-five *Panzerkampfwagen* (PzKw) I training tanks, on November 1, 1933. Eight months later it established the Command of the Tank Forces (*Kommando der Panzertruppen*) with General Lutz at its head. In July 1935 the army's ordnance office organized a demonstration of armored elements at the training area of Kummersdorf. A month later it held an exercise with a provisional armored division to demonstrate the command of large, rapidly moving armored units as well as cooperation between armored, infantry, and artillery forces.[59]

On October 15, 1935, the army raised three *Panzer* divisions. Each included a tank brigade; a motorized infantry brigade containing one truck-borne regiment and one motorcycle battalion; a motorized artillery regiment; an antitank battalion; a reconnaissance battalion; an engineer company (soon expanded to a battalion); and signal and service units. Maneuvers indicated that the initial organization lacked sufficient infantry. As a result, in 1938–1939 the infantry element of the *Panzer* division grew to four battalions. Moreover, the division's tank battalions were reorganized into one medium and two light companies.[60]

Smith learned of the three *Panzer* divisions shortly after arriving in Berlin but was informed that they were off-limits to foreign officers. Although he did not receive permission to visit a *Panzer* unit until 1937, he learned a great deal about their organization and equipment from his sources within the *Wehrmacht*.[61] Because of the secrecy that the Germans accorded the divisions and the fluidity of their organization, however, it took two years for Smith and his staff to understand fully their organization and missions.

Smith and Crockett attended the *Wehrmacht*'s 1935 autumn maneuvers in Silesia. Although the army treated the Americans well, Smith felt that they had been "so conducted as to befog the attachés in matters of details. In consequence there was a general air of camouflage surrounding the entire maneuvers." In fact, the exercise was insignificant compared with others under way at the same time. Smith subsequently heard about experiments in Westphalia and Hanover "to determine the efficiency of the tank as a strategical weapon for achieving decisive battle successes."[62] What he saw nonetheless convinced him of the magnitude of the changes under way within the *Wehrmacht*. As he later wrote,

59. Deist et al., *Germany and the Second World War*, 433.

60. Addington, *Blitzkrieg Era*, 35; Matthew Cooper and James Lucas, *Panzer: The Armoured Force of the Third Reich* (London: Macdonald and Jane's, 1976): 80.

61. Smith, "Activities of the Office of the Military Attaché," 9.

62. MID 2016–1220/274 "Silesian Maneuvers 1935," September 11, 1935, *Military Intelligence Division Correspondence, 1917–1941*, Box 627, RG 165, NA, 1.

they "indicated that the Germans were developing new organizations, introducing new weapons and altering their previous system of tactics." His experience as an instructor at the Infantry School at Fort Benning had highlighted the differences between the German and American approaches to armored warfare.[63] As he now saw it, the German military was "conducting a revolution in military methods."[64]

In 1936 the German army established three additional types of armored units. It formed independent *Panzer* brigades to support infantry units, raised Light Divisions to execute traditional cavalry missions such as reconnaissance and screening, and equipped several infantry units with tanks and motorized transportation to form Motorized Infantry divisions. By the outbreak of World War II, the *Wehrmacht* had four Light divisions and five Motorized Infantry divisions.[65]

In September 1936 the German army conducted its largest maneuvers since 1914.[66] It invited all accredited foreign attachés, including Smith and his two assistants. The exercise included a regiment of PzKw I tanks. Smith's fifty-two-page report on the exercise shows real insight into German concepts for the employment of armor. As one German officer with tank experience told him:

> Infantry and artillery can today always break a front line as they always did in the World War. The tank, however, is the weapon of the attack to throw in when the infantry-artillery attack begins to bog down. It is then irreplaceable and fills the role which the heavy cavalry filled in the seventeenth and eighteenth century. The infantry tank is an exploitation weapon—not a front line breaking weapon.[67]

Smith and his staff followed German writings on armored warfare closely. The office paid particular attention to Lutz and Guderian, whom Smith identified as "Germany's [J. F. C.] 'Fuller.'" In November 1936, for example, Crockett translated Guderian's "Armored Troops and Their Cooperation with Other Arms." Given Guderian's position as commander of the 2nd *Panzer* Division, Crockett felt that the article "may be accepted as official German tactical and organizational doctrine for armored troops." In fact, Guderian represented one school of thought on armored warfare, albeit the one that eventually dominated

63. Smith, "Activities of the Office of the Military Attaché," 8.
64. Robert Hessen, ed., *Berlin Alert: The Memoirs and Reports of Truman Smith* (Stanford, Calif.: Hoover Institution Press, 1984): 29.
65. Addington, *Blitzkrieg Era*, 41.
66. Citino, *Path to Blitzkrieg*, 234.
67. Koch, "Watching the Rhine," 221.

the German army. Based on Guderian's writings, Crockett concluded that the German army believed that tanks should not be used as infantry support vehicles. Rather, they should have separate organizations and missions. He also believed that the Germans felt that auxiliary arms should be organic to the *Panzer* division and should have speed and mobility equal to that of tanks. Finally, he predicted that German armored attacks would rely on speed, mass, and surprise to overwhelm and demoralize the defender.[68] Each of these predictions proved to be accurate.

The German army continued to refine its concepts of armored warfare during the late 1930s. In April 1937 it formed Group Command 4 to control its mechanized units, including *Panzer* Divisions and Brigades, Light Divisions, and Motorized Infantry Divisions. That year's autumn maneuvers, which included the 3rd *Panzer* Division and 1st *Panzer* Division's 1st *Panzer* Brigade, demonstrated the employment of the *Panzer* division as an integral unit.[69]

By November 1937, Smith had accumulated sufficient information to draft a fifteen-page report outlining the development of the German armored corps, highlighting the importance of the *Panzer* division. He wrote that:

> The German Panzer Division is the most important development (from an organizational standpoint) of the entire German rearmament program. Originally conceived of as a German parallel to the British mechanized force, it has been now for two years passing through a variety of transformations, until today, the autumn of 1937, the Panzer Division has become a unique organization, without exact or even close parallel in other European countries.[70]

The report described the organization and equipment of the division and identified its mission as being to:

(1) Break rapidly into the interior of a hostile country at the outbreak of the war.

(2) Form the spear head of a major enveloping movement, aiming at a strategic division.

68. MID 2016–1248/2, "Armored Troops and Their Cooperation with Other Arms," November 24, 1936, *Military Intelligence Division Correspondence, 1917–1941*, Box 627, RG 165, NA, 1.

69. Guderian, *Panzer Leader*, 46.

70. MID 2016–1206/35, "The Panzer Division," November 24, 1937, *Military Intelligence Division Correspondence, 1917–1941*, Box 626, RG 165, NA, 3.

(3) Operate independently in a country of great expansion, such as Poland and Russia [*sic*].[71]

Smith's report became the basis of the U.S. Army's understanding of the *Panzer* division. MID cited it repeatedly in response to requests by Army organizations for information on German armor developments.[72]

Information that Wedemeyer gained during his term at the *Kriegsakademie* supplemented Smith's reports. In April 1938 he filed a seventy-five-page report on the *Panzer* division that enumerated the organization, equipment, and approximate manpower of the division. The report described the planning and execution of an armored attack, including the anticipated rates of advance of tank forces.[73]

By mid-1938, MID thus possessed an accurate picture of the composition, equipment, and doctrine of the German tank force. Military attachés sent MID detailed reports of German concepts and organizations for combined-arms warfare. U.S. Army officers, including students at the *Kriegsakademie*, forwarded information on German tank construction as well. The quality of these reports was testimony to the skill and expertise of the officers the Army assigned to Germany. Prior to the outbreak of World War II, however, it was unclear what value, if any, this information had. The contingencies of greatest interest to the Army, such as the defense of the Philippines and the Panama Canal Zone, did not require tank forces. Moreover, because the United States did not anticipate fighting Germany, the Army's need to develop countermeasures to armored warfare seemed doubtful.[74]

Although the U.S. Army managed to assemble an accurate picture of the German army's prewar approach to armored warfare, the magnitude of Germany's success during the early campaigns of World War II shocked both participant and observer alike. On September 1, 1939, five German armies composed of fifty-two divisions invaded Poland. Army Group North, under General Fedor von Bock, and Army Group South, under General Gerd von Runstedt, formed the claws of a giant pincer converging on Warsaw. The deployment of Polish forces along the border with Germany gave the *Wehrmacht* a tremendous advan-

---

71. Ibid., 2.

72. Cameron, "Comprehending the Tank," 18n.

73. MID 2016–1004/47, "The German Armored Division," April 7, 1938, *Military Intelligence Division Correspondence, 1917–1941*, Box 620, RG 165, NA.

74. On the development of armor in the U.S. Army, see David E. Johnson, *Fast Tanks and Heavy Bombers: Innovation in the U.S. Army, 1917–1945* (Ithaca: Cornell University Press, 1998).

tage. Moreover, Polish equipment was largely of World War I vintage. Besides being deficient in antitank weapons, the Poles possessed little motorized transportation and only a few companies of tanks. Poland was thus ill-equipped to deal with even the light PzKw I and II tanks that formed the bulk of the German armored force.

During the campaign, the Germans used armored divisions as the spearhead of four of their five armies. Armored units played a key role in Walter von Reichenau's advance on Warsaw and in Wilhelm von Thoma's night infiltration through some fifty miles of undefended but thickly wooded country to turn the Polish flank at the Jablunka pass. The General Staff dismissed the idea of a deep strategic penetration by armor, however, because of the small number of tanks available.[75]

U.S. military attachés in Berlin witnessed portions of the campaign firsthand. The German army permitted American officers to visit the front, a privilege they extended to only three other countries.[76] The Germans allowed Black to accompany the Second Army Corps to Warsaw and to observe their assault upon Modlin.[77] They later allowed Lieutenant Colonel Hohenthal and Majors Kramer and Partridge to tour the front.[78]

The Army launched a systematic effort to collect and to disseminate the lessons of the war in Europe soon after the attack on Poland. MID began to issue a *Tentative Lessons Bulletin* containing analyses of the organization, tactics, and battlefield performance of the belligerents. A majority of the 170 bulletins issued between May 1940 and November 1941 dealt with the German army.[79] MID distributed the reports throughout the Army. Students at the Army War College, for example, studied and analyzed the reports.

The performance of German armored units in Poland convinced many in the U.S. Army of the need to develop an analogous capability. The Chief of Cavalry, Major General John K. Herr, advocated transforming the 7th Cavalry Brigade (Mechanized) into a replica of the *Panzer* division.[80] His office sent Black, the acting military attaché, an exhaustive list of questions regarding the performance of German armor during the invasion. Many of the questions reflected ongoing

75. Cooper and Lucas, *Panzer*, 25.

76. Hungary, Finland, and Japan.

77. Maj. Percy Black, "Germany," notes of lecture at the Army War College, Washington, D.C., December 6, 1939, MSS G-2 #28 1940, USAMHI, 7.

78. MID 2016–1297/64, "Visit to Polish Theatre of Operations," October 31, 1939, *Military Intelligence Division Correspondence, 1917–1941*, Box 630, RG 165, NA.

79. Cameron, "Americanizing the Tank," 561.

80. Ibid., 462–65.

debates within the U.S. Army regarding the employment of tanks, including the vulnerability of armored units to ambush, measures to coordinate infantry and armor, and the impact of weather on operations. Black's response stressed that the Germans had solved many of the problems that still plagued the U.S. Army's armored forces. Asked whether the speed of advance of armored forces was held to that of infantry, Black replied that mechanized units were given independent missions to allow them to use their speed to full effect. He also noted the value of the *Panzer* division's reconnaissance battalion as a means of seizing and holding territory to avoid ambush.[81]

In February 1940, MID distributed a comprehensive assessment of the German campaign in Poland based on attaché dispatches from Berlin and Warsaw. The report observed that the German army had not deviated from its peacetime training and doctrine during the campaign, implying that such training and doctrine provided a reliable indicator of future wartime performance. The report correctly concluded that the campaign's outcome was attributable not to Polish ineptitude, but rather to superior German arms and doctrine.[82]

In November, Lieutenant Colonel Sumner Waite filed a report on German tactics based on discussions with Polish officers. His account was reminiscent of Conger's observations of the *Reichswehr's* 1926 maneuvers. He noted that German penetrations of Polish lines, which he compared to the tines of a fork, exposed the flanks of defending forces to rapid and powerful envelopment by light formations and motorized units supported from the air. While armored units concentrated in the area of the penetration during the breakthrough, in the exploitation they "*avoided combat* and were *pushed forward as far and as rapidly as possible*, breaking up enemy formations, disrupting his communication, and destroying his establishments and reserve depots of materiel and personnel [emphasis in original]."[83]

Attachés returning to the United States shared their insights with their fellow officers on German armor developments. Truman Smith, who returned to the United States in April 1939, gave a talk on the Pol-

---

81. "Statement by Major Percy G. Black, Field Artillery, Who Recently Returned From Germany Where He Has Been on Duty as Assistant Military Attaché," December 5, 1939, in The Willis D. Crittenberger Papers, USAMHI, 1–5.

82. "The German Campaign in Poland, September 1—October 5, 1939," February 1, 1940, Special (Bulletins), Operations in European War, A.W.C. File 236-F, Copy No. 1, Part 1, USAMHI, 52–53; War Department, *Digests and Lessons of Recent Military Operations: The German Campaign in Poland, September 1 to October 5, 1939* (Washington, D.C.: Government Printing Office, March 31, 1942).

83. Koch, "Watching the Rhine," 223–24.

ish campaign to the 2nd Division in early 1940.[84] He subsequently published a report on the operations of an armored-car platoon during the campaign in the cavalry's official journal.[85] Percy Black spoke at the Army War College in December 1939, three months after his return from Germany. He noted, correctly, that the German attack on Poland employed a strategy of envelopment: while German infantry engaged Polish units, mechanized forces moved around their flanks and encircled them. He used a football analogy to explain the cooperation between the arms of the German army:

> The air corps and the mechanized troops received most of the publicity, just as in a football game the backfield men have their names in the headlines in the papers, but the German infantry was the line and it was the German infantry divisions, attacking on a broad front, which rolled up the Poles and herded them into areas where they were surrounded and destroyed.[86]

He noted that armored troops were able to sustain deep penetrations of Polish lines because they had an organic infantry regiment to protect their line of march and seize and hold positions.[87]

General Adna Chaffee asked Black to address the staff of the Army's only mechanized unit, the 7th Cavalry Brigade (Mechanized), because he "had been allowed to accompany the German army in Poland, where he had had an exceptional opportunity to view the usage of the German mobile mechanization [*sic*]."[88] After his talk in early February 1940, Chaffee wrote to Marshall, commending Black and noting that he had "brought to the Mechanized Brigade many ideas concerning the organization, training, and combat of the highly developed German army."[89]

On May 10, 1940, 135 German divisions supported by 2,750 aircraft and airborne forces launched an attack on France, Belgium, and the Netherlands. General Georg von Küchler's Eighteenth Army advanced into the Netherlands behind a large airborne operation. A second landing allowed the Germans to capture the Belgian fortress Eben Emael

84. Bland, ed., *The Papers of George Catlett Marshall*, volume 2, *"We Cannot Delay", July 1, 1939—December 6, 1941* (Baltimore: The Johns Hopkins University Press, 1986): 162.

85. Lieutenant Colonel Truman Smith, Infantry, "Operations of a German Armored Car Platoon in the Pursuit of the Polish Army," *The Cavalry Journal* 48, no. 6 (November-December 1939): 475−76.

86. Black, "Germany," 10.

87. Ibid., 12−13.

88. Bland, *The Papers of George Catlett Marshall* 2, 120.

89. Koch, "Watching the Rhine,", 125.

covering the approaches to the Maastricht Appendix. General Gerd von Rundstedt's army group struck Allied forces through the Ardennes. Three days later, Guderian's *Panzer* corps opened up a sixty-mile gap in the Allied center and breached French positions guarding the Meuse. A hole in the Belgian defenses farther north created a second gap. A week later, the first German unit reached the English Channel coast, splitting Allied forces. German forces occupied Paris on June 14, and a cease-fire took effect on June 25. The entire campaign lasted forty-six days but was effectively decided in ten. In less than two months, the German army achieved something it had not been able to do in four years during World War I. The Allies lost half of their forces on the continent, as well as three-quarters of their first-line equipment.[90] The speed and magnitude of the defeat stunned participants and onlookers alike.

MID accumulated substantial information on the fall of France from both sides of the conflict. In December 1940, the Division issued a description of the campaign by General Frère, commander of the French Seventh Army. Frère, whose force consisted of six or seven infantry divisions backed by two understrength armored divisions, had been assigned to block the roads to Paris from Ham and Abbeville.[91] His report contained a vivid and accurate portrayal of Germany's use of combined-arms doctrine against France.[92]

General Requin, who commanded the French Fourth Army, gave MID a more extensive analysis of the campaign. His status as an acknowledged authority on military doctrine lent additional weight to his assessment. The campaign convinced Requin, like Frère, that the combination of tanks and aviation had become the epitome of land warfare. As he saw it, the key to the success of the German army had been its ability to exploit penetrations in French lines rapidly. As Requin described it, *"The development of this strategical exploitation is so rapid,* that the reorganization of a constituted front in order to limit the effects thereof, becomes impossible even when the classical general reserve of Large Units and Artillery, are still available to attempt such action [emphasis in original]."* He concluded that *"The decisive breakthrough,* tactically possible, but strategically an utopia during the last

90. Addington, *Blitzkrieg Era,* 97–109; Cooper, *The German Army,* 217.

91. General André Beaufre, *1940: The Fall of France,* trans. Desmond Flower (London: Cassel, 1967): 194.

92. "Operations of the French Seventh Army, May 10–June 24, 1940," December 9, 1940, Special (Bulletins), Operations in European War, A.W.C. File 236-H, Volume 1, US-AMHI, 3–4.

war of 1914–1918, has become a reality thanks to the use of Large Armored Units and Aviation for the *exploitation* [emphasis in original]."[93] The fact that prior to the war he had been an exponent of the French doctrine of the methodical battle, which declared such penetration and exploitation to be impossible, made his conversion to combined-arms warfare all the more poignant.

Throughout the campaign, the German army continued to provide U.S. military attachés information. It also invited them to tour the front in Belgium and France.[94] The assistant military attaché in Berlin filed a report describing the campaign in the west based on conversations with the commander of a reconnaissance car platoon that had taken part in the invasion.[95]

The rapid collapse of the French army in May 1940 prodded the U.S. Army into forming its own armored divisions. In July it created an Armored Force composed of the 1st and 2nd Armored Divisions and a headquarters reserve battalion. The Army also gave the Armored Force responsibility for developing the tactics and technology for mechanized units. General Chaffee assumed command of the I Armored Corps.

In forming the Armored Force, the Army drew heavily on prewar intelligence regarding the composition and doctrine of German armored forces. As George C. Marshall wrote to the Secretary of War on March 29, 1941, "The data gradually being collected, on a factual basis, as a result of the incredible happenings in Belgium and France, made clear the necessity for certain changes in organization, notably the Armored Force and increased motorization throughout the Service."[96] The Armored Force sent the U.S. attaché in Berlin, Colonel Bernard Peyton, sixty-one questions regarding the combat performance of German armored forces in northern France. Among the topics of interest were the coordination of artillery and tactical aviation and the effectiveness of armored forces absent air superiority.[97] The Armored Force used his responses to refine U.S. armored doctrine and training.

93. "General Requin's 'Lessons and Conclusions' from Operations of French Fourth Army," October 11, 1940, Special (Bulletins), Operations in European War, A.W.C. File 236-H, Volume 1, USAMHI, 3, 4.

94. "German Principles of Employment of Armored Forces," August 30, 1940, *Tentative Lessons from the Recent Active Campaign in Europe* 1, AWC File 236-F, USAMHI.

95. MID 2016-1254/10, "German Reconnaissance Car Platoon in Combat—May, 1940," July 29, 1940, *Military Intelligence Division Correspondence, 1917–1941*, Box 627, RG 165, NA.

96. Bland, *The Papers of George Catlett Marshall* 2, 460.

97. Koch, "Watching the Rhine," 231–32.

Former military attachés also played a vital role in the development of U.S. armored forces. Black served as the Armored Force's first intelligence officer.[98] When he moved on to MID's German Section in 1941, James Crockett, another veteran of the military attaché office in Berlin, replaced him.[99]

The organization and doctrine of German tank forces influenced the development of the Armored Force in several significant ways. First, the *Panzer* division served as the benchmark for American armored divisions. As Brigadier General Alvan C. Gillem put it, "Our Armored Division should be organized and equipped to be at least the equal of, but preferably superior to, the German Armored Division."[100] Indeed, the structure of the U.S. armored division was nearly identical to that of the prewar German *Panzer* division.[101] When the United States received information that the *Wehrmacht* had changed the infantry and artillery components and supply echelon of the *Panzer* division, the Army altered the composition of its armored divisions accordingly.[102]

Second, American armored doctrine bore many similarities to that of the German tanks corps. In part, this represented a continuation of a cavalry tradition that emphasized speed, maneuver, and initiative. It was also the result of an effort to emulate German doctrine because of its success on the battlefield. The War Department's *Training Circular No. 4*, issued in September 1940, described the armored division as "a self-sustaining unit of specially equipped elements of the combined arms and services. It has great offensive power and mobility but only a limited and temporary capacity for the defense." Army doctrine envisioned using armored divisions against objectives deep in the enemy rear. The armored divisions would seize critical areas, envelop and encircle enemy units, and pursue retreating forces. Tactical aircraft would

98. In that role, Black published insightful articles on foreign armored doctrine and its implications for the United States. See Lieutenant Colonel Percy G. Black, G.S.C., "The U.S. Armored Force: The Possibilities of Its Strategical and Tactical Employment," *The Cavalry Journal* 49, no. 5 (September–October 1940); "The Armored Force and Its Development," *The Cavalry Journal* 49, no. 6 (November–December 1940).

99. Cameron, "Americanizing the Tank," 565.

100. Ibid., 542.

101. Each 1940 U.S. armored division included a reconnaissance battalion; an armored brigade with two light and one medium tank regiments, a field artillery regiment, and an engineer battalion; an infantry regiment; a field artillery battalion; and service and maintenance units. Each 1935 *Panzer* division included a reconnaissance battalion; tank brigade; motorized artillery regiment; engineer battalion; motorized infantry brigade; antitank battalion; and signal and service units. On the composition of the U.S. armored division, see Cameron, "Americanizing the Tank," 495. On the composition of the *Panzer* division, see Addington, *Blitzkrieg Era*, 35.

102. Cameron, "Americanizing the Tank," 542.

support their forward movement while motorized infantry units would consolidate their gains.[103]

In some cases, the Armored Force attempted to copy German tactics explicitly. Crockett sent the force a translation of a German textbook on the training and tactics of a tank platoon, including lessons derived from the campaign in France. The Armored Force duplicated the document, replaced the illustrations of German tanks and vehicles with their American counterparts, and used it as a basis of a field manual governing tank platoons.[104]

Although the Armored Forced was influenced by the *Panzer* division, it also bore the mark of the mechanized cavalry as well as novel features.[105] The Armored Force, like the mechanized cavalry before it, did not expect to get into a slugging match with enemy armored vehicles. It therefore acquired tanks that emphasized speed at the expense of armor and firepower. As a result, American tanks were often inferior to their German counterparts, especially the Mark V Panther and Mark VI Tiger that appeared in the later stages of the war.[106]

American armored doctrine also approached antitank operations much differently from that of the Germans. The U.S. Army planned to use independent antitank units composed of fast, lightly armored "tank destroyers," held in reserve to counter massed armor attacks. Indeed, the infantry used the promise that tank destroyers could free the battlefield from the threat of tanks to argue against expanding armored forces and reorganizing around the tank.[107] Battlefield realities, however, soon demonstrated that the weapon best suited to destroying a tank was another tank. American forces rarely met massed German armored formations, so tank destroyers were rarely used in the role envisioned.[108]

U.S. Intelligence and German Armored Warfare

This case demonstrates that it is possible to detect and characterize foreign military innovation before it appears on the battlefield. Two

---

103. Cameron, "Americanizing the Tank," 545–46.

104. Ibid., 565.

105. Johnson, *Fast Tanks and Heavy Bombers*, 220–22; William O. Odom, *After the Trenches: The Transformation of U.S. Army Doctrine, 1919–1939* (College Station: Texas A&M University Press, 1999).

106. Martin Blumenson, *Breakout and Pursuit* (Washington, D.C.: U.S. Army Center of Military History, 1961): 44–45.

107. Cameron, "Americanizing the Tank," 610, 887.

108. Charles M. Baily, *Faint Praise: American Tanks and Tank Destroyers during World War II* (Hamden, Conn.: Archon Books, 1983): 6.

years before the outbreak of World War II and four years before U.S. involvement in the war, U.S. Army leaders possessed detailed, accurate intelligence describing the German approach to armored warfare. That the Army did not immediately put this information to work had more to do with the priorities of the U.S. armed forces than with the quality of U.S. intelligence.

The use of tanks in the final campaigns of World War I had triggered widespread speculation as to their proper employment in the years that followed. Tanks also drew the attention of intelligence services around the world. MID, like its foreign counterparts, was thus keen to find out what the Germans were up to.

Despite the close relationship between the *Reichswehr* and the U.S. Army, Germany concealed its early experimentation with tanks. Although MID learned of cooperation between Germany and the Soviet Union involving armored warfare, including the existence of the armored training center at Kazan, the Division was unable to determine what the center was doing in any detail. Not until the German army formed its first *Panzer* units was MID was able to put all of the pieces together. Despite Berlin's attempts to restrict the flow of information on its armored forces, U.S. military attachés reported German armored doctrine accurately and determined the organization and missions of the *Panzer* division. By November 1937, the Army possessed authoritative information on the organization of the *Panzer* division and its role within the German concept of mobile warfare. The observation of the German campaigns in Poland and France allowed MID to refine its views of armored warfare. The United States was in a privileged position in both campaigns, for it was able to collect intelligence from both sides.

U.S. military intelligence officers disseminated information regarding German armored operations throughout the Army. The German campaigns against Poland and France demonstrated the need for the Army to form armored divisions of its own. The campaigns also convinced the service of the superiority of the German approach to armored warfare. The Army went on to model its armored divisions on the *Panzer* division, and German doctrine influenced that of the Armored Force.

U.S. estimates of German tank technology, doctrine, and organization compared favorably with those of other intelligence services. MID developed a more sophisticated understanding of German tank organizations and doctrine than that of British military intelligence. In fact, British military attachés gathered only fragmentary information on German armor. As a result, British military intelligence lacked a coherent view of Germany's approached to armored warfare before World

War II. Reports from British attachés portrayed armored warfare in a future war as a replay of World War I.[109] French intelligence also followed the evolution of German military doctrine, including its emphasis on mobility and on armored warfare. However, the French viewed German armor developments through the lens of French army doctrine, which envisioned the tank as an adjunct to the infantry. As a result, the French were skeptical of the potential effectiveness of combined-arms warfare.[110]

Tactical Aviation and Rocketry

Tactical aviation also played a prominent role in Germany's success during the early campaigns of World War II. While the American and British air forces pursued strategic bombing in the years following World War I, Germany emphasized the use of air forces to support ground units and devised methods to coordinate air and ground operations. As a result, in World War II the *Luftwaffe* formed an integral part of combined-arms operations. The challenge facing U.S. military intelligence was recognizing the emergence of an approach to air warfare considerably different from American or British orthodoxy.

The Versailles Treaty prohibited Germany from possessing an air force and placed restrictions on its aviation industry. German aircraft manufacturers were forced to close, to move overseas, or to diversify their production. The German army took several steps to circumvent the treaty, however. The government secretly funded flying schools and clubs to train pilots. Some aircraft manufacturers opened offices abroad to elude the restrictions and to increase their business; those companies included Junkers in Switzerland, Rohrbach in Holland, Dornier in Switzerland and Italy, and Heinkel in Sweden. In addition, between 1924 and 1927, Junkers operated an airframe and engine plant at Fili near Moscow.[111] Workers at Fokker-Flugzeugwerke MBH at Schwerin disassembled much of the factory's machinery, hid it from Allied inspectors, and smuggled it to Holland in some 350 railroad

---

109. Harris, "British Military Intelligence," 405; T. Harrison Place, "British Perceptions of the Tactics of the German Army, 1938–40," *Intelligence and National Security* 9, no. 3 (July 1994): 496–99.

110. Peter Jackson, *France and the Nazi Menace: Intelligence and Policy Making, 1933–1939* (Oxford: Oxford University Press, 2000): 117–18, 342–3.

111. Edward L. Homze, *Arming the Luftwaffe: The Reich Air Ministry and the German Aircraft Industry, 1919–1939* (Lincoln, Neb.: University of Nebraska Press, 1976), 10, 11, 13–14.

cars. Fokker subsequently reopened as Nederlandische Vliegtuigen-fabriek NV.[112]

Allied governments shared information on German attempts to circumvent the Versailles Treaty with MID. On May 25, 1924, the military attaché in Paris forwarded information from the *Deuxième Bureau* listing the foreign subsidiaries of German aircraft manufacturers, including Fokker's Rotterdam works and Junkers factories in the Soviet Union.[113] In early October 1926, the military attaché in Riga submitted a report describing the construction of Junkers aircraft at Fili.[114]

Germany's most successful attempt to elude Allied scrutiny took place in the Soviet Union. In 1924, the German army opened an air training center on the western Russian steppe at Lipetsk, some 250 miles south of Moscow and far from Allied intelligence services. The base initially received fifty Fokker DXIIIs, one of the highest-performance fighters of its day. Over time, additional aircraft supplemented them.[115] At Lipetsk, German pilots practiced fighter and ground-attack tactics and coordinated ground and air operations. By the time Hitler ordered the base closed in 1933, the facility had trained some 120 fighter pilots and one hundred observers.[116]

After the Paris Air Agreement loosened restrictions on the German air industry in 1926, the army's Ordnance Office issued requirements for four new military aircraft: a fighter, a reconnaissance aircraft, a night fighter/reconnaissance aircraft, and a long-range reconnaissance bomber. By 1932, the requirements had been filled by the He-46 close-support and reconnaissance aircraft, He-45 light bomber and reconnaissance aircraft, Ar65 fighter, and Do-11 medium-range bomber. The army shipped these aircraft to Lipetsk for testing and evaluation.[117]

The Polish military intelligence service collected a great deal of intelligence regarding both Germany and the Soviet Union.[118] In February

112. Barton Whaley, *Covert German Rearmament, 1919–1939: Deception and Misperception* (Frederick, Md.: University Publications of America, 1984), 12–14.

113. MID 2016–941/3, May 25, 1924, *Military Intelligence Division Correspondence, 1917–1941*, Box 618, RG 165, NA.

114. MID 2090–163/3, "Types of Military Planes in Use," October 7, 1926, *Correspondence of the Military Intelligence Division Relating to General, Political, Economic, and Military Conditions in Russia and the Soviet Union, 1918–1941*, Roll 20, RG 165, NA.

115. Hanfried Schliephake, *The Birth of the Luftwaffe* (Chicago: Henry Regnery Co., 1971): 16–21, 62.

116. Homze, *Arming the Luftwaffe*, 21; Zeidler, *Reichswehr und Rote Armee*, chaps. 9–12.

117. Ibid., 21, 25–26.

118. See, for example, Richard A. Woytak, *On the Border of War and Peace: Polish Intelligence and Diplomacy in 1937–1939 and the Origins of the Ultra Secret* (New York: Columbia University Press, 1979).

1931, the Poles gave the military attaché in Warsaw, Major Emer Yeager, a roster of fifty-six German officers who had been discharged from the *Reichswehr* only to rejoin it after receiving pilot training in Russia.[119] A year later, British journalist Cecil Melville published a nearly complete account of cooperation between the *Reichswehr* and the Soviet army. The book included a description of the German facility at Lipetsk, where, Melville wrote, "special courses for German officer pilots were being held to train them in the handling and piloting of high-power scouting machines."[120]

With Hitler's appointment as chancellor in January 1933, the German government began to acknowledge air rearmament publicly. In 1934 the air force began to recruit heavily, and several hundred army personnel transferred to the Air Ministry. Indeed, Hitler and other German leaders exaggerated the country's air strength to deter Poland and France from launching a preemptive attack.[121] On March 10, 1935, Hermann Göring, the head of the Reich Air Ministry (*Reichsluftfahrtministerium*, or RLM), revealed the existence of a separate air service, the *Luftwaffe*, during an interview with the *London Daily Mail*. Two weeks later, Hitler boasted that the German air force had already achieved parity with the Royal Air Force. Although Hitler's bluff was widely believed, in fact only eight hundred of the 2,500 aircraft in the German air force were operational.[122]

When Truman Smith arrived in Germany in the summer of 1935, the *Luftwaffe* was expanding aircraft factories, constructing airfields, and recruiting personnel. The government nonetheless attempted to deny foreign observers the ability to collect information on the air force. As Smith later recalled, "Such a situation stirred up endless speculation and quite often, it must be admitted, wild guesses on the part of the American attachés. On one matter, however, the attachés all agreed: both the German army and the *Luftwaffe* construction programs were gigantic."[123]

U.S. military attachés had much less access to the air force than to the army. Although Smith and his staff enjoyed good relations with officers at the Air Ministry, including many former *Reichswehr* officers, the U.S. delegation accumulated fewer contacts within the *Luftwaffe*, which contained many Nazi Party members, who were less sympathetic to the

119. MID 2016–1109/10, "German-Soviet Cooperation," February 19, 1931, *Military Intelligence Division Correspondence, 1917–1941*, Box 624, RG 165, NA.

120. Melville, *The Russian Face of Germany*, 79.

121. Williamson Murray, *Strategy for Defeat: The Luftwaffe, 1933–1945* (Maxwell AFB, Ala.: Air University Press, 1983): 14.

122. Homze, *Arming the Luftwaffe*, 50, 98.

123. Hessen, *Berlin Alert*, 80.

United States.[124] Similarly, although U.S. Army officers studied at the *Kriegsakademie*, none attended the air force equivalent, the *Luftkriegsakademie*.

Monitoring German air developments was the primary responsibility of the assistant military and naval attachés for air matters. Between 1933 and 1939, the assistant military attachés for air, Captain Theodore J. Koenig and Major Arthur Vanaman, and their naval counterparts, Lieutenant Commander Ben H. Wyatt, Commander F. M. Maile, and Lieutenant Commander Paul E. Pihl, followed German aircraft developments closely. One way they did so was by visiting factories. In September 1934, for example, Wyatt inspected the Junkers factory at Dessau.[125] A year later, Koenig toured the same facility. Although his hosts showed him only a small portion of the operation, he did get to see examples of the Ju-160 transport and the Ju-86 bomber.[126] Wyatt's replacement, Lieutenant Harry A. Guthrie, visited the factory again in May 1936.[127]

Attachés also visited air force units in the field. In late May 1935, Koenig arranged to visit the *Richthofen Geschwader* at Döberitz. The following April, he and Smith became the first foreign attachés to visit the experimental testing station at Rechlin in Pomerania. There they examined the Ju-86 and He-111 bombers, Hs-123 and He-50 dive-bombers, and the He-70 reconnaissance aircraft and bomber.[128]

Every September, the assistant military and naval attachés for air matters submitted an "Aviation Statistics" report according to a format MID and ONI had developed. The reports estimated the number and types of aircraft in the German air force as well as their characteristics and performance; the number and types of air units; and the number and levels of training of pilots. The office filed the first such report in 1932, three years before the German government renounced the Versailles Treaty. The assistant military and naval attachés also filed reports on individual aircraft designs and engine types; military airfields and the squadrons assigned to them; and aircraft and engine factories.

---

124. Ibid., 123.

125. A-1-i 17474 B, "Junkers Airplanes, Junkers Factory, etc.," September 14, 1934, *Naval Attache Reports, 1886–1939*, Box 44, RG 38, NA.

126. MID 2082–768/2, "Junkers Aircraft and Engine Works," October 4, 1935, *Military Intelligence Division Correspondence, 1917–1941*, Box 858, RG 165, NA.

127. They were not, however, shown the Do-17 bomber, which was just beginning to enter the force. A-1-i 17474 B, "Junkers Airplanes, Junkers Factory, etc.," May 29, 1936, *Naval Attache Reports, 1886–1939*, Box 44, RG 38, NA.

128. MID 2082–883/1, "Air Force Experimental Station, Rechlin," April 7, 1936, *Military Intelligence Division Correspondence, 1917–1941*, Box 859, RG 165, NA.

Keeping abreast of German air expansion proved to be more difficult than gauging the growth of the German army. In part, this was because air intelligence was still a young discipline. The Army Air Corps had not, for example, developed many of the techniques of estimating industrial production that it would use to assess the effectiveness of the strategic bombing campaign during World War II.[129] The nature of the German buildup posed an even more fundamental challenge. The *Luftwaffe* was in many ways built from scratch during the second half of the 1930s. As a result, U.S. military attachés lacked experience with which they could gauge the likely pace of rearmament. Nor was this a uniquely American phenomenon: French and British intelligence organizations also had difficulty estimating the scope of German air rearmament.[130]

The assistant military attaché for air matters, Koenig, spoke German well and knew some of the leaders of the *Luftwaffe* and aircraft industry, including Erhard Milch, the State Secretary for Aviation; Ernst Udet, the head of the Air Ministry's Technical Office; and Gerd von Massow, the commander of the *Luftwaffe*'s elite fighter squadron and later the head of the air force training program. Koenig's lack of understanding of aeronautics and intelligence methods, however, hampered his ability to assess accurately the rapid expansion of the German air force.[131]

The secrecy that surrounded the expansion of the air force and the absence of any baseline against which German air developments could be measured meant that attachés had difficulty estimating the scope and pace of German rearmament. In November 1934—four months before the announcement of the *Luftwaffe*—a report based on tentative data estimated that Germany possessed one thousand bomber, pursuit, and reconnaissance aircraft; its actual frontline strength was approximately six hundred aircraft.[132] The 1935 annual air statistics report was better, estimating that the German air force possessed three fighter,

129. See, for example, Major General Haywood S. Hansell Jr., USAF (retired), *The Air Plan That Defeated Hitler* (Atlanta: Higgins-MacArthur, 1972): 50–53.

130. Wesley K. Wark, *The Ultimate Enemy: British Intelligence and Nazi Germany, 1933–1939* (Ithaca: Cornell University Press, 1985): chaps. 2–3; Donald Cameron Watt, "British Intelligence and the Coming of the Second World War in Europe" in *Knowing One's Enemies: Intelligence Assessment before the Two World Wars,* ed. Ernest R. May (Princeton, N.J.: Princeton University Press, 1984): 256.

131. Hessen, *Berlin Alert,* 108.

132. MID 2082–822/4, "Estimate of Pilots and Airplanes in Germany," November 10, 1934, *Military Intelligence Division Correspondence, 1917–1941,* Box 859, RG 165, NA; Deist et al., *Germany and the Second World War,* 484.

four reconnaissance, nine heavy bomber, and three naval air squadrons, underestimating the number of reconnaissance squadrons by one and overestimating the number of bomber squadrons by four.[133]

Considerable debate occurred within the *Wehrmacht* and *Luftwaffe* over the proper employment of air power. General Ludwig Beck, for example, believed that the primary mission of air forces was to support ground operations. Other officers argued that Germany needed long-range bombers to allow it to strike an adversary's homeland.[134] Göring and others touted the air force as an instrument of strategic bombardment. Moreover, the Air Ministry began to develop two heavy bombers, the Do-19 and Ju-89.

The *Luftwaffe*'s primary doctrinal publication—Air Force Regulation 16, *The Conduct of the Air War*—emphasized that victory in warfare required the combined efforts of the army and air force. It declared that the primary mission of air forces was the defeat of the enemy's air force. The heart of the doctrine was strategic attack on the sources of enemy power, including production, power, railroad, military, and government facilities.[135]

After the death of General Walther Wever, the first chief of the *Luftwaffe*, in June 1936, the German air force increased its emphasis on the use of air power to support ground forces. The *Wehrmacht*'s 1937 maneuvers included the use of a dedicated air group to provide close support to ground forces.[136] The *Luftwaffe* had halted work on the heavy-bomber program by the end of April 1937 because of slow progress in developing engines for the aircraft, the low priority of the aircraft in a continental war, and resource constraints. Instead, it emphasized medium bomber and dive-bomber programs.[137]

Germany's pursuit of a long-range bombing capability had important implications for the United States. If Germany were to develop the

133. MID 2082–812/9, "Aviation Statistics," February 8, 1936, *Military Intelligence Division Correspondence, 1917–1941*, Box 859, RG 165, NA; Schliephake, *Birth of the Luftwaffe*, 35.

134. Corum, *The Luftwaffe: Creating the Operational Air War, 1918–1940* (Lawrence: University Press of Kansas, 1997): 128–34.

135. Horst Boog, *Die Deutsche Luftwaffenführung, 1935–1945: Führungsprobleme, Spitzengliederung, Generalstabsausbildung* (Stuttgart: Deutsche Verlags-Anstalt, 1982): 164–72; Corum, "The Luftwaffe's Army Support Doctrine, 1918–1941," *The Journal of Military History* 59, no. 1 (January 1995): 58.

136. Corum, *The Luftwaffe*, 247.

137. Homze, *Arming the Luftwaffe*, 124–25; R. J. Overy, "From 'Uralbomber' to 'Amerikabomber': The Luftwaffe and Strategic Bombing," *Journal of Strategic Studies* 1, no. 2 (September 1978): 154–78.

ability to carry out long-range strategic bombardment, then its bombers would be able to threaten the United States. If, however, it were to focus on the battlefield use of airpower, its aircraft could threaten its neighbors but not the United States. Koenig consistently argued that Germany was intent on building a strategic bomber force.[138] Such a conclusion was reasonable, given public statements by Göring and others, along with Germany's long-range bomber programs. Still, such an assessment bore the imprint of mirror-imaging. Army Air Corps doctrine during the interwar period emphasized strategic bombing, paying scant attention to the use of aircraft to support ground forces.[139] In Koenig's case, at least, U.S. air doctrine appears to have served as a lens that lent coherence to German air developments.

In May 1936, Smith invited Charles Lindbergh to inspect the German air force. He hoped that the *Luftwaffe* would reveal its secrets to Lindbergh because of his status as one of the world's foremost aviators. He also believed that bringing Lindbergh to Germany would enhance his own stature in the eyes of the Air Ministry, thereby increasing the ability of his office to gather intelligence.

Lindbergh's visit between July 22 and August 2, 1936, yielded a treasure trove of information on the German air force. Lindbergh, accompanied by Koenig, visited the *Richthofen Geschwader*, the *Luftwaffe*'s elite fighter group. Colonel von Massow, the unit's commander, admitted that the unit's He-51 biplanes were obsolescent but told Lindbergh that he was expecting new Bf-109 fighters to replace them and gave him accurate figures for the aircraft's speed, armament, and flight ceiling. Lindbergh also toured the Heinkel factories at Rostock and Warnemünde. These visits yielded the first close-up examination of the He-111 medium bomber, the He-112 fighter, He-70 observation aircraft, and the He-118 dive-bomber. Koenig subsequently transmitted detailed and accurate reports on each of these aircraft to MID. Lindbergh and Koenig also visited the Junkers factory at Dessau, where they saw the Ju-86 medium bomber and were among the first foreigners to get a close-up look at the Ju-87 ("Stuka") dive-bomber.[140] Lindbergh met

---

138. Hessen, *Berlin Alert*, 98.

139. See, for example, David MacIsaac, "Voices from the Central Blue: The Air Power Theorists" in *Makers of Modern Strategy: From Machiavelli to the Nuclear Age*, ed. Peter Paret (Princeton: Princeton University Press, 1986): 633–34. See also Hansell, *The Air Plan That Defeated Hitler*, chap. 2.

140. Hessen, *Berlin Alert*, 94–98; MID 2082–768/3, "The Junkers Aircraft and Engine Works," August 28, 1936, *Military Intelligence Division Correspondence, 1917–1941*, Box 858, RG 165, NA.

with Smith regularly throughout his visit, educating him on German aeronautical developments.

Although Koenig had developed contacts throughout the *Luftwaffe*, Smith became increasingly dissatisfied with his performance as an intelligence officer. In early 1936 he asked Colonel Charles Burnett, the head of MID's Military Attaché Section, to replace him with a more qualified officer. Major Arthur Vanaman took over in April 1937. Vanaman was a respected member of the Air Corps and later rose to the rank of major general. Moreover, he used his contacts within the U.S. aviation community to gather intelligence regarding German aircraft programs. He arranged for J. H. Kindelberger, the president of North American Aviation Company, to visit several German aircraft factories. Kindelberger's expertise in aircraft production gave Vanaman insight into the German air industry. As Vanaman later recalled, "When Dutch Kindelberger walked through a plant, he could tell you right off the reel what their production was, what it could be and what they could build up to."[141]

Vanaman's appointment also led to a reevaluation of German air doctrine. By the fall of 1937, Vanaman had concluded that the purpose of the *Luftwaffe* was not strategic bombardment, but support of ground forces.[142] His assessment was not based on an analysis of German doctrine, but rather on the fact that Germany was producing only a handful of prototype four-engine bombers.

The volume of intelligence collected during Lindbergh's trip led Smith to arrange a second visit between October 11 and 25, 1937. On this occasion, Lindbergh visited the Rechlin air testing station, the Focke Wülf and Henschel aircraft factories, and the Daimler-Benz engine factory. He inspected the He-111 medium bomber, Do-17 light bomber and reconnaissance aircr aft, Bf-109 fighter, Fieseler *Storch* liaison aircraft, and Hs-123 and Ju-87 dive-bombers. He also viewed demonstration flights of the Do-17, Bf-109, and Ju-87. He was one of the first foreigners to be given the opportunity to examine the Bf-109 in detail. Given the aircraft's characteristics and his understanding of German aeronautics research and development, Lindbergh predicted that the Germans would next field a twin-engine fighter with 1,200-

141. Hall, "Truman Smith: United States Military Attaché," 119.

142. As Smith later wrote, "Scarcely had Major Vanaman taken over air activities of the office than he began to stress in his reports that Goering's Luftwaffe was not a long-range air force in the American sense, but rather an air arm, primarily designed to support the German air forces." Hessen, *Berlin Alert*, 120.

horsepower engines. This turned out to be an accurate description of the Bf-110, which was then in prototype development.[143]

The German air force was more anxious than ever to display its achievements during Lindbergh's third and final tour in October 1938.[144] While in Germany, Lindbergh visited the Heinkel factory at Oranienburg, where his hosts allowed him to sit in the cockpit of an He-111 bomber. He also got to fly the Focke Wülf FW-200 four-engine transport. At the main Junkers factory at Dessau, he inspected the Ju-90 four-engine transport, Ju-86 two-engine bomber, and Ju-87 dive-bomber. He also examined the Do-17 light bomber at the Dornier plant at Ludwigshafen. At Rechlin, he got to inspect two Bf-109s and a Bf-110 and to fly a Bf-109 for forty minutes.[145] He was also one of the first foreigners to see the then-secret Ju-88 bomber, although his guides naively asked that he and Vanaman not tell anyone that they had seen the aircraft.[146] As a result of these inspections, Vanaman drafted a special report on the Ju-88 and revised his previous report on the Bf-109.[147]

Although the military attaché's office produced a prodigious number of reports, little of this information reached the leaders of the Army or the Air Corps. As late as 1940, Brigadier General Hap Arnold, the Air Corps Assistant Chief was not on the distribution list for intelligence on the German air force.[148] Lindbergh himself gave the Air Corps leaders more information on the German air force than MID. Arnold met with Lindbergh after his third trip to Germany, later writing that this discussion had given him "the most accurate picture of the Luftwaffe, its equipment, leaders, apparent plans, training methods, and present defects" he had received.[149]

Although Lindbergh's trips yielded valuable insight into the German air force, his final visit proved costly to Smith. The spectacle of a prominent American touring Germany during the Sudeten crisis angered President Roosevelt and inflamed public opinion. Moreover, the visit culminated in Göring presenting Lindbergh a medal in a well-staged event. The incident reflected poorly on Smith, who had

143. Wayne S. Cole, *Charles A. Lindbergh and the Battle against American Intervention in World War II* (New York: Harcourt Brace Jovanovich, 1974): 36; Hessen, *Berlin Alert*, 112.

144. Charles A. Lindbergh, *The Wartime Journals of Charles A. Lindbergh* (New York: Harcourt Brace Jovanovich, 1970): 93–111.

145. Hessen, *Berlin Alert*, 131–36.

146. Lindbergh, *The Wartime Journals of Charles A. Lindbergh*, 107.

147. Hessen, *Berlin Alert*, 136.

148. Hansell, *The Air Plan That Defeated Hitler*, 49.

149. General H. H. Arnold, *Global Mission* (New York: Harper & Brothers, 1949): 188–89.

arranged the visit. Roosevelt took a personal dislike to Smith, blocking repeated requests that he be promoted.[150]

Despite the intelligence gathered during Lindbergh's tours, Smith continued to be concerned about his office's limited grasp of German air developments. He opened the 1938 annual air statistics report with a caveat:

> An annual report of this type contains perforce much accurate information, many real estimates, and some wild guesses. I consider the information herein contained as to . . . details of manufacturing establishments and processes [and] performance data of airplanes and motors as reasonably ACCURATE. I consider the data presented herewith as to the number of planes on hand and as to rates of plane production as a *Good Estimate*. I believe the data as to the "Order of Battle" of the Air Corps should be regarded as a Fair Estimate. I consider all personnel information contained in this report as a *Wild Guess* and believe such has no place in a serious Military Intelligence Report [emphasis in original]."[151]

In October 1935 the German Air Ministry began to evaluate the Bf-109 and He-112 as replacements for the He-51 biplane fighter. The following month the military attaché reported that Messerschmitt was developing a "new, very fast pursuit plane" with a speed of 490 kilometers per hour. The report was filed less than two months after the first Bf-109 prototype made its initial flight and more than a half year before the fighter's first public appearance during the 1936 Summer Olympics.[152] In mid-March 1937, Koenig filed a sketchy report on the aircraft.[153] Five months later Vanaman provided a more extensive assessment, based on information gained during Lindbergh's second visit to Germany. This update correctly identified the engines used in the Bf-109D and -E and provided dimensions as accurate as could be gained by visual inspection (see Table 6).[154]

Although U.S. attachés obtained good information on German military aircraft, they were less successful at uncovering more sensitive

150. Forrest C. Pogue, *George C. Marshall: Organizer of Victory, 1943–1945* (New York: The Viking Press, 1973): 120.

151. MID 2082–812/52, "Forwarding Annual Aviation Report for 1938," August 30, 1938, *Military Intelligence Division Correspondence, 1917–1941*, Box 859, RG 165, NA.

152. MID 2082–871/1, "New German Pursuit Airplane," November 25, 1935, *Military Intelligence Division Correspondence, 1917–1941*, Box 860, RG 165, NA.

153. MID 2082–812/24, "Pursuit—Bf 109," March 17, 1937, *Military Intelligence Division Correspondence, 1917–1941*, Box 860, RG 165, NA.

154. MID 2082–812/24, "BFW—Bf 109," October 27, 1937, *Military Intelligence Division Correspondence, 1917–1941*, Box 859, RG 165, NA.

Table 6   MID Estimate of the Characteristics of the Messerschmitt
Bf-109, 1937.

	Estimate	Actual
Weight	Unknown	4,421 lbs empty 5,523 lbs loaded
Wingspan	30 ft. (estimated)	32 ft., 4.25 in.
Wing area	200 sq. ft. (estimated)	174 sq. ft.
Maximum speed	325 mph	354 mph
Engine	Daimler-Benz DB 600 or 601 12-cylinder	DB 601A
Armament	Unknown	4 MG 17 machine guns

Actual. Figures are for the Bf-109E-1. J. R. Smith and Antony L. Kay, *German Aircraft of the Second World War* (Baltimore: The Nautical and Aviation Publishing Company of America, 1972): 492.

Estimate. MID 2082-812/24, "B FW-Bf 109," October 27, 1937,
Military Intelligence Division Correspondence, 1917–1941, Box 859, RG 165, NA.

projects. In the years leading up to World War II, the German military conducted research into a number of advanced weapons, including jet aircraft, rocket artillery, and ballistic and cruise missiles.[155] U.S. intelligence collected little information about Germany's progress in these areas. Although attachés produced several reports on experimental helicopter designs, for example, they did not obtain any information on German jet aircraft research and development.

The United States also failed to collect information on Germany's cruise and ballistic missile programs. While two German companies, Askania and Siemens, began conducting research on "flying bombs" in the early 1930s, it was an independent inventor, Paul Schmidt, who first developed the pulse-jet engine needed to power an airbreathing missile Schmidt began work on a pulse-jet in 1928 and received a patent on the device three years later. In 1934, Schmidt and a business partner proposed developing a pulse-jet-powered "flying bomb" for the German government. Although the military wanted the device, it shelved the project because of problems involving range, accuracy, and

155. Ian V. Hogg, *German Secret Weapons of the Second World War: The Missiles, Rockets, Weapons, and New Technology of the Third Reich* (London: Greenhill Books, 1999).

costs. Four years later, however, the Argus company began its own pulse-jet program; two years later Schmidt joined Argus.[156]

Although Germany's cruise missile program originated in private industry, its covert ballistic missile program was sponsored by the Ballistics and Munitions Branch of the German army's Ordnance Department. During the early 1930s, the army established a cadre of talented rocket scientists, including Werner von Braun. It also constructed a rocket test facility at Kummersdorf.[157]

In March 1936, scientists began drawing up plans for the A-4 rocket, the weapon that would eventually be known as the V-2 ballistic missile. Two and a half years later, the commander in chief of the German army, General Walther von Brauchitsch, approved the rocket's development. The first test of its engine occurred in the spring of 1939. The rocket's long range demanded that the army establish a new proving ground, however, and in early 1937 the rocket program began operating at Peenemünde, on Borkum Island in the North Sea. In the years that followed, the facility became the hub of German rocket and missile research, development, and testing.

The German army managed to conceal its rocket programs from U.S. intelligence. For example, U.S. officers did not learn of the existence of Peenemünde prior to World War II.[158] Although Smith managed to gather circumstantial evidence of German interest in military rocket development, he failed to pursue it. During Lindbergh's first visit to Germany, the aviator mentioned to Smith that German scientists had been unwilling to talk about rocket research. Smith also heard rumors of German interest in rockets on two other occasions. Nonetheless, because of both competing priorities and German secrecy, he failed to explore the matter further.[159] The fact that Smith was otherwise an outstanding attaché makes his dismissal of the information all the more striking.

The Spanish Civil War provided a testing ground for the *Luftwaffe*. During the conflict, the German air force refined its doctrine on close air support, experimented with dive-bombing tactics, and developed measures to coordinate ground and air forces.[160] Although Smith tried

---

156. Kenneth P. Werrell, *The Evolution of the Cruise Missile* (Maxwell AFB, Ala.: Air University Press, 1996): 41.

157. See Michael J. Neufeld, *The Rocket and the Reich: Peenemünde and the Coming of the Ballistic Missile Era* (New York: The Free Press, 1995); Dieter Hölsken, *V-Missiles of the Third Reich: The V-1 and V-2* (Sturbridge, Mass.: Monogram, 1994): chap. 1.

158. Indeed, the British learned of the facility through the so-called Oslo Report in November 1939. See R. V. Jones, *Most Secret War* (London: Hamish Hamilton, 1978): 69.

159. Hessen, *Berlin Alert*, 96, 165.

160. Corum, "The Luftwaffe and the Coalition Air War in Spain, 1936–1939", *Journal of Strategic Studies* 18, no. 1 (March 1995): 83.

to follow the war from Berlin, the secrecy with which the German military treated its intervention in Spain hampered his efforts.[161] Instead, the bulk of intelligence on the conflict came from the attachés in Spain, Britain, France, Italy, and the Soviet Union.

German aircraft and aviators were responsible for much of the success of Nationalist forces during the war.[162] On August 14, 1936, several Ju-52 bombers launched an attack against the Republican battleship *Jaime I*, becoming the first German aircraft to conduct a combat mission since World War I.[163] In November, the *Luftwaffe* formed the Condor Legion under the command of General Hugo von Sperrle. The legion included *Jagdgruppe* 88 (J/88), *Kampfgruppe* 88 (K/88), *Aufklärungsstaffel* 88 (A/88), and *See-Aufklärungsstaffel* 88 (AS/88), as well as staff, radio, anti-aircraft artillery, and maintenance detachments.[164] The unit initially possessed Ju-52 bombers, He-51 fighters, He-45 light bomber and reconnaissance aircraft, He-59 attack and reconnaissance aircraft, and He-60 naval floatplanes. In December 1936, Hauptmann Rudolf Freiherr von Moreau, commander of K/88, recommended establishing an experimental bomber group—*Versuchsbomberstaffel* (VB/88)—equipped with the latest bomber types for operational evaluation. Early the next year, Germany sent four He-111B-1s, three or four Do-17E-1s, and four Ju-86D-1s to Spain. The Condor Legion also established an experimental fighter squadron—VJ/88—equipped with Ju-87, Bf-109, and He-112 prototypes. Both units were treated with the utmost secrecy.[165]

Although Army Air Corps officers studied the war closely, their concepts of air warfare hampered their ability to draw meaningful conclusions from the conflict. Hap Arnold received regular reports on the war but dismissed them as irrelevant. He argued against drawing lessons from the conflict since strategic bombardment—the primary use of air power, according to Air Corps doctrine—had not occurred in Spain.[166] Moreover, the *Luftwaffe*'s concentration on interdiction and close air support was not apparent. Indeed, Arnold admitted that as late as May 1939, "Goering's neglect of strategic bombardment and logistics was

161. Indeed, Smith counted his office's inability to gather information on the air war in Spain as one of his greatest failures as attaché. See Hessen, *Berlin Alert*, 122, 166.

162. Corum, "The Luftwaffe and the Coalition Air War," 82–83.

163. Schliephake, *Birth of the Luftwaffe*, 42.

164. Gerald Howson, *Aircraft of the Spanish Civil War, 1936–1939* (London: Putnam, 1990): 27.

165. Ibid., 118–19, 184–85, 211, 232.

166. Corum, "The Spanish Civil War: Lessons Learned and Not Learned by the Great Powers," *Journal of Military History* 62, no. 2 (April 1998): 318.

not yet apparent."[167] British reports on the German air force during the war were similarly inconclusive, indicating that the *Luftwaffe* would have both a tactical and a strategic role.[168] Moreover, they tended to discount the conflict as an example of modern war because Spain offered few major industrial and population centers for air attack and because Republican forces had little anti-aircraft protection.[169]

Information from attachés in France and Britain allowed the United States to assess the performance of German weapons. In April 1938, Captain Ellis Stone, the U.S. naval attaché in Paris, sent ONI a French Air Ministry analysis of a Bf-109 captured in Spain. The report, prepared by aeronautical engineers, described in meticulous detail the flight characteristics of the aircraft.[170] In January 1940, he forwarded a report describing a second Bf-109 that the French had acquired and flown.[171] The assistant naval attaché in Paris, Lieutenant Commander C. D. Glover, provided additional insight into the capabilities of the Bf-109 through conversations with a French aviator who had faced them in combat.[172]

U.S. Intelligence and German Aviation

Collecting intelligence on the German air force proved to be more difficult than gathering information on the army's development of armored warfare. Although U.S. attachés possessed a range of sources within the War Ministry and *Wehrmacht*, they had fewer contacts within the Air Ministry and *Luftwaffe*. Moreover, the German air force attempted to conceal the extent of its expansion. Such efforts were at least partially successful, in that MID was denied an accurate understanding of the German air order of battle.

Nonetheless, by mid-1940 the War Department possessed a reasonably good understanding of German military aircraft. The department's recognition manual for German aircraft contained accurate, though incomplete, data on most models, based largely on attaché re-

---

167. Arnold, *Global Mission*, 174, 189.

168. Wark, "British Intelligence on the German Air Force and Aircraft Industry," *The Historical Journal* 25, no. 3 (1982): 642.

169. Ibid., 79.

170. A-1-i 22529, "Messerschmidt Airplanes," *Intelligence Division, Secret Reports of Naval Attachés, 1940–1946*, Box 6, RG 38, NA.

171. A-1-i 22529, "Messerschmidt Airplanes," January 12, 1940, *Intelligence Division, Confidential Reports of Naval Attachés, 1940–1946*, Box 21, RG 38, NA.

172. A-1-i 22529, "Messerschmidt Airplanes," December 13, 1939, *Naval Attaché Reports, 1886–1939*, Box 48, RG 38, NA.

ports from Berlin.[173] The 1941 version of the manual contained more comprehensive data, including that obtained from the British.[174]

Understanding German concepts for war in the air proved to be a greater challenge. U.S. concepts of warfare shaped the way attachés viewed German air doctrine. Throughout the mid-1930s, MID believed that the German air force was pursuing a strategic bombing capability similar to that which formed the cornerstone of Air Corps doctrine. Although some German air force leaders publicly advocated such a doctrine, others saw the air force as a means of supporting ground units. U.S. air doctrine served as a filter that allowed attachés to make sense out of this contradictory data. It was not until 1937 that attachés began to report that the main role of the *Luftwaffe* was interdiction and close air support. As late as 1939 Air Corps leaders such as Hap Arnold continued to believe that German air doctrine emphasized strategic bombing. It was not until the campaigns in Poland and France that the role of the German air force became apparent.

Foreign intelligence services confronted similar challenges. During the interwar period, British intelligence viewed the *Luftwaffe* as an instrument of strategic bombing, not a force designed for tactical support of ground forces.[175] Similarly, until the outbreak of World War II French intelligence was convinced that the *Luftwaffe* had been designed for strategic bombing.[176] Both services fell victim to mirror-imaging, attributing to Germany doctrine favored by their own air forces.

UNDERSTANDING GERMAN INNOVATION

In general, American attachés in Berlin enjoyed much better access to the German armed forces than their counterparts in Tokyo did to the Japanese armed forces. Moreover, the cultural divide separating the United States and Germany was much narrower than that between the United States and Japan. Beyond that, however, the two militaries represented different intelligence problems. U.S. intelligence organizations studying Japan faced the challenge of recognizing the gradual emergence of a regional power capable of manufacturing sophisticated

173. War Department, Field Manual 30–35, *Military Intelligence: Identification of German Aircraft* (Washington, D.C.: U.S. Government Printing Office, July 5, 1940).

174. War Department, Field Manual 30–35, *Military Intelligence: Identification of German Aircraft* (Washington, D.C.: U.S. Government Printing Office, July 5, 1941).

175. Wark, "British Intelligence on the German Air Force and Aircraft Industry," 627, 642, 646.

176. Jackson, *France and the Nazi Menace,* 127–28, 271–72.

weapons and developing innovative doctrine. U.S. intelligence services in Germany had to assess the rapid reemergence of an established power that had exploited advanced, unproven technology and doctrine.

U.S. intelligence did a good job of understanding German military developments between the two world wars. This success was the result of two sets of circumstances. The first was that the United States enjoyed privileged access to the German military throughout much of the period because of cordial relations between Washington and Berlin. U.S. attachés attended exercises and visited facilities that were beyond the reach of other foreign intelligence services. The legacy of close relations between the American and German armies endured even after diplomatic relations between the two governments cooled. That is not to say that collecting intelligence regarding German military developments was not at times difficult. During the Weimar years, gathering information on the army's covert tank and aircraft programs proved challenging; during the Nazi era, collecting intelligence on the *Panzer* divisions was hard.

The second reason for the U.S. success was the quality of the men who served as attachés in Germany during the interwar period. The U.S. Army assigned a number of highly capable officers to Germany. Foremost among these was Truman Smith, who possessed not only a wide range of contacts within the German armed forces, but also the depth of knowledge to allow him to translate the disparate bits of information gleaned from his sources into a comprehensive and largely accurate portrait of German rearmament.

Despite the German army's attempts to conceal details of its armor developments, by the end of 1937 Smith was able to describe accurately both German armored doctrine and the units designed to carry it out. Attaché reports were credible enough to convince portions of the Army that the *Wehrmacht* had developed a much different form of warfare than that which had characterized World War I. Moreover, information collected during the campaigns in Poland and France persuaded the Army to emulate Germany.

ONI and MID collected less information regarding the expansion of German air power because of secrecy and a lack of sources within the German air force. Moreover, much of the information regarding German air doctrine was contradictory. Under such circumstances, the Army Air Corps' strategic bombing doctrine seemingly acted as a filter that allowed attachés to make sense out of inconsistent statements regarding German air doctrine. Despite statements indicating that the German air force planned to emphasize support of ground forces, attachés in Germany and leaders of the Army Air Corps believed that Germany was intent on building a strategic air force. The accumulation of additional evidence, however, forced attachés to reassess German air doctrine. The image of the *Luftwaffe* as an instrument of strategic bombing nonetheless proved durable: not until the dramatic employment of German air power in the campaigns against Poland and France did Army Air Corps leaders recognize German air doctrine.

Organizational culture also helps explain why MID placed a low priority on gathering information regarding new technologies and organizations. Smith, for example, did not investigate German rocket programs despite evidence that the German armed forces were interested in the area. That even such a capable officer as Smith failed to identify German progress in this area demonstrates the difficulty of uncovering new ways of war.

[5]

Great Britain
Watching a Once and Future Ally

American intelligence organizations did not confine themselves to operations against potential adversaries; both the Army and the Navy monitored military developments in friendly nations as well. Britain was a particularly attractive target. Both the Army and the Navy were eager to learn as much as they could about Britain's development of advanced weaponry. Many intelligence reports from London dealt with technical subjects ranging from scientific breakthroughs to the design of new weapons. London was also a logical location from which to gather information about the British Empire. U.S. attachés in London monitored events not only in the British Isles, but also in Afghanistan, Australia, Canada, Egypt, India, Iran, Iraq, and New Zealand.[1] London also offered a vantage point from which U.S. intelligence services could report on events in other areas of interest. Before Washington's recognition of the Soviet government in 1934, information from Britain was vital to understanding military developments in the Soviet Union. After the outbreak of World War II, London offered a vantage point from which American military officers could study German weapons and tactics.

U.S. intelligence operations in Great Britain suffered from several handicaps, however. First, intelligence in London was a low priority throughout the interwar period because neither the Army nor the Navy believed that the United States would go to war with Britain.[2] As a result, there was little impetus for a systematic collection effort, such

1. In 1919, Sherman Miles, then the Army Assistant Chief of Staff, G-2, recommended establishing military attaché offices in Canada, India, and Australia or New Zealand and possibly in Egypt and South Africa. The recommendation was never acted on, however, presumably because of the drawdown in U.S. forces after World War I. See MID 2345–819, September 23, 1919, *Military Intelligence Division Correspondence, 1917–1941,* Box 1301, Record Group (RG) 165, National Archives (hereafter referred to as NA).

2. The services did, however, develop plans for a war with Britain. See William R. Braisted, "On the American Red and Red-Orange Plans, 1919–39" in *Naval Warfare in the*

as that directed against Japan. Attempts to gather technical intelligence were tempered by the possibility that the discovery of such efforts could damage relations between London and Washington.

British security posed another obstacle. In some areas, such as observing army maneuvers, attachés in London faced greater restrictions than their counterparts in Tokyo and Berlin. In addition, British officers were tight-lipped about military matters. Lieutenant Commander H. F. Kingman complained in a 1930 letter to the Director of Naval Intelligence that it had proven "almost impossible to pick up any information from conversation with British naval officers on duty at the Admiralty in London." The British officers were reluctant to talk to foreigners and refused to discuss naval developments. Salesmen were more useful. In Kingman's words, "Sooner or later their ambition to sell you something will make them talk too much, to your benefit."[3]

Although intelligence operations in Britain faced constraints, U.S. attachés could count on the press to provide valuable information on military developments. Attachés spent considerable time collecting newspapers and journals and transmitting them to MID and ONI in Washington; they spent less time assessing the accuracy and meaning of these reports.

U.S. MILITARY INTELLIGENCE AND BRITAIN

Neither the Army nor the Navy developed a dedicated cadre of experts on British military affairs during the interwar period. Whereas intelligence officers routinely spent two or even three tours of duty in Japan, with few exceptions officers were stationed in London but once. In part, this was driven by the absence of any unique qualifications for duty in Great Britain. Unlike their counterparts in Germany and Japan, attachés in Great Britain required no specialized language training. Moreover, life in London was quite comfortable. As a result, the attaché posts in London tended to be perks reserved for senior officers.

The Military Attaché's Office

The Army generally assigned a colonel or senior lieutenant colonel to London. Seven of the nine officers who served as military attaché

Twentieth Century, 1900–1945, ed. Gerald Jordan (London: Croom Helm, 1977); Thaddeus Holt, "Joint Plan Red," *Military History Quarterly* 1, no. 1 (autumn 1988).

3. E-9-a 20747, "Obtaining Intelligence Information in London," September 26, 1930, *Naval Attaché Reports, 1921–1939,* Box 820, RG 38, NA, 1–2.

Table 7   U.S. Military Attachés in London, 1917–1941

Military Attaché	Tour of Duty
Lt. Col. S. L. Slocum	October 1917–May 1919
Col./Maj. Oscar N. Solbert*	May 1919–April 1924
Lt. Col./Col. Kenyon A. Joyce	April 1924–August 1927
Col. John R. Thomas	August 1927–August 1931
Lt. Col./Col. Cortlandt Parker	August 1931–May 1935
Lt. Col./Col. Raymond E. Lee	June 1935–April 1939
Lt. Col. Bradford G. Chynoweth	April 1939–September 1939
Brig. Gen. Sherman Miles	September 1939–June 1940
Col./Brig. Gen. Raymond E. Lee	June 1940–December 1941

Source: Registers of Communications Received from Military Attachés and Other Intelligence Officers ("Dispatch Lists"), 1889–1941, Roll 3, RG 165, NA.

*Oscar Solbert began his tenure in London as a colonel; in 1920, in the wake of demobilization following World War I, his rank was reduced to that of major.

there did so for a single tour; two—Stephen Slocum and Raymond Lee—served two tours each for a total of three and five years, respectively.[4] The military and naval attachés shared offices at No. 6 Grosvenor Gardens next to the U.S. Embassy.[5] By the standards of the 1920s and 1930s, the office was well equipped: in a time in which the military intelligence community experienced steep reductions in funding and personnel, the attaché in London maintained an airplane, two cars, and a stable of horses.[6]

The military attaché had the benefit of a large staff. Indeed, the attaché office in London managed to grow in a period in which Congress limited the overall size of the attaché corps. In 1927, for example, there were three assistant military attachés assigned to London; by 1934 there were six. The office also had an assistant dedicated to monitoring British aeronautical developments. One officer, Martin F. Scanlon, held the post twice during the 1930s.

In 1927, the Army began assigning officers to Europe to gather information on foreign advances in weaponry. From July 1936 to October 1940 the Ordnance Department assigned Captain René R. Studler, an expert in small arms, as an assistant military attaché in London. The

4. Slocum's first tour in London was from January 1911 to June 1912. He had previously served as military attaché in Russia.

5. MID 2521–219/1, October 19, 1920, *Military Intelligence Division Correspondence, 1917–1941,* Box 1455, RG 165, NA.

6. MID 2521–283/2, "Request for Procurement Authority F/Y 1922," August 1, 1921, *Military Intelligence Division Correspondence, 1917–1941,* Box 1455, RG 165, NA.

Army equipped him with a detailed list of intelligence requirements, including information on high-velocity ammunition, ammunition loading techniques, and tracer round manufacture.[7] Although based in London, he made frequent trips to the Continent, reporting on foreign technological developments.[8]

While British officers served in U.S. Army units and attended service schools, no American officers were seconded to the British army.[9] Nor did cooperation between British and American air services get off the ground. During the mid-1920s, the U.S. Army Air Corps sought an exchange of officers with the Royal Air Force, proposing to send two American aviators to the RAF's Staff College while admitting two British officers to the Air Corps Tactical School. The British were anything but receptive, replying flatly that foreigners were not allowed to attend their staff colleges.[10]

The Naval Attaché's Office

The job of naval attaché in London was the most desirable post in naval intelligence, and it was generally held by one of the Navy's most senior intelligence officers. Four of the eleven attachés to serve in London during the interwar period were former Directors of Naval Intelligence and one—Alan Kirk—assumed the post after his tour. The naval attaché in London studied British naval technology closely, sending the Navy Department blueprints and equipment samples. His efforts were aided by the fact that the U.S. and British navies maintained good relations throughout the period despite periodic strains in Anglo-American relations.[11]

The naval attaché had several relatively high-ranking assistants, usually lieutenant commanders or commanders. Because the Navy, like the Army, was interested in British technology, it accredited a succession of Construction Corps officers to London. The vast majority of the

7. "Proposed Travel Abroad of Captain René R. Studler," February 1, 1935, The René Studler Papers, U.S. Army Military History Institute (hereafter referred to as USAMHI).

8. Constance McLaughlin Green, Harry C. Thomson, and Peter C. Roots, *The Ordnance Department: Planning Munitions for War* (Washington, D.C.: Office of the Chief of Military History, Department of the Army, 1955): 208.

9. Col. Bruce W. Bidwell, USA (retired), *History of the Military Intelligence Division, Department of the Army General Staff: 1775–1941* (Frederick, Md.: University Publications of America, 1986): 385.

10. MID 2257-ZZ-93/1 "Interchange of Students with the English Air Force Staff College," October 8, 1926, *Military Intelligence Division Correspondence, 1917–1941*, Box 1049, RG 165, NA.

11. Stephen Roskill, *Naval Policy between the Wars* 1 (Annapolis, Md.: U.S. Naval Institute Press, 1976): 157.

Table 8   U.S. Naval Attachés in London, 1919–1942

Naval Attaché	Tour of Duty
Capt. Walton Roswell Sexton	October 1919–August 1921
Rear Adm. Nathan Crook Twining	August 1921–February 1922
Capt. Charles Lincoln Hussey	March 1922–September 1924
Capt./Rear Adm. Luke McNamee	September 1924–March 1926
Capt. William Carleton Watts	March 1926–July 1928
Capt. William Winton Galbraith	July 1928–September 1931
Capt. Arthur Leroy Bristol Jr.	September 1931–February 1934
Capt./Rear Adm. Walter Stratton Anderson	February 1934–January 1937
Capt. Russell Willson	January 1937–May 1939
Capt. Alan Goodrich Kirk	May 1939–February 1941
Capt. Charles Lockwood	March 1941–March 1942

Source: *Register of the Commissioned and Warrant Officers of the United States Navy and Marine Corps* (Washington, D.C.: Government Printing Office, various years).

one hundred and four reports filed by Commander Ralph T. Hanson between July 1 and December 31, 1931, for example, were on such subjects as British naval construction, materials, and guns.[12]

ARMORED WARFARE

Tanks first appeared on the battlefield during World War I, shielding the infantry's advance across no-man's-land by crushing obstacles and destroying machine-gun nests. Although the British army first employed armored vehicles during the Battle of the Somme in 1916, their massed use at Cambrai in November 1917 was what captured the imagination of many observers.[13] During the battle, a force of nearly five hundred British tanks achieved a spectacular breakthrough in German lines. By the end of the war, a handful of British officers, such as J. F. C. Fuller and Giffard LeQuesne Martel, had begun arguing that tanks could transform warfare.

In 1918, Great Britain led the world in tank technology and doctrine. On Armistice Day, the British tank corps could muster twenty-five battalions, eighteen of which were deployed in France.[14] In the years that

12. E-9-a 20606, "Chronological List of Reports Submitted by the Assistant Naval Attaché (London) for Construction," *Naval Attaché Reports, 1921–1939*, Box 820, RG 38, NA.

13. Brian Holden Reid, "Fuller and the Revolution in British Military Thought" in Reid, *Studies in British Military Thought: Debates with Fuller and Liddell Hart* (Lincoln: University of Nebraska Press, 1998): 54.

14. A. J. Smithers, *Rude Mechanicals: An Account of Tank Maturity during the Second World War* (London: Leo Cooper, 1987): 1.

followed, the British army, like its counterparts around the world, sought to determine the most effective use of the tank on the battlefield. Although most officers believed that the tank was a valuable weapon, the organization and training of armored forces spawned considerable debate. Armor enthusiasts argued that the tank had brought about a radical change in the conduct of warfare. In the words of Robert H. Larson, they sought nothing short of "a revolution in military thought, a comprehensive philosophy of war explicitly designed to destroy the theoretical and practical foundations of the strategy of attrition that grew out of the experience of the Napoleonic Wars and dominated the strategic doctrines of the postwar period."[15] Fuller saw the development of the tank as "the greatest revolution that has ever taken place in the history of land warfare" and believed that independent, fast-moving tank units would restore strategic mobility to the battlefield through a combination of firepower, shock, and protection unattainable by traditional combat arms.[16]

Although armor enthusiasts were vocal, they did not represent the views of most British army leaders. Most officers, especially those from infantry and cavalry regiments, viewed armor as a means to enhance the effectiveness of traditional combat arms. Recalling the success of the tank in World War I, many believed that armor should support the advance of the infantry. Others advocated using tanks to carry out traditional cavalry missions such as reconnaissance and screening.[17] Not surprisingly, an officer's branch affiliation strongly affected his views of armored warfare: an overwhelming number of officers from the infantry and cavalry opposed mechanized forces, while many from the technical branches favored them.[18] Infantry and cavalry officers looked down on tankers, while the "rude mechanicals," as they were known, regarded officers from the traditional combat arms as obstructionist and unprogressive.

The U.S. Army expressed considerable interest in Great Britain's development of tank technology and doctrine. On at least one occasion, the Army dispatched a tank expert to serve as attaché in London: Lieutenant Colonel Bradford Chynoweth, who served in London in 1939,

15. Robert H. Larson, *The British Army and the Theory of Armored Warfare, 1918–1940* (Newark: University of Delaware Press, 1984): 82.

16. J. F. C. Fuller, *Armored Warfare: An Annotated Edition of Lectures on F.S.R. III* (Harrisburg, Pa.: Military Service Publishing Co., 1943): 2.

17. Brian Bond, *British Military Policy between the Two World Wars* (Oxford: Clarendon Press, 1980): 130–32.

18. Barton C. Hacker, "The Military and the Machine: An Analysis of the Controversy over Mechanization in the British Army, 1919–1939" (Ph.D. thesis, University of Chicago, 1969): 86–87.

had been one of the Army's earliest exponents of armored warfare.[19] The military attaché in London sent the War Department a steady stream of reports on British tank technology, including track and track-laying mechanisms, transmissions, suspension systems, engines, and wheels. By studying British tank programs, the War Department hoped to identify systems that the Army could copy or buy. The Army also looked to Britain for concepts for employing tanks.

On September 1, 1923, the British army established the Royal Tank Corps (RTC), with its headquarters at Wool, and assigned a tank battalion to each of the four infantry divisions based in the British Isles.[20] The following year, the army adopted the Vickers Medium Tank Mark I (commonly known as the Vickers Medium). Faster than existing models and equipped with a revolving turret, the Vickers Medium remained the army's standard tank until 1937. It was protected by eight millimeters of riveted plate armor and had a 47mm 3-pounder cannon with a muzzle velocity of 1,750 feet per second—enough to penetrate inch-thick armor at a range of 500 yards. Its secondary armament consisted of two Vickers water-cooled machine guns in ball mounts for use against infantry. The tank was equipped with an Armstrong-Siddeley air-cooled V8 engine that gave it a maximum road speed of fifteen miles per hour.[21]

Although the Military Intelligence Division was eager to learn about British tank technology, the British were reluctant to share such information. When foreign attachés visited RTC headquarters in the spring of 1924, for example, all that their hosts were willing to show them were World War I-vintage machines such as the Mark V, Mark V Star, and Medium C.[22] When Lieutenant Colonel Kenyon Joyce inquired about the Vickers Medium at the War Office several months later, he was told that the government's policy was that "the specifications of . . . the new Vickers tank may not be communicated to Foreign Powers."[23] Nevertheless, by October 1925 he and his staff had pieced together relatively accurate technical specifications for the tank, including the muzzle velocity of its cannon and the thickness and com-

19. David E. Johnson, *Fast Tanks and Heavy Bombers, Innovation in the U.S. Army, 1917–1945* (Ithaca: Cornell University Press, 1998): 70–71, 74–75.

20. Bond, *British Military Policy*, 132–33.

21. David Fletcher, *Mechanised Force: British Tanks between the Wars* (London: HMSO, 1991): 9–10.

22. MID 2881-A-60, "Visit to Royal Tank Corps Centre, Wool," April 30, 1924, *Military Intelligence Division Correspondence, 1917–1941*, Box 1147, RG 165, NA.

23. MID 2881-A-60/2, "Mark I Vickers Tank," July 8, 1924, *Military Intelligence Division Correspondence, 1917–1941*, Box 1147, RG 165, NA.

position of its armor.[24] His successor, Colonel John Thomas, reported the characteristics of the Mark IIA and Mark III tanks as well.[25]

As in Germany, attachés used field exercises to gain insight into the evolution of British armored doctrine. The most interesting of the RTC's early exercises were those held between September 21 and 25, 1925, on Salisbury Plain, which brought together the four infantry divisions stationed in England, the army's cavalry division, and two tank battalions. It pitted a smaller, more mobile force against a larger, less mobile force. The Eastern Force under Lieutenant General Sir Philip Chetwode consisted of three infantry divisions, while the Western Force under General Sir Alexander Godley included one infantry division and the cavalry division. Each had one battalion of tanks. Although the maneuver was mostly routine, on the third day Godley organized his tank battalion, a mechanized field artillery battalion, and a truck-mounted infantry battalion into a mobile force that he ordered to flank the enemy force and strike its rear. The tanks covered thirty-three miles in the dark in less than five hours, but the other units were unable to keep up. Because the tanks launched their attack without support, the umpires ruled it a failure.[26]

The innovative use of armor caught the attention of Joyce, who attended the exercises. His report to MID highlighted the British army's use of tanks, noting that:

> Contrary to the generally accepted principle of tank tactics, that the main use for tanks in the attack is to assist the advance of Infantry, this arm was used very little for this purpose by either force during the maneuvers. Instead . . . they were employed mainly in making wide detours, usually accompanied by other mobile troops such as Cavalry, Motorized Artillery, or Motorized Infantry, for the purpose of outflanking enemy troops.

Joyce judged such a strategy to be sound "because the increased mobility of this weapon would be sacrificed if they were tied down to slow moving Infantry [sic]." Still, he stopped short of advocating independent tank operations. Rather, he saw the tank as "a most formidable auxiliary."[27]

---

24. MID 2881-A-56/18, "New Data on the Vickers Mark I and the Dragon Mark II," October 8, 1925, *Military Intelligence Division Correspondence, 1917–1941*, Box 1147, RG 165, NA.

25. MID 2881-A-69/10, "British 10-ton Tanks, Mark IIA and III," July 16, 1928, *Military Intelligence Division Correspondence, 1917–1941*, Box 1147, RG 165, NA.

26. Larson, *The British Army and the Theory of Armored Warfare*, 122–23.

27. MID 2017–748/12, "Army Maneuvers, September 21st to 25th," October 9, 1925, *Military Intelligence Division Correspondence, 1917–1941*, Box 638, RG 165, NA, 37, 38.

The Army received Joyce's report with great interest. Colonel James H. Reeves, the Assistant Chief of Staff, G-2, sent extracts to the Army Chief of Staff. The summary emphasized the use of tanks to support infantry attacks, however, and omitted all references to their independent use.[28] Whether the Army considered the latter heretical or merely uninteresting is difficult to determine.

Despite periodic experiments, it was not until 1926 that the British army took its first tentative steps toward establishing tank forces as an independent branch. That year, the incoming chief of the Imperial General Staff (CIGS), Field Marshal Sir George F. Milne, authorized an Experimental Mechanize Force (EMF) to assess the performance of large armored formations. The unit included a light tank battalion for reconnaissance, a medium tank battalion for assault, a machine-gun battalion for security, five motorized or mechanized artillery batteries, and a motorized engineer company.[29] The EMF's 1927 and 1928 maneuvers demonstrated the effectiveness of armored formations. Particularly in its 1927 exercises, the mechanized force acquitted itself well against infantry and cavalry units. The maneuvers were hardly an unblemished success, however: they also revealed the difficulty of coordinating infantry, cavalry, tank, and air forces.[30] Indeed, they strengthened the conviction among many tank corps officers that armor should be employed separately from traditional combat arms.[31]

The British government did not permit U.S. military attachés to observe the EMF's maneuvers. When Thomas asked to visit the force in September 1927, the army politely informed him that the British chief of staff had "decided that this mechanized force is in such a nebulous state that it would not be practicable to permit foreign Attaches to visit it this year."[32] Attachés learned of the EMF's maneuvers through articles in the popular press and through professional journals such as the *Royal Tank Corps Journal*. The authors' attitudes toward tank war-

28. MID 2017–748/13a, "The British Maneuvers," October 22, 1925, *Military Intelligence Division Correspondence, 1917–1941*, Box 639, RG 165, NA, 4–5.

29. Capt. Jonathan M. House, USA, *Toward Combined Arms Warfare: A Survey of 20th-Century Tactics, Doctrine, and Organization*, Combat Studies Institute Research Survey No. 2 (Fort Leavenworth, Kan.: U.S. Army Command and General Staff College, August 1984): 48.

30. Bond, *British Military Policy*, 144; Harold R. Winton, *To Change an Army: General Sir John Burnett-Stuart and British Armored Doctrine, 1927–1938* (Lawrence: University Press of Kansas, 1988): 80–81.

31. House, *Toward Combined Arms Warfare*, 48.

32. MID 2017–807/16, "The Mechanized Force," September 7, 1927, *Military Intelligence Division Correspondence, 1917–1941*, Box 639, RG 165, NA, 1.

fare influenced their coverage of the exercises: although tank enthusiasts such as Basil H. Liddell Hart praised the maneuvers, more conser-
vative observers stressed the problems they had revealed.

Lectures were another source of information on the EMF. In December 1927, for example, Thomas attended a talk by the force's commander, Colonel R. J. Collins, at the Royal Artillery Institution. As
Collins saw it, the formation of tank battalions and changes to British
field service regulations deposing the infantry as the sole winner of
battles:

> represent a revolution in military thought, the results of which will not of
> course be seen for decades yet, but which will have an increasing effect on
> military organization. . . . It is far too soon to say what its final form will
> be, but, even in the short time the Force has been in training, much has
> been learned, enough it might fairly be said to justify the cost of the ex-
> periment to date.[33]

He did not, however, describe an overall concept of armored warfare,
nor did he assess the effectiveness of tanks against conventionally
equipped forces. He believed that rather than answering questions
about the effectiveness of armored warfare, the EMF had raised new
ones regarding the vulnerability of tanks to enemy artillery and anti-
tank guns.[34]

Although the British army excluded U.S. military attachés from the
EMF's maneuvers, it permitted them to attend divisional maneuvers in
which tanks carried out their traditional role of supporting the infantry.
In September 1926, for example, Joyce joined the 1st Battalion of the
Seaforth Highlanders for their annual maneuvers near Aldershot, the
first time that the War Office had allowed a U.S. observer to serve with
a British unit since World War I.[35] The following month, he and an assistant observed the 2nd Division's maneuvers.[36] More often than not,
however, the British restricted U.S. observers. American officers rarely

33. MID 2017–807/58, "The Experimental Mechanized Force," April 19, 1928, *Military Intelligence Division Correspondence, 1917–1941*, Box 639, RG 165, NA, 1.

34. Larson, *The British Army and the Theory of Armored Warfare*, 141.

35. MID 2017–807, "Final Maneuvers of the 1st Division Near Aldershot, on September 1st, 2nd, and 3rd, 1926," September 14, 1926, *Military Intelligence Division Correspondence, 1917–1941*, Box 639, RG 165, NA.

36. MID 2017–807/2, "Final Maneuver of the Present Training Season of the Second
Division, British Army," October 5, 1926, *Military Intelligence Division Correspondence,
1917–1941*, Box 639, RG 165, NA.

received copies of field orders, nor did their hosts allow them to attend the critiques that followed the exercises.[37]

Attaché reports on the EMF circulated throughout the U.S. Army. The cavalry, infantry, field artillery, signal corps, and engineers all requested information from MID. The Assistant Chief of Staff, G-2, Colonel Stanley H. Ford, emphasized the importance of the British experiments in a lecture at the Army War College in 1929.[38] The maneuvers also aroused the interest of American armor advocates such as Adna R. Chaffee. Chaffee sought information on British developments from his friend Major Charles G. Mettler, who was serving as an assistant military attaché in London. Chaffee questioned Mettler about British armor development when he visited Washington in 1927. As Mettler later recalled, Chaffee "loaded me with a terrible list of things he wanted to know and expected me to find out for him when I returned to London."[39]

In 1927, Secretary of War Dwight F. Davis witnessed a demonstration of the EMF at Aldershot. Impressed by the performance of British tank forces, he asked the General Staff to undertake similar experiments.[40] The Army assembled a mixed brigade-sized force at Fort Meade, Maryland, in 1928; it formed a second experimental force at Ft. Eustis, Virginia, two years later. The cost of the project, along with doctrinal disputes, organizational politics, and limitations of contemporary tank technology, conspired to end the experiment, however. In May 1931, Army Chief of Staff Douglas MacArthur ordered the force disbanded and directed one cavalry and one infantry regiment to incorporate tanks into their existing organizations. He hoped that the mechanized cavalry unit, the 1st Cavalry (Mechanized), would serve as a laboratory for tactical and doctrinal experimentation.[41]

The War Department's interest in British tank technology continued into the 1930s. In the fall of 1930, an ordnance officer assigned to London sent MID classified minutes of the tenth meeting of the War

37. MID 2017–993/8, "War Office Exercise with Troops—September 16–17," September 25, 1929, *Military Intelligence Division Correspondence, 1917–1941*, Box 643, RG 165, NA.

38. Col. Stanley H. Ford, "The Military Intelligence Division, War Department General Staff," lecture, G-2 course no. 3, November 29, 1929, #362A-3, USAMHI, 17.

39. Timothy K. Nenninger, "The Experimental Mechanized Forces," *Armor* 78, no. 3 (May-June 1969): 35.

40. Ibid., 33.

41. In December 1931 the War Department ordered the First Cavalry subordinated to the newly activated Seventh Cavalry Brigade (Mechanized). The Thirteenth Cavalry was subsequently mechanized and subordinated to the same brigade.

Office's Mechanical Warfare Board, which reviewed the trials and performance of various classes of mechanical vehicles and outlined experiments for the coming year. He noted that he had obtained the report "in a most confidential way and with the expressed understanding that the information contained therein is for the exclusive use of the United States and is not to be revealed to the attaches from other countries, or otherwise given publicity."[42] While he did not specify the source of the report, it presumably came from inside the British government.

In 1929 Colonel C. N. F. Broad had attempted to distill the lessons learned from the EMF in *Armoured and Mechanized Formations*, known as the "Purple Primer" because of the color of its cover. The primer, while provisional, provided a conceptual underpinning for future armored efforts. Although U.S. attachés did not acquire the confidential document, in October 1928 Thomas had reported on a talk Broad gave at the Royal Artillery Institution during which he outlined his concept of armored warfare. Broad stressed the need to mechanize infantry to allow it to keep up with the tank rather than slowing down the tank to match the pace of the infantry. He also stressed the importance of equipping tanks with radios to improve tactical communication.[43]

On April 1, 1931, Broad was promoted to brigadier and given command of the 1st Brigade, RTC, to test the concepts he had outlined in the "Purple Primer." The maneuvers represented the first time since the EMF had been disbanded that the British army employed tanks in greater than battalion strength. Broad used the maneuvers to develop a common system of armored tactics. The brigade, composed of the 2nd, 3rd, and 5th battalions of the RTC, practiced methods for conducting deep penetrations of an adversary's lines.[44] Throughout the exercise, the unit's flexibility, mobility, and firepower proved superior to that of more conventional forces.[45]

The maneuvers demonstrated the use of radios to control tank units.[46] As Lieutenant Colonel Cortlandt Parker reported to his superiors in Washington, radio allowed the tactical commander to exercise

---

42. MID 2881-A-197/1, "Mechanical Warfare Board Proceedings," September 10, 1930, *Military Intelligence Division Correspondence, 1917–1941*, Box 1148, RG 165, NA.

43. MID 2281-A-151/1, "Tactics of Armoured Fighting Vehicles," January 16, 1929, *Military Intelligence Division Correspondence, 1917–1941*, Box 1148, RG 165, NA.

44. Captain B. H. Liddell Hart, *The Tanks: The History of the Royal Tank Regiment and its Predecessors: Heavy Branch Machine-Gun Corps, Tanks Corps, and Royal Tank Corps, 1914–1945*, volume 1, *1914–1939* (London: Cassel and Co., 1959): 292–94.

45. Larson, *The British Army and the Theory of Armored Warfare*, 156–57.

46. Winton, *To Change an Army*, 118.

greater control over units. However, the sets employed in early exercises were difficult to hear above the noise of the tank's engine. Only one operator could talk at a time, and his transmission was broadcast to all.[47]

British newspapers published numerous reports of the exercises, including many by Liddell Hart. As Parker explained, although the army attempted to conceal their mechanized developments from foreign intelligence services, "in order to stimulate public support they permit the British public to view maneuvers of the Tank Brigade and allow the press to publish many details."[48] Press articles, especially those written by retired army officers, were generally detailed, accurate, and insightful.[49]

In January 1932, Parker filed a report analyzing the armored brigade's maneuvers. He hoped that the assessment would be useful not only as a description of British tactical doctrine, but also as a source of "ideas on which to organize tactical exercises for the 1st U.S. Cavalry [Regiment]." In his view, the exercises showed that while an army could use tanks to support the infantry, it could employ them more effectively against the enemy's rear. "The tactics advocated by the British do not seek a decision by attacking the enemy's infantry from the front. The tactics seek to paralyze the enemy by attacking his command areas and artillery from the rear, avoiding his infantry and anti-tank guns, and leaving the area attacked when the damage had been done." Parker likened the tactic to a cavalry raid, noting, however, that a tank attack could prove far more decisive than a traditional cavalry raid.[50]

While German doctrine emphasized combined-arms organization and operations, the Royal Tank Corps and many British armor enthusiasts advocated the formation of units composed entirely of tanks. Tank Corps officers fostered the belief that large armored formations operating independently held the key to victory on the battlefield. The officers emphasized the mobility of tanks over their striking power while ignoring their substantial shortcomings. Although such an approach greatly simplified the task of developing armored doctrine,

47. MID 2280-A-112/1, "Communications within a Tank Brigade", September 22, 1931, *Military Intelligence Division Correspondence, 1917–1941*, Box 1147, RG 165, NA.

48. MID 2281-A-87/7, "The Tank Brigade—A Summary of Organization, Communications, and Tactics," January 27, 1932, *Military Intelligence Division Correspondence, 1917–1941*, Box 1148, RG 165, NA, 1.

49. See, for example, MID 2017–1107/16, "Tank versus Tank," April 29, 1932, *Military Intelligence Division Correspondence, 1917–1941*, Box 645, RG 165, NA.

50. "The Tank Brigade—A Summary of Organization, Communications, and Tactics," 4, 6.

the neglect of combined-arms tactics limited the flexibility of tank formations.[51]

In November 1933 the army authorized the permanent formation of the 2nd, 3rd, and 5th battalions of the Royal Tank Corps into the 1st Tank Brigade and appointed Brigadier Percy Hobart as its commander. Hobart, an advocate of independent tank operations, used the opportunity to test these concepts. In a series of exercises beginning in August 1934, his brigade consistently beat infantry and cavalry units. A mechanized infantry brigade, mechanized artillery brigade, and other units then joined the tank brigade to form what was in essence an armored division.[52]

Near the end of Parker's tour, he compiled a massive treatise on British mechanization efforts, titled "Mechanization and Motorization of the British Army." He was highly critical of the British army's exploration of independent tank operations, believing—correctly—that they ignored the need for cooperation between tanks and other arms. In his words:

> While a prophecy concerning warfare may be hazardous, it appears that, should a European war break out in the near future, defensive fronts will be as difficult to break as in the World War. . . . The solution to breaking a defensive front appears to lie in the direction of an attack in which tanks and infantry are closely associated and in which the infantry advances with the same mobility as the fast tanks, and in close association with the tanks.[53]

He believed that the British, "overimpressed . . . with the increased speed . . . of the Vickers 12-ton tank [sic]," had developed tactics involving independent action by tank units.[54] Parker was thus able to diagnose one of the main weaknesses of British armored doctrine four years before the outbreak of World War II.

During the 1930s British tank technology lagged behind that of other major powers. In 1936 the army formulated a requirement for a new generation of tanks to replace the Vickers Medium, including cruiser and medium tanks for the Tank Brigade, a light tank for mechanized

---

51. House, *Toward Combined Arms Warfare*, 48–49; Richard M. Ogorkiewicz, *Armor: A History of Mechanized Forces* (New York: Frederick A. Praeger, 1960): 58.

52. Kenneth Macksey, *Armoured Crusader: A Biography of Major-General Sir Percy Hobart* (London: Hutchinson & Co., 1967): 111–12.

53. MID 2017–807/129, "Mechanization and Motorization of the British Army," May 27, 1935, *Military Intelligence Division Correspondence, 1917–1941*, Box 640, RG 165, NA, 172.

54. Ibid., 205.

cavalry units, and an infantry or assault tank for army tank battalions.[55] Years of neglect had seriously eroded Britain's manufacturing base. The Cruiser Tank Mark I—also known as the A9—was designed in 1934 but did not enter even limited production until 1937.[56]

Gathering information on the British tank corps was a high priority for U.S. military intelligence throughout the 1930s, even though the British army was reluctant to share its secrets.[57] The Royal Tank Corps Centre remained off-limits to U.S. personnel until June 1936, when Colonel Raymond E. Lee and Lieutenant Colonel Hayes Kroner visited it.[58] Similarly, when the U.S. Army's Ordnance Department proposed increasing the flow of information between the United States and Great Britain on tank technology, the military attaché in London responded that the War Office had never permitted any foreigner to see the inside of a British tank.[59] Despite such constraints, Captain Studler, the office's ordnance expert, monitored British tank developments closely. During his tenure in London he gathered accurate design information on the Light Tank Mark VI and VII, Cruiser Tank Mark VI, and Infantry Tank Mark II and III.

In 1937 the army took its first step toward mechanizing its cavalry by forming a "Mobile Division" composed of two mechanized cavalry brigades, a tank brigade, and divisional troops. Like the horse cavalry, the mobile division was designed for reconnaissance and screening rather than assault. The army also consolidated tank units for infantry support into Army Tank Brigades composed of three tank battalions each.[60] It began to procure fast, lightly armored "cruiser" tanks for cavalry roles and slow, heavily armored "infantry" tanks for infantry support.

In early 1939 the army reorganized the Mobile Division and renamed it the 1st Armoured Division. Its composition reflected the tank corps' emphasis on tank-heavy formations: it included two tank brigades and a mixed brigade of infantry and artillery.[61] The unit nonetheless re-

55. Larson, *The British Army and the Theory of Armored Warfare*, 191.

56. Winton, *To Change an Army*, 185.

57. MID 9771–249/149, "Exchange of Information," November 28, 1936, *Military Intelligence Division Correspondence, 1917–1941*, Box 2193, RG 165, NA.

58. MID 2281-A-85/5, "Visit to the Royal Tank Corps Centre," June 15, 1936, *Military Intelligence Division Correspondence, 1917–1941*, Box 1147, RG 165, NA.

59. Green, Thomson, and Roots, *The Ordnance Department*, 212.

60. Ibid., 58.

61. Ogorkiewicz, *Armor*, 59. The organization and equipment of the division was reported to MID by the military attaché in MID 2017–822/78, "1st Armored Division, British Army," December 18, 1939, *Military Intelligence Division Correspondence, 1917–1941*, Box 641, RG 165, NA.

mained undermanned and inadequately equipped; when World War II erupted, the organization existed largely on paper.

At the outbreak of World War II, Britain's only other armored division was in Egypt. In 1932 the army had sent a battalion of tanks to North Africa to meet the threat of Italian aggression. Under the command of Lieutenant General John Burnett-Stuart, the 6th Battalion, RTC, practiced cooperation with air units and developed methods of night fighting.[62] In 1938 the army dispatched Percy Hobart to Egypt to oversee the formation of an armored division. Despite considerable resistance, he assembled the 7th Armoured Division, later dubbed the "Desert Rats."[63]

As the threat of war with Germany and Italy grew, the British government reconsidered its traditional reluctance to share information with the United States. In 1938 the army offered to let U.S. attachés inspect the Mark I Cruiser Tank. This time it was Washington that balked: the Ordnance Department recommended that the attaché decline, both because the office lacked an ordnance expert and because the British would expect an invitation to inspect U.S. tanks in return. Despite the rebuff, British openness grew. In July 1939, Lieutenant Colonel Bradford Chynoweth received a tour of the Armored Fighting Vehicle School at Bovington, where he saw the full range of British tanks and rode in several.[64]

By the outbreak of World War II, MID had thus managed to accumulate an accurate understanding of British armor developments. Military attachés had described both British armored doctrine and the tank corps' more innovative experiments. Although the British army frequently denied attachés permission to attend field exercises, U.S. officers nonetheless managed to glean substantial information from newspapers and professional journals. U.S. intelligence had less success collecting information on British tank designs. Although U.S. officers obtained performance characteristics of British vehicles, British security prevented them from gathering detailed technical data that would have been useful to the designers of U.S. tanks.

The outbreak of World War II in Europe gave U.S. Army officers an opportunity to evaluate the performance of British forces in combat.

62. Winton, *To Change an Army*, 142–54. The military attaché in London described the Sixth Battalion, RTC, in MID 2281-A-87/15, "Tank Corps Reorganization in Egypt," July 1, 1933, *Military Intelligence Division Correspondence, 1917–1941*, Box 1148, RG 165, NA.

63. Macksey, *Armoured Crusader*, 156. MID's description of the division is contained in MID 2017-744/15, "British Armoured Division in Egypt," November 19, 1940, *Military Intelligence Division Correspondence, 1917–1941*, Box 638, RG 165, NA.

64. Brig. Gen. Bradford Grethen Chynoweth, USA (retired), *Bellamy Park* (Hicksville, N.Y.: Exposition Press, 1975): 165.

The Army had stationed twenty-four military observers in England by the end of 1940. It also expanded its network of attachés and observers in British colonies: in December 1941, it had officers posted in Australia, Canada, Egypt, Ireland, and South Africa and observers in Iraq, Malaya, and India.[65]

Although the onset of war restricted the amount of information that U.S. military intelligence could gather on Japanese and German forces, it also yielded greater cooperation between Britain and the United States. Attachés provided important links between the British and American armed forces and intelligence services. As the British government realized that Washington was committed to assisting it, the British army began to grant U.S. attachés greater access to their units.[66] In mid-February 1940, Brigadier General Sherman Miles visited the 1st Armoured Division. Although the unit had been in existence for a year and a half, Miles reported that the unit's commander, Major General Roger Evans, described it as experimental and unable to carry out its assigned missions.[67]

When Germany invaded France, the only armored forces attached to the British Expeditionary Force (BEF) were the 4th and 7th battalions of the Royal Tank Regiment, which formed part of the 1st Army Tank Brigade. The unit's only major action occurred when seventy lightly armed, slow, and heavily protected infantry tanks—mostly A11 "Matilda I's"—struck at Rommel's 7th Panzer Division at Arras on May 21. The attack broke down because infantry and artillery were unable to keep up with the tanks. The 1st Armoured Division did not embark for France until ten days after the Germans had launched their offensive, by which time Guderian's tanks had already reached the Channel coast.[68]

Besides getting reports from U.S. Army officers who observed the fall of France from both sides of the conflict, Washington received information from London. In March 1941, Major General Giffard Martel, the commanding officer of the Royal Armoured Corps, gave the U.S. military attaché, Brigadier General Raymond E. Lee, a report documenting lessons learned from the BEF's experience in France.[69] Martel

---

65. Bidwell, *History of the Military Intelligence Division*, 386, 389.

66. Green, Thomson, and Roots, *Ordnance Department*, 261.

67. MID 2017–822/80, "1st Armored Division, British Army," February 27, 1940, *Military Intelligence Division Correspondence, 1917–1941*, Box 641, RG 165, NA, 2.

68. Liddell Hart, *The Tanks*, 6.

69. Not only was Martel a tank enthusiast, he had also commanded the 50th Territorial Army Division in France. His division had been involved in the failed Allied counterattack at Arras.

noted that the British armored division lacked the flexibility of the combined-arms *Panzer* division, which "always had the right tool available to deal with whatever opposition appeared before them."[70] He thought it was too late for Britain to adopt German methods, however; the best hope was to adapt to the situation. The primary roles of Army Tank Brigades became protecting infantry from the threat of attack, engaging in set-piece battles against defensive positions, and supporting attacks on enemy units in mobile warfare.[71]

The failure of the British tank corps in France was partially offset by its success in North Africa. Between December 1940 and February 1941, forces under General Archibald Wavell defeated the numerically superior Italian 10th Army under Marshal Rodolpho Graziani in Operation *Compass*. Using tactics that went against British army doctrine, General Richard O'Connor used his tank assets—the 7th Armoured and 4th Indian divisions—to envelop the Italians at Sidi Barrani between December 9 and 11, 1940. O'Connor pursued the Italians into Libya, besieging and then taking Bardia and Tobruk before annihilating the remainder of the enemy force at Beda Fomm between February 5 and 7, 1941.[72]

The British thought the campaign demonstrated that infantry divisions accompanied by infantry tanks should fight together, with armored divisions engaging enemy armor on the flanks.[73] Unfortunately, cooperation between separate units proved difficult. As the British would learn in coming campaigns, the Germans could exploit this weakness to separate and destroy British formations.

On January 9, 1941, Miles, now the Assistant Chief of Staff, G-2, sent Lee a confidential cablegram instructing him to "obtain for staff use available British documents [concerning the] employment [of] armored divisions in normal and Egyptian operations [sic]." Lee responded by sending MID a copy of the War Office's analysis of the first phase of the campaign in North Africa. His preface to the report included the caveat that the lessons of the campaign "although generally applicable in principle . . . may require variation to a greater or lesser degree when applied to operations against a first class enemy in a European theatre of war [sic]." The British assessment of the army's performance at Sidi Barrani was, not surprisingly, positive. According to the report, the tank attack was so effective "that it was possible for infantry to be brought forward in [motorized transport] to debussing points within

70. MID 2017–822/109, "Lessons in Employment of Armoured Units," March 12, 1941, *Military Intelligence Division Correspondence, 1917–1941*, Box 641, RG 165, NA, 1.
71. Ibid., 2–3.
72. Correlli Barnett, *The Desert Generals* (London: William Kimber, 1960): chaps. 1–3.
73. Macksey, *Armoured Crusader*, 196.

small arms range of the enemy position and to be employed in a 'mopping up' role only."[74] The battle had, however, demonstrated the need to strengthen the infantry and artillery element of armored divisions.

Major Bonner Fellers, the U.S. military attaché in Cairo, sent MID regular reports on the campaign, including Wavell's official account of the planning and execution of Operation *Compass* and lessons learned from the Battle of Sidi Barrani.[75] Reports on the campaign showed that a flexible commander could solve problems of infantry-tank coordination so evident in prewar exercises. The campaign also demonstrated the need for an armored unit to possess sufficient recovery vehicles: during the Battle of Sidi Barrani, the 7th Battalion lost approximately half its strength during the three days it was in action, mostly because of mechanical problems. British reports on the campaign also noted the demoralizing effect on an infantry force of being confronted by tanks that were virtually immune to their fire. The British questioned whether the campaign would have gone as well as it did had they faced German rather than Italian troops.[76] It was an apt question, and one that would soon be answered when General Alan Cunningham's 8th Army faced Rommel's *Afrika Korps* outside Tobruk.

U.S. Military Intelligence and British Armored Warfare

The Army gathered a great deal of accurate data regarding British armored developments throughout the period. Moreover, the sources of information available to attachés complemented one another: when attachés were unable to observe exercises firsthand, they were often able to obtain accounts from the press. Reports on Britain's development of armored forces received wide distribution within the Army. Indeed, the success of the Experimental Mechanized Force provided ammunition for American advocates of independent armored operations and spurred the creation of an analogous organization within the U.S. Army.

74. MID 2017–744/17, "Lesson from the Western Desert (Mechanized Forces in Africa)," January 10, 1941, *Military Intelligence Division Correspondence, 1917–1941*, Box 638, RG 165, NA, 1–2.

75. Fellers also inadvertently gave the Italians and Germans insight into British dispositions in North Africa. Fellers transmitted intelligence from the British to the War Department using the Black Code, which had already been broken by both the Italians and the Germans. The German *Wehrmacht* OKW/Chi transmitted the decoded reports to Rommel's headquarters. See Gerhard L. Weinberg, *A World at Arms: A Global History of World War II* (Cambridge: Cambridge University Press, 1994): 350, 550–51.

76. MID 2017–744/26, "British Campaign in the Western Desert," May 1, 1941, *Military Intelligence Division Correspondence, 1917–1941*, Box 638, RG 165, NA, 11, 12, 15, 20.

The legacy of World War I permeated assessments of British armor developments from 1918 to the early 1930s, perpetuating the view that tanks were an auxiliary to the infantry. Although attachés recognized that the mobility of armored forces was an asset, they had difficulty understanding how independent armored operations might unfold on the battlefield. Rather, their assessment of armored operations often rested on the assumption that the proper measure of armor's effectiveness was its contribution to an infantry attack.

By the early 1930s, however, attachés began to recognize independent armor operations as a new form of warfare. Indeed, such a view became widely held. Even so, attachés continued to have difficulty characterizing the impact such operations would have on the battlefield. Instead, the attachés tended to portray a tank attack as a more effective version of a cavalry raid. It was not until World War II that the Army was able to assess the effectiveness of British tank forces. Combat in North Africa against the Italian army served as a concrete demonstration of the effectiveness of armored forces. It also allowed MID to conduct an informal net assessment of the British and Italian armies. Even under such circumstances, however, drawing conclusions could prove perilous: although British forces were victorious against the Italians, they were considerably less successful against the Germans until the Battle of El Alamein on July 1, 1942.

INTEGRATED AIR DEFENSE

Although the success of British armor was at best mixed, London's development of an integrated air defense system utilizing radar played a decisive role in the Battle of Britain. The RAF's ability to maintain air superiority over the British Isles helped convince Hitler that an invasion of Great Britain would be impossible. The success of the RAF was in turn attributable to the integrated air defense system.

The key to the system's effectiveness was not merely the use of radar for early warning, but also the development of organizations and procedures that allowed the RAF to act on warning rapidly and effectively. Radar and ground observers allowed controllers to plot the path of incoming raids and vector fighters to intercept them.[77] Radar stations detected the position of each raid, the number of aircraft in it, their altitude, and their direction of flight and transmitted the information to a

---

77. Additional information on impending attacks came from intelligence sources such as the high-frequency direction-finding network operated by the Y-Service. Decryption

Group Headquarters filter room by telephone. This information was plotted on a map and then was passed simultaneously to Fighter Command, Group, and Sector operations rooms. Group Headquarters allocated targets to particular Sector Headquarters, which then organized and controlled intercepts.[78]

The barriers to understanding the development of integrated air defenses were considerable. Britain's radar program was shrouded in secrecy and its potential contribution to air defense largely theoretical. Moreover, the success of the British air defense system was the result of synergy between technology, doctrine, and organization. To fully appreciate British air defenses, U.S. intelligence officers would have had to both uncover British radar developments and understand how the procedures that RAF developed to filter and to distribute information increased the effectiveness of radar.

The air defense system that operated during World War II had its origins in the mid-1920s. On January 1, 1925, the Air Defence of Great Britain Command was formed, with Air Marshal Sir John Salmond its commander. Over the next several years, the organization developed procedures to filter incoming contact reports to prevent them from overwhelming the system.[79] By 1928, it had established a system that supported both fighter aircraft and anti-aircraft artillery (AAA) with a system of ground observers and dedicated telephone lines.[80]

In the command's first air defense exercise, conducted in July 1927, an attacking force of nine bomber squadrons faced twelve fighter squadrons deployed around London. Umpires ruled only twelve of the thirty-two daylight raids the attackers launched successful. In exercises conducted the following August, only nine of fifty-seven raids launched by the enemy reached their targets without interception. By the early 1930s, however, the increasing speed of bombers had begun to complicate the task of interception. Unless fighters were very fast, they had little time to intercept attacking bombers before they came into the range of their targets.[81]

---

of coded *Luftwaffe* traffic through ULTRA could provide warning as well. See Peter Calvocoressi, *Top Secret Ultra* (New York: Pantheon Books, 1980), chaps. 1–3.

78. The British Isles were divided into four Groups, numbered 10 to 13. See Francis K. Mason, *Battle Over Britain* (London: McWhirter Twins, 1969): 95–97.

79. Neil Young, "British Home Air Defence Planning in the 1920s," *Journal of Strategic Studies* 11, no. 4 (December 1988): 499–501.

80. Stephen Peter Rosen, *Winning the Next War: Innovation and the Modern Military* (Ithaca: Cornell University Press, 1991): 16.

81. Young, "British Home Air Defence Planning," 502–503, 505.

American attachés followed British air exercises through reports in newspapers and journals such as the *Journal of the Royal United Service Institute*.[82] On November 22, 1932, for example, the assistant military attaché for air matters, Major Martin F. Scanlon, reported on an RAF exercise, during which one-third of bombers were judged to have reached their target unscathed. The umpires ruled that bombs from those aircraft would have destroyed their targets. To the British, the exercise reinforced the view that strategic bombing would prove devastating in a future war. Scanlon, however, questioned the ability of an attacking force to remain effective in the face of such losses.[83] It was an insightful observation, one that foreshadowed the impact of the British air defense system on the *Luftwaffe* during the Battle of Britain.

The development of radar (which the British called "Radio Direction Finding," or RDF), together with the organization of filter centers to process and disseminate reports, made effective air defense possible. In February 1935, Robert Watson Watt, the superintendent of the Radio Research Station at Slough, submitted a proposal to the Air Ministry to use radio waves to detect approaching aircraft.[84] The British government subsequently constructed a prototype radar station at Bawdsey Manor and opened the Air Defence Research and Development Establishment at Christchurch.[85] In September 1935, Air Chief Marshal Sir Hugh Dowding proposed the construction of a line of radar stations that was to become the Chain Home (CH) radar defense system. The Air Ministry envisioned a network of twenty stations that would be able to detect and to locate aircraft approaching the British coast at an altitude of three thousand feet or higher at a range of up to forty miles.[86] In December of that year, the Air Ministry earmarked £100,000 (approximately $300,000) to build the first five stations.[87]

Early British designs employed meter-wave radar technology. Chain Home stations, consisting of four 360-foot wooden transmitter towers

82. See, for example, A-1-z 20441, "British Air Maneuvers, 1930," *Naval Attaché Reports, 1921–1939*, Box 180, RG 38, NA.

83. MID 203–1329/11, "R.A.F. Air Exercises 1932," November 22, 1932, *Military Intelligence Division Correspondence, 1917–1941*, Box 868, RG 165, NA.

84. E. G. Bowen, *Radar Days* (Bristol: Adam Hilger, 1987): 6.

85. Ibid., 22; Reg Batt, *The Radar Army: Winning the War of the Airwaves* (London: Robert Hale, 1991): 27.

86. Basil Collier, *The Defence of the United Kingdom* (London: HMSO, 1957): 39.

87. Alan Beyerchen, "From Radio to Radar: Interwar Military Adaptation to Technological Change in Germany, the United Kingdom, and the United States" in *Military Innovation in the Interwar Period*, eds. Williamson Murray and Allan R. Millett (Cambridge: Cambridge University Press, 1996): 283.

and an equal number of 240-foot receivers, provided long-range detection of high-altitude aircraft. Chain Home Low (CHL) sets optimized to detect low-flying aircraft supplemented their coverage.[88] In addition, the army began to develop Gun Laying (GL) radar to direct anti-aircraft artillery against bombers at night or in cloudy weather.

The RAF also harnessed radar technology to improve the ability of its fighters to intercept night bombers. Initial air interception (AI) radar designs featured a transmitter on the ground and a receiver aboard the fighter aircraft. In the autumn of 1937, the British fielded self-contained airborne radar.[89] They also developed Air-to-Surface-Vessel (ASV) radar sets to allow aircraft to detect ships at sea. ASV radar was installed aboard Coastal Command's Lockheed *Hudson* patrol aircraft. Although the original purpose of ASV had been to detect surface ships, Coastal Command later realized that radar enabled it to locate submarines running on the surface.[90]

During August and September 1936, the RAF examined the feasibility of using radar to intercept attacking aircraft in an exercise conducted around the experimental radar station at Bawdsey Manor. The demonstration lasted three days and involved about a hundred aircraft: some fifty bombers made simulated attack runs against the manor, while an equal number of fighters attempted to intercept the bombers under direction of the radar site. The trial was hardly a success: because the radar was unable to detect bombers until they had closed to within ten to fifteen miles of the target, controllers were unable to direct the fighters to make an intercept before the bombers reached their target.[91]

Despite the disappointing exercise, construction of the Chain Home network continued. By the Munich crisis in the autumn of 1938, five stations had become operational, supplemented by mobile radar sets. In October, Fighter Command established its first filter center at Bentley Priory. When war broke out in Europe, the British radar network included eighteen stations stretching from the Channel coast to the Scottish border.[92]

U.S. military intelligence did not collect any information on the development of radar by Great Britain before World War II. Although

---

88. Bowen, *Radar Days*, 50; Gordon Kinsey, *Bawdsey: Birth of the Beam* (Lavenham, Suffolk: Terence Dalton, 1983): 22.

89. Beyerchen, "From Radio to Radar," 284.

90. Bowen, *Radar Days*, 75–76, 98, 108.

91. Ibid., 24.

92. Beyerchen, "From Radio to Radar," 284.

ONI asked Alan G. Kirk, the naval attaché in London, to gather information on the British radar program, it was never a high priority. Moreover, he lacked the technological expertise to ask the right questions or to evaluate the accuracy of any information he might have received. In any event, British secrecy prevented American attachés from learning about London's radar research and development.[93] Attaché reporting on British research and development often amounted to nothing more than a recounting of statements that the secretary of state for war gave to Parliament. Nor did a reciprocal exchange of information appear beneficial to the U.S. armored forces. Because the U.S. services believed that the United States led Great Britain in radar technology, they were reluctant to give the British access to American secrets.[94]

Intelligence regarding the British, like that on the Germans, emphasized the familiar over the novel. Although the Army and Navy neglected intelligence on radar research and development, they paid considerable attention to the RAF's development of fighter aircraft. Information from the Air Ministry, aircraft manufacturers, and press reports yielded generally accurate—though incomplete—information on both the Supermarine *Spitfire* and Hawker *Hurricane* fighters one to two years before they entered production (see Table 9). In some cases, attachés were able to call on civilian experts for assistance. In June 1936, for example, the American aviation pioneer Glenn Martin and several coworkers toured the Hawker aircraft plant at Kingston, near London. Martin and an associate each provided the naval attaché's office with a detailed assessment of the methods being employed to manufacture the *Hurricane*.[95]

As the clouds of war gathered over Europe, Britain sought to increase collaboration with the United States. In August 1939, the British Air Ministry proposed to ship a *Spitfire* to the Army Air Corps at Wright Field, Ohio, for test and experimentation in exchange for an XP-40 *Warhawk* fighter, then in development. The British crated a *Spitfire* and loaded it onto the cargo vessel *American Importer* bound for North America. The State Department objected to the transaction, however, claiming that it violated the Neutrality Act of 1939. As a result, the

93. "The Reminiscences of Alan Goodrich Kirk", Part I, Oral History Research Office, Columbia University, 1962, OA/NHC, 133.

94. James R. Leutze, *Bargaining for Supremacy: Anglo-American Naval Collaboration, 1937–1941* (Chapel Hill, N.C.: University of North Carolina Press, 1977), 57, 65.

95. "Notes on Visit to Hawker Aircraft Plant," June 7, 1938, A-1-i 17439, "Aviation Plant of the Hawker Engineering Company at Kingston, near London, England," *Naval Attaché Reports, 1921–1939*, Box 44, RG 38, NA.

Table 9 Estimated Characteristics of British Fighter Aircraft, 1936

Characteristic	Supermarine Spitfire I		Hawker Hurricane I	
	Estimate	Actual	Estimate	Actual
Weight	– – –	5,784 lbs	– – –	9,600 lbs
Wingspan	36'	36'10"	40'	40'
Length	– – –	29' 11"	– – –	31' 5"
Maximum speed	345 mph	355 mph	315 mph	324 mph
Engine	RR Merlin V 1,135 hp	RR Merlin II 1,030 hp	RR Merlin V 1,135 hp	RR Merlin II 1,030 hp
Armament	8 × .303 guns	8 × .303 guns	8 × .303 guns	8 × .303 guns

Actual. John Frayn Turner, *British Aircraft of World War 2* (New York: Stein and Day, 1975): 32–3, 46–7.

Estimate. MID 2083-794/48, "Annual Aviation Intelligence Report," September 28, 1936, *Military Intelligence Division Correspondence, 1917–1941,* Box 864, RG 165, NA.

British were forced to unload the aircraft in Belfast.[96] The two governments subsequently arranged a test of the two aircraft at Uplands Airport, Ottawa, with British pilots flying the XP-40 and Americans the *Spitfire.*[97]

The outbreak of World War II also led to greater cooperation between Britain and the United States in the area of radar technology. Even so, each side limited what it was willing to share. As Alan Kirk later put it, "In no case was there what you might call wide-open exchange. Our side was very, very cautious, and so were they."[98] London's need for American aid forced Britain to reveal its progress in radar technology.[99] In early 1940, Sir Henry Tizard—chairman of the Aeronautical Research Committee—suggested that Britain share its secrets with the United States in exchange for technical and production assistance. The proposal was unpopular; Watson Watt and others felt that Britain could go it alone.[100] Tizard nonetheless prevailed, and on August 29, 1940, he

96. MID 2574–1463/3, "Exchange of U.S. Bell 2-Engined Fighter and Supermarine 'Spitfire'," August 23, 1939, *Military Intelligence Division Correspondence, 1917–1941,* Box 1517, RG 165, NA.

97. MID 2574–1463/9, "Visit to Canada to Inspect Supermarine Spitfire," May 6, 1940, *Military Intelligence Division Correspondence, 1917–1941,* Box 1517, RG 165, NA.

98. Kirk Reminiscences, 133.

99. The definitive work on Anglo-American cooperation in the early phases of World War II is Leutze, *Bargaining for Supremacy.*

100. Bowen, *Radar Days,* 150.

and several colleagues sailed for the United States with instructions to give Washington information on British advances in jet engines, rocketry, and radar in exchange for assistance. Over the next few weeks the mission discussed British scientific and technical advances with General J. O. Mauborgne, the Army's Chief Signal Officer; Admiral Harold Bowen, the Director of the Naval Research Laboratory; and Dr. Vannevar Bush of the National Defense Research Council (NDRC).[101]

The U.S. government responded by appointing its own liaison group. On July 12, 1940, Rear Admiral Robert L. Ghormley, the Assistant Chief of Naval Operations, was designated Special Naval Observer and was attached to the U.S. embassy in London.[102] Shortly thereafter, Major General Delos C. Emmons, the Commanding General of the General Headquarters (GHQ) Air Force, and Brigadier General George V. Strong were designated special military observers. The group, officially called the Anglo-American Standardization of Arms Committee, was chartered to explore Anglo-American cooperation. In October they were joined by Major General Eugene Chaney and Captain Gordon P. Saville, who were ordered to observe air developments. In particular, "Major General Chaney received orders to investigate the efficiency of foreign aircraft, power plants, instruments, equipment, and methods of operation, and to familiarize himself with the operation of foreign aircraft."[103] He was assisted by Colonel Homer Case, who had served as chief of the British Empire Section of MID from 1938 to 1940.[104]

By the summer of 1940, the Navy had assigned a 130-man unit of naval aviators to observe air operations in Britain. The head of the group, Commander Ralph A. Ofstie, had served as assistant naval attaché for aviation in Tokyo and would go on to head the Navy section of the U.S. Strategic Bombing Survey. Naval aviators, including Commander William E. G. Taylor, USNR, accompanied RAF pilots on missions and observed their methods for intercepting German bombers; Marine aviators, including Edward C. Dyer and Walter G. Farrel, observed British air operations in North Africa and the Mediterranean.[105]

---

101. Ibid., 157–58.

102. Mark Skinner Watson, *Chief of Staff: Prewar Plans and Preparations* (Washington: Office of the Chief of Military History, Department of the Army, 1950): 114.

103. Capt. S. J. Thurman et al., "SPOBS: The Special Observer Group Prior to the Activation of the European Theater of Operations," Historical Section, European Theater of Operations, October 1944, The Charles L. Bolte Papers, USAMHI, 2–3.

104. Bidwell, *History of the Military Intelligence Division*, 386.

105. Jeffery M. Dorwart, *Conflict of Duty: The U.S. Navy's Intelligence Dilemma, 1919–1945* (Annapolis, Md.: U.S. Naval Institute Press, 1983), 154.

The military attaché's office began to receive information on British radar developments in the summer of 1940. Studler, an assistant attaché, followed British radar developments the closest; the military attaché, Colonel Raymond E. Lee,[106] was involved only peripherally.[107] In August, Studler visited the radar site at Manor Bier and got to inspect Gun Laying radar. He obtained accurate figures for the detection range of the radar as well as its elevation and bearing accuracy. His report also mentioned the existence of air interception radar, but noted that "to date, none of our personnel has had an opportunity to examine [it]."[108]

Later that month, the office sent MID additional information on ASV and AI radar systems. One report described the use of radar for air interception as well as the installation of ASV sets in Coastal Command's aircraft. Lee wrote that the British were "working very hard on a scientific detector [air-interception radar] which will enable their fighters to shoot these Boche raiders down at night. If they evolve this soon they will have gone a great way toward winning the war [sic]."[109] (In fact, radar-equipped fighters had claimed their first kill of a German bomber on the night of July 22–23, 1940.) Another report described the operation and detection range of the air interception radar.[110]

In November, a delegation including Ghormley, Emmons, Lee, Studler, and Major G. Bryan Conrad toured an air defense radar site and inspected Chain Home, Chain Home Low, and Gun Laying units. Although the officers tried to avoid attracting attention by dressing in civilian clothes, their attire had the opposite effect. As one British scientist later wrote, the Americans looked like characters straight out of a gangster movie: "The secret visitors were dressed in long-jacketed lightish blue suits and broad-brimmed trilby hats which were then typical of American attire as seen in Hollywood films."[111] Nor did the delegation possess the skills needed to gather technical intelligence on British radar systems. Their report to MID did, however, include such characteristics as the maximum detection range of the radar systems. It

---

106. On September 28, 1940, Lee was promoted temporarily to the rank of brigadier general to increase his prestige.

107. James Leutze, ed., *The London Journal of General Raymond E. Lee, 1940–1941* (Boston: Little, Brown and Company, 1971): 118.

108. MID 2728-A-22/1, "British Fire Control," August 15, 1940, *Military Intelligence Division Correspondence, 1917–1941*, Box 1801, RG 165, NA, 2.

109. Leutze, *The London Journal of General Raymond E. Lee*, 94.

110. MID 2728-A-22/3, "Radio Detection," August 26, 1940, *Military Intelligence Division Correspondence, 1917–1941*, Box 1801, RG 165, NA.

111. Batt, *The Radar Army*, 82.

also described the procedures employed by the radar site to transmit data to the Plotting Room at Fighter Command Headquarters.[112]

U.S. military attachés paid particular attention to Gun Laying radar designs; development of similar radar was a top priority for the U.S. Army.[113] In July 1941, Lieutenant Colonel W. Q. Jeffords Jr., an assistant military attaché, wrote a report that contained specifications for the GL Mark II radar, including its wavelength, power, detection range, and range and bearing accuracy.[114] Both Jeffords and Frank D. Lewis, scientific liaison officer with the NDRC mission, witnessed radar training at the Air Defence Research and Development Establishment at Christchurch. Lewis subsequently filed a secret report on the GL Mark III radar set, including information on its power output, detection capability, and range and bearing error.[115]

U.S. military intelligence began to gather information on British command and control arrangements for air defense as well. Lee received a tour of one of the RAF's filter centers, writing in his diary that he "had no idea the British could evolve and operate so intricate, so scientific and rapid an organization [*sic*]."[116] In addition, the Air Ministry gave the United States a copy of its manual for observer centers in exchange for information on U.S. air interception tactics.[117]

U.S. Intelligence and British Integrated Air Defense

U.S. military intelligence failed to understand the British air defense system until its effectiveness was demonstrated in war. Before World War II ONI and MID lacked data on important aspects of the system, including data on radar programs and on air defense organizations and procedures.

The failure of U.S. military intelligence was the product of two mutually supporting factors. On the one hand, the U.S. Army and Navy displayed a marked lack of curiosity regarding Britain's development of radar. Collecting intelligence regarding radar was a low priority for U.S. attachés throughout the period. On the other hand, the British

112. MID 2728-A-22/4, "Radio Detection," September 26, 1940, *Military Intelligence Division Correspondence, 1917–1941*, Box 1801, RG 165, NA.

113. Beyerchen, "From Radio to Radar," 293.

114. MID 2728-A-22/30, "Notes on G.L. Mk. II," July 11, 1941, *Military Intelligence Division Correspondence, 1917–1941*, Box 1801, RG 165, NA.

115. MID 2728-A-22/32, "10cm G.L. Mk. III," July 29, 1941, *Military Intelligence Division Correspondence, 1917–1941*, Box 1801, RG 165, NA.

116. Leutze, *The London Journal of General Raymond E. Lee*, 30.

117. MID 2083–937/8, "Instructions for Observer Centres—1938," n.d., *Military Intelligence Division Correspondence, 1917–1941*, Box 865, RG 165, NA.

maintained tight security over their radar program. It is therefore doubtful that U.S. attachés would have been able to collect meaningful information on the British radar program even if they had been looking harder.

The lack of data on the British air defense system reinforced the tendency for preconceptions about warfare to shape intelligence collection. In essence, MID focused on gathering information on familiar weapons—such as fighter aircraft—while ignoring innovative technology and doctrine. Even after the British government revealed the existence of its air defense system, military attachés focused on collecting data on weapon systems involved in air defense. They paid much less attention to the organizational arrangements that lay at the heart of the effectiveness of the British air defense system.

IDENTIFYING BRITISH INNOVATION

Great Britain was a relatively benign environment for intelligence collection during the interwar period. Certainly the United States was closer culturally to Britain than to Germany or Japan, and it was much easier for American attachés to blend into British society than those of Germany or Japan. Moreover, Britain was not a potential foe but a once and future ally. The Army and Navy sought information on the British armed forces not because they feared they would face them on the battlefield, but because they suspected that the British armed forces possessed technology that was potentially useful to the United States. They were also interested in studying how the British services were approaching emerging combat areas, such as armored warfare.

U.S. intelligence gathering in Britain yielded mixed results. American attachés did a good job of tracking technology and doctrine that had already proven to be militarily effective. The U.S. Army, for example, looked to Britain for insight on tank technology and armored doctrine. Although the British were reluctant to share the technical characteristics of their weapon systems with the United States, MID nonetheless managed to collect a large volume of data on British military developments. In some cases, U.S. attachés gathered information firsthand by observing British military exercises or by inspecting installations and factories. In others, they had to rely on the press. Such information was generally accurate and insightful, in part because the British press corps included talented military correspondents, such as B. H. Liddell Hart. MID reports on British armor development enjoyed wide dissemination within the U.S. Army. Moreover, reports on British experiments regarding independent armored operations led the secretary of war to establish an experimental armored force in the Army and influenced armor advocates such as Adna Chaffee.

Even though U.S. military attachés monitored the British army's development of armored warfare, they tended to view it through the lens of the last war. Until the mid-1930s, most attachés, reflecting current U.S. Army doctrine, believed that tanks were an auxiliary to the infantry and that the proper measure of armor's effectiveness was its contribution to the infantry's advance. British security, which denied U.S. attachés access to the army's most innovative tank maneuvers, reinforced this tendency. As a result, attachés often had difficulty understanding how independent armored operations might unfold on the battlefield.

Although collecting information regarding armored warfare was a top priority throughout the interwar period, the same cannot be said of radar. Indeed, U.S. Army and Navy attachés paid little attention to Britain's development of radar, a tendency that strict British security abetted. To the extent that U.S. attachés monitored the British air defense system, they concentrated on proven weapons, such as fighter aircraft, and ignored novel technology, such as radar. Attachés also paid little attention to the organizational arrangements and operational concepts that made air defense feasible. It was not until the British began literally handing radar technology to the United States that attachés began systematically to collect information on British radar.

[6]

Implications for a New Interwar Period

Most previous studies of American intelligence in the interwar period portray ineffective and inept—even incompetent—organizations handicapped by small staffs and meager budgets. According to the orthodox view, the United States, lacking accurate intelligence, slumbered in blissful ignorance of the growing threat posed by Nazi Germany and Imperial Japan until roused by the attack on Pearl Harbor.

This book has painted a much different picture. Far from being a haven for incompetents, ONI and MID housed many capable intelligence officers: some served for a single tour, others throughout their careers. Despite limited personnel and scarce resources, ONI and MID did a creditable job of collecting and analyzing information on foreign military forces. Indeed, they excelled at the particularly difficult task of identifying and characterizing the development of new ways of war by friend and enemy alike.

CASE SUMMARY

Previous chapters have examined nine cases of innovation in the period between the two world wars. In four cases, U.S. intelligence organizations recognized the emergence of new ways of war; in two they were partially successful; and in three they failed (see Table 10).

Japan's development of massed carrier air strikes can best be characterized as a genuine surprise. Given the sources and methods of the day, detecting this innovation would have been difficult for any intelligence service. While Washington devoted considerable resources to monitoring the Japanese navy, the Japanese government enacted extensive security measures to conceal its experimentation with carrier aviation. Moreover, because the navy adopted the most important changes in its organization and tactics on the eve of the Pacific War, ONI had few opportunities to collect intelligence that could have alerted the U.S. Navy to Japan's interest in carrier air strikes.

Table 10 Summary of Cases

Category	Cases
Failure	
Genuine Surprises	Japanese Carrier Aviation
Overlooked Innovations	German Rocketry
	British Integrated Air Defenses
Partial Success	
Imperfect Recognition	Japanese Surface Warfare
	German Tactical Aviation
Success	
Recognition of Similar Practices	Japanese Amphibious Warfare
	British Armored Warfare
Recognition of Dissimilar Practices	German Armored Warfare
	British Tank Experiments

Washington collected little information regarding Germany's development of ballistic and cruise missiles and Britain's radar program as well. However, in these cases the failure of ONI and MID can be attributed to preconceptions about warfare that prevented the Army and Navy from identifying and monitoring these developments. Attachés emphasized information on established ways of war and neglected emerging warfare areas. The U.S. military attaché in Berlin, for example, received indications of Germany's interest in rocketry but failed to pursue them. Similarly, neither the military attaché in London nor his naval counterpart took much interest in collecting information on the development of radar by the British armed forces. In both cases, the legacy of World War I shaped assumptions about future wars and steered attachés away from exploring emerging military technology.

Preconceptions about warfare both shaped the activities that ONI and MID chose to monitor and influenced the interpretation of the information they gathered. In some cases, U.S. intelligence detected the development of new ways of war by foreign armed forces but failed to recognize fully their significance. In the case of ONI's analysis of Japanese naval surface warfare tactics and MID's assessment of German air doctrine, preconceptions about warfare skewed intelligence assessments. These assumptions operated differently in the two cases, however. In the case of Japanese naval surface warfare, U.S. naval concepts filled holes in the information that ONI had gathered. In that of German tactical aviation, Air Corps doctrine lent consistency to statements that were often contradictory. In both cases, attachés emphasized similarities and ignored differences with U.S. doctrine.

Other cases represent successes. With Britain's development of armored warfare and Japan's development of amphibious capabilities, ONI and MID detected and recognized practices that resembled existing U.S. doctrine. In these instances the existence of analogous American concepts helped U.S. intelligence to characterize foreign developments. Attachés were able to determine which practices were likely to succeed and which were likely to fail on the battlefield, often offering cogent critiques of foreign activities in the process.

Recognizing foreign practices that differed significantly from American concepts should have been a considerably more difficult task. Yet U.S. intelligence succeeded in doing so in two cases: MID's assessment of German armored doctrine and of British experiments with independent tank operations. In these instances the quantity and quality of information U.S. attachés collected was apparently sufficient to override any preconceptions they had regarding the conduct of warfare; the information also convinced them that Britain and Germany were developing new military practices much different from those employed by the U.S. armed forces. U.S. intelligence sources were aided by the fact that the U.S. Army had yet to develop strong beliefs about armored warfare. Rather, it looked abroad for ideas about how best to employ tanks.

Taken as a whole, these cases demonstrate that although recognizing foreign military innovation is a challenge, it is not insurmountable. Indeed, U.S. intelligence achieved at least partial success in two-thirds of the cases examined. Because the development of new ways of war unfolds over the course of years or decades, it frequently yields various indicators. Averting technological and doctrinal surprise is thus a more tractable problem than preventing surprise attack. This record is all the more remarkable given the small size and limited resources of the Army and Navy intelligence services.

Not only did the Army and Navy detect foreign innovations, but in several significant cases intelligence actually shaped U.S. doctrine, organization, and equipment. Among the U.S. military services, the Army followed foreign experimentation the most closely. During the 1920s, it looked to both France and Great Britain for insight into armored warfare; the Army likewise monitored Germany after that country formed its first *Panzer* divisions in 1935.[1] The British Experimental Mechanized Force inspired the Army to form an analogous unit to ex-

---

1. On the influence of French armored doctrine on the U.S. Army, see Robert S. Cameron, "Americanizing the Tank: U.S. Army Administration and Mechanized Development within the Army, 1917–1943" (Ph.D. dissertation, Temple University, 1994): 200, 285–86, 296.

amine the feasibility of armored operations. Similarly, the doctrine, tactics, and organization of the German *Panzer* corps influenced the development of the Armored Force in 1940–1941. Nor was the Navy, the most traditional of the services, above looking overseas for ideas. Study of the Sino-Japanese War allowed the Marine Corps to refine its concepts of amphibious warfare and influenced the design of U.S. landing craft.

Foreign concepts had the least influence on the youngest arm of the armed forces, the Army Air Corps. In part, this was because of the Air Corps's lack of a dedicated intelligence organization. Instead, it was MID, dominated by infantry, cavalry, and artillery officers, that monitored foreign air forces. As a result, the development of foreign air forces was a lower priority than that of armies. The Air Corps's strong preconceptions about future war also stifled its curiosity regarding foreign air developments. Because it had a coherent vision of future warfare based on strategic bombing, the Air Corps had limited interest in what foreign services were doing.[2] As Williamson Murray has written:

> [American] bomber proponents either disregarded combat experience in Europe or interpreted it in light of American doctrinal preferences. . . . When American airmen, some of whom were to lead the army air forces after Pearl Harbor, went to England in 1940 to study European air war at first hand, their reports doubted that British or German experiences applied to U.S. forces.[3]

This book also sheds light on why ONI and MID succeeded in some cases and failed in others (see Table 11). First, the services were more inclined to monitor the development of established weapons than to search for new military systems. The tank and the airplane had demonstrated their value during World War I, while the aircraft carrier had proven promising. By the end of the war, all three had become accepted as valuable—though not necessarily dominant—elements of military power. The war did not, however, provide definitive answers to their most effective employment. It was thus only natural for military organizations in the interwar period to study how others were adapting to

---

2. Robert Frank Futrell, *Ideas, Concepts, and Doctrine: Basic Thinking in the United States Air Force, 1907–1960*, volume 1 (Maxwell AFB, Ala.: Air University Press, 1989): chap. 3; David MacIsaac, "Voices from the Central Blue: The Air Power Theorists" in *Makers of Modern Strategy: From Machiavelli to the Nuclear Age*, eds. Peter Paret, Gordon A. Craig, and Felix Gilbert (Princeton, N.J.: Princeton University Press, 1986): 624–47.

3. Williamson Murray, "Strategic Bombing: The British, American, and German Experiences" in *Military Innovation in the Interwar Period*, eds. Murray and Allan R. Millett (Cambridge: Cambridge University Press, 1996): 126.

Table 11 Conditions Influencing Detection of Foreign Military Innovation

Cases	Established Practice?	Demonstrated in War?	United States Interested?
Failure			
Japanese Carrier Aviation	×		×
German Rocketry			
British Integrated Air Defenses			×
Partial Success			
Japanese Surface Warfare	×	×	×
German Tactical Aviation	×	×	×
Success			
Japanese Amphibious Warfare		×	×
British Armored Warfare	×	×	×
German Armored Warfare	×	×	×
British Tank Experiments	×	×	×

the demands of modern warfare. U.S. attachés were thus expected to monitor other countries' tank, aircraft, and carrier programs.

By contrast, ONI and MID paid little attention to truly new weapons, such as missiles and radar. Even though both the Army and the Navy were developing radar during the 1930s, it did not become an essential element of war on land and at sea until World War II. The services thus accorded low priority to gathering intelligence on foreign radar programs. Similarly, they paid little attention to the development of rocketry, an area that would—with the development of the intercontinental ballistic missile—revolutionize warfare. The low priority that ONI and MID attached to collecting intelligence regarding new technology made it all the easier to ignore the small amount of information that they did receive.

A related point is that it was easier to detect technology and doctrine that had been demonstrated in war than weapons and concepts that had not seen combat. One reason the Army paid so much attention to foreign armored doctrine was that the tank had been used with reasonable success during the closing campaigns of World War I. By contrast, the disastrous landings at Gallipoli indicated to many observers that future amphibious operations would be doomed. Therefore, Army and Navy intelligence paid little attention to foreign amphibious warfare developments. Not until the Japanese army's successful landings along the China coast during the early campaigns of the Sino-Japanese War did U.S. intelligence begin to focus on amphibious warfare.

The ability to observe firsthand new ways of war played an important role in determining whether the United States would detect an innovation. U.S. intelligence organizations gathered firsthand evidence of innovation in each of the six successes or partial successes; they lacked similar opportunities in any of the three cases of failure. In the case of Japanese surface warfare operations and British independent tank experiments, attachés observed experimentation with new approaches to warfare in realistic field exercises. In the cases of German tactical aviation and Japanese amphibious warfare, they witnessed the use of new technology and doctrine on the battlefield. In the cases of British and German armored warfare, they witnessed exercises and use on the battlefield. These opportunities often provided a convincing demonstration of the effectiveness of new ways of war.

Assessing new weapons is nonetheless a considerable challenge, as the battle debut of a weapon may not indicate its full potential. During the Vietnam War, for example, beyond-visual-range air-to-air missile such as the AIM-4 *Sparrow* were notoriously unreliable. Over time, however, their electronics were improved and rules of engagement for their use were developed. As a result, in the Gulf War the *Sparrow* and its successor, the AIM-120 Advanced Medium-Range Air-to-Air Missile (AMRAAM), scored an impressive number of kills. Similarly, the laser-guided bombs employed in Vietnam possessed significant operational limitations, including an inability to maintain guidance through fog, rain, and clouds. As a result, evaluations of their future utility based on their initial employment would have considerably underestimated their potential effectiveness.[4]

Analytical constructs based on experience may yield an inaccurate characterization of new weapons and doctrine as well.[5] Models used to explain mature systems that have well-understood combat utility can yield misleading results when applied to emerging weapon systems. For example, most early machine guns—including the Gatling gun— were too like artillery pieces in their appearance and logistic requirements to be viewed as infantry weapons. The U.S. Army implicitly measured the effectiveness of the machine gun as an artillery piece and, not surprisingly, found it wanting.[6] Similarly, in the 1920s and 1930s, the U.S. Navy treated carrier aviation as if it were long-range

---

4. I am indebted to Barry D. Watts for these insights.

5. James G. Roche and Barry D. Watts, "Choosing Analytic Measures," *Journal of Strategic Studies* 14, no. 2 (June 1991): 165.

6. David A. Armstrong, *Bullets and Bureaucrats: The Machine Gun and the United States Army, 1861–1916* (Westport, Conn.: Greenwood Press, 1982): 15, 23, 210.

naval gunfire, modeling effectiveness of carrier air strikes using Lanchester equations. Such an approach ignored the ability of air strikes to produce a pulse of power, which generated qualitatively different results from that of past approaches to naval combat.[7] Assessing the merit of novel practices is thus likely to prove extremely difficult.

In addition, identifying innovation during the interwar period proved to be easier in areas that one's own services were exploring than in those that they had not examined, were not interested in, or had rejected. In part, the neglect of innovative approaches to warfare was the result of mirror-imaging. Another factor was that the U.S. armed forces wanted to learn how foreign services were exploiting new warfare areas. Throughout the interwar period, the Army—in particular the cavalry—was interested in determining how other armies planned to employ tanks on the battlefield. As a result, the Army tasked attachés in Berlin, London, and elsewhere to follow the development of tanks and armored doctrine. Similarly, one reason ONI devoted attention to Japan's landings on the China coast was that the Marine Corps was experimenting with amphibious warfare. The Navy's interest in carrier aviation led ONI to pay attention to foreign carrier programs as well.

By contrast, ONI and MID had difficulty identifying and assessing technologies that the Army and Navy had yet to field or were not interested in pursuing. They paid little attention to Britain's development of radar and to Germany's development of rocketry. Although naval attachés in Tokyo collected accurate intelligence on Japan's development of the Type 93 oxygen-propelled torpedo and the Type 0 fighter plane, naval engineers dismissed the reports because they failed to conform to U.S. design practices.

In several cases, preconceptions about technological superiority blinded U.S. intelligence to foreign developments. The belief that the United States led Great Britain in radar technology dampened efforts to learn what the British were doing. Similarly, the fact that the United States had been unable to produce a torpedo as fast as or with as long a range as the Type 93 *Long Lance* caused the Navy to dismiss accurate information on the weapon.

The tendency to concentrate on the familiar at the expense of the novel carries with it the danger of mirror-imaging. In the case of ONI's assessment of Japanese naval tactics and MID's assessment of Germany's air doctrine, the paucity of information regarding new forms of

---

7. Captain Wayne P. Hughes Jr., USN (retired), *Fleet Tactics: Theory and Practice* (Annapolis, Md.: Naval Institute Press, 1986): chaps. 3–4.

warfare abetted the tendency to ignore emerging practices that differed from service doctrine. When intelligence organizations possessed incomplete information, they used assumptions derived from U.S. doctrine to fill in gaps in their understanding of foreign practices. When faced with contradictory information, they paid attention to the facts that were in accord with U.S. practice and ignored the rest. As a result, ONI believed Japanese naval tactics resembled those of the U.S. Navy, and MID initially characterized the *Luftwaffe* as a strategic air force similar to that advocated by the Army Air Corps.

Officers with expertise in a particular country generally did a better job of identifying and characterizing attempts to develop new ways of war than generalists. Officers who combined foreign area expertise with an understanding of U.S. technology and doctrine proved most adept at identifying innovation. Although many officers characterized the Japanese armed forces as second-rate, attachés with firsthand experience rated them more highly. Similarly, attachés in both Berlin and London were able to identify doctrinal and technological innovations that set the German and British armed forces apart from their U.S. counterparts.

Many cases in this book exhibit a common pattern that suggests a set of indicators of innovation (see Table 12). In the first stage of the process, which may be termed speculation, military innovators identify novel ways to solve existing operational problems or to exploit the potential of emerging technology. The most visible indicators of innovation during this phase are often books, journal articles, speeches, and studies advocating new approaches to warfare. These sources may offer the first warning that a state is interested in acquiring new capabilities. In the years immediately following the end of World War I, for example, a handful of European and American military officers speculated on how armored vehicles, aircraft carriers, and land- and sea-based aviation would change the shape of future wars.[8] Debates over the proper composition and employment of tank formations raged on in British journals such as the *Journal of the Royal United Service Institute, Army Quarterly, Journal of the Royal Artillery, Royal Engineers Journal,* and even the *Cavalry Journal.* During the same period, service journals contained numerous articles discussing the proper employment of air power and the relative merit of the battleship and aircraft carrier.

The primary challenge that intelligence agencies faced at this stage was detecting foreign interest in new approaches to combat. Predicting a service's actions based on speculative writings in military journals is,

8. See the essays in Murray and Millett, eds., *Military Innovation in the Interwar Period.*

Table 12 Potential Indicators of Innovation

Phase	Potential Indicators of Innovation
I. Speculation	• Publication of concept papers, books, journal articles, speeches, and studies regarding new combat methods. • Formation of groups to study the lessons of recent wars. • Establishment of intelligence collection requirements focused on foreign innovation activities.
II. Experimentation	• Existence of an organization charged with innovation and experimentation. • Establishment of experimental organizations and testing grounds. • Field training exercises to explore new warfare concepts. • War gaming by war colleges, the defense industry, and think tanks regarding new warfare areas. • Experimentation with new combat methods in wartime.
III. Implementation	• Existence of a formal transformation strategy. • Establishment of new units to exploit, counter innovative mission areas. • Revision of doctrine to include new missions. • Establishment of new branches, career paths. • Changes in the curricula of professional military education institutions. • Field training exercises to practice, refine concepts.

however, a hazardous undertaking. Determining which—if any—statements are authoritative can be exceedingly difficult. Although British armor advocates such as B. H. Liddell Hart and J. F. C. Fuller argued publicly in favor of establishing independent tank formations, they were a minority within the British army. Rarely do military professionals agree on the effectiveness of unproven weapons and concepts. Without in-depth knowledge of both the formal and informal hierarchy of foreign military organizations, it is difficult to tell whether an author's opinions are merely his own, or whether they reflect a consensus within his service.

Nor do all discussions of new forms of warfare take place in public. In 1920, for example, Germany's shadow general staff, the Troop Office (*Truppenamt*), established fifty-seven secret committees to study the lessons of World War I. The army subsequently used their conclusions to develop its doctrine.[9] Great Britain, for its part, developed its integrated air defense system in utmost secrecy. In these instances, early detection of innovation would have required precisely targeted clandestine collection.

Experimentation

If the seeds of innovation fall on fertile soil, then speculation regarding emerging warfare areas may grow into experimentation with organizations and doctrine to carry out the experiments. Military services may, for example, establish experimental units. Between 1926 and 1928, for example, the British army formed an Experimental Mechanized Force (EMF) to explore armored operations. The U.S. Army created its own experimental forces in 1928 and 1930.[10]

Services also conducted exercises to examine new concepts. During the 1920s and 1930s, the British, French, German, Soviet, and American armies all held maneuvers to explore the effectiveness of armored formations.[11] In several cases, they sought to determine the value of new organizations by pitting them against standard formations. During the same period, the U.S. Navy used its fleet exercises to examine concepts for the offensive use of carrier aviation.

War games represented another form of experimentation. During the interwar period, for example, war games at the U.S. Naval War College explored the role of carrier aviation in a future conflict. One exercise in the fall of 1923 depicted an engagement between a U.S. naval force with five aircraft carriers—more than any navy possessed at the time—against an opponent with four. During the game, the U.S. force launched two hundred aircraft armed with bombs and torpedoes in one strike at the enemy fleet, crippling its carriers and a battleship.[12]

9. James S. Corum, *The Roots of Blitzkrieg: Hans von Seeckt and German Military Reform* (Lawrence: University of Kansas Press, 1992): 37–38.

10. John T. Hendrix, "The Interwar Army and Mechanization: The American Approach," *Journal of Strategic Studies* 16, no. 1 (March 1993): 78–82; Timothy K. Nenninger, "The Experimental Mechanized Forces," *Armor* 78, no. 3 (May–June 1969).

11. On the development of armored warfare during the interwar period, see Captain Jonathan M. House, USA, *Toward Combined Arms Warfare: A Survey of 20th-Century Tactics, Doctrine, and Organization*, Combat Studies Institute Research Survey No. 2 (Fort Leavenworth, Kan.: U.S. Army Command and General Staff College, August 1984); Richard M. Ogorkiewicz, *Armor: A History of Mechanized Forces* (New York: Frederick A. Praeger, 1960).

12. Stephen Peter Rosen, *Winning the Next War: Innovation and the Modern Military* (Ithaca: Cornell University Press, 1991): 69.

In addition, military services used foreign wars to try out new concepts. For example, Germany, Italy, and the Soviet Union used their participation in the Spanish Civil War to test concepts of armored and air warfare. Indeed, the German Condor Legion established experimental bomber and fighter squadrons to evaluate new aircraft types under operational conditions.[13] Japan's war in China offered a testing ground for its development of amphibious warfare and carrier aviation.

Experimental activities such as these offered clear indicators of foreign interest in new warfare areas. Yet without a clear understanding of the objectives of foreign maneuvers, it is easy to misinterpret their results. The U.S. Marine Corps, for example, began conducting amphibious exercises in the early 1920s, only to halt them in 1926. An observer could have easily concluded that the corps had abandoned the idea of amphibious landings as unfeasible. Indeed, a Marine report describing these early exercises found them "woefully theoretical."[14] In fact, the Marine Corps remained committed to the seizure of advanced bases, but had been forced to suspend exercises because of commitments in Asia and Latin America. Conversely, military organizations do not always adopt promising experimental concepts. Indeed, both the British and American armies disbanded their experimental mechanized forces, even though they had enjoyed considerable success. It is therefore important to understand the level of bureaucratic support for experimentation within a foreign military organization.

Implementation

Successful experimentation with new approaches to combat led military services to adopt concepts and organizations tailored to carry out the new approaches. Following the British Experimental Mechanized Force's maneuvers, for example, Colonel C. N. F. Broad wrote *Armoured and Mechanized Formations*, the British army's first doctrinal publication to discuss armored warfare. In 1931, he assumed command of the 1st Brigade of the Royal Tank Corps to test methods for conducting deep penetrations of an adversary's lines.[15] In November 1933,

13. Gerald Howson, *Aircraft of the Spanish Civil War, 1936–1939* (London: Putnam, 1990): 118–19, 184–85, 211, 232.

14. Allan R. Millett and Peter Maslowski, *For the Common Defense: A Military History of the United States of America* (New York: The Free Press, 1984): 376.

15. Captain B. H. Liddell Hart, *The Tanks: The History of the Royal Tank Regiment and Its Predecessors: Heavy Branch Machine-Gun Corps, Tanks Corps, and Royal Tank Corps, 1914–1945*, volume 1, *1914–1939* (London: Cassel and Co., 1959): 292–94.

the army authorized the permanent formation of the 1st Tank Brigade and appointed Brigadier Percy Hobart as its commander. Hobart, an advocate of independent tank operations, used the opportunity to test and refine concepts of armored warfare. Mechanized infantry and artillery brigades and supporting units joined the tank brigade to form what was in essence an armored division.

Various indicators appeared at this stage. The establishment of new military formations and the promulgation of doctrine to govern their employment demonstrated a service's commitment to novel combat methods. In some cases, services established new branches, specialties, and career paths to support these methods. The services also conducted exercises and training in these areas. The curricula of professional military education institutions changed to reflect new doctrine as well.

In some cases, the processes of experimentation and doctrinal development overlapped. In 1934, for example, the U.S. Marine Corps issued the first draft of its *Tentative Manual for Landing Operations*. Beginning in 1936, the Marines began holding fleet landing exercises to examine a panoply of new amphibious tactics, techniques, and technology. The corps used the results of these exercises to refine the *Manual*.[16]

The key intelligence problem at this stage was not detecting or recognizing innovation, but evaluating the merit of practices that had only theoretical potential. Predicting the battlefield impact of new weapons and concepts during peacetime is extremely difficult. Information was often fragmentary and ambiguous—and thus unlikely to challenge prevailing assumptions about warfare. Instead, it sometimes reinforced the tendency to ignore new combat methods.

Nor did the value of new ways of warfare necessarily become apparent when they appeared on the battlefield in an embryonic form. Wars are discrete events, and the lessons of one conflict may have limited applicability to another. All too often, military services pay attention to evidence that accords with previously held beliefs and ignore contrary evidence. Although tanks had seen use in various conflicts—the Spanish Civil War, border clashes between Japan and the Soviet Union, and Italy's war in Ethiopia—many observers had difficulty drawing meaningful lessons from these conflicts. Rather, they saw in

16. Millett, "Assault from the Sea: The Development of Amphibious Warfare Between the Wars—the American, British, and Japanese Experiences" in Murray and Millett, eds., *Military Innovation in the Interwar Period*, 76–77.

them what they wanted to. As one 1939 commentary in the U.S. Army's cavalry journal put it:

> Unquestionably from accumulated incidents which have taken place in China, Ethiopia, Spain, and now eastern Europe, the conclusion has been drawn that the machine has proven supreme. Has it been overlooked that in each of these theaters of operations the machine has been pitted against the forces of impoverished and unprepared peoples? Has it, in reality, been so much the supremacy of the machine as the exertion of over-whelming strength against peoples completely dominated by opposing forces in every phase of modern warfare?[17]

The longer an activity went on, the easier it was to observe. In cases where ONI and MID got to accumulate evidence over years, they were generally successful. Other developments, particularly short-notice improvisations, proved more difficult to detect (see Table 13). The Japanese navy, for example, developed the concept of launching concentrated carrier air strikes only months before the attack on Pearl Harbor.[18] Similarly, the Japanese army began to study jungle warfare less than a year before its attack on Southeast Asia.[19] These developments proved much more difficult to detect.

Foreign governments attempted to conceal their development of new ways of war from U.S. attachés in every case examined in this book. Their task proved easiest in the early stages of development and grew increasingly difficult as new weapons and new doctrine entered operational use. Moreover, concealing the development of new technology was easier than concealing the doctrine and organizations necessary to employ the technology effectively.

IMPLICATIONS

As this book has shown, detecting and characterizing military innovation is often difficult, especially in its early stages. In some cases, intelligence agencies overlook innovative technology, doctrine, and organizations because of a focus on current forms of warfare. In other cases, the agencies collect information indicating innovation but fail to recog-

17. "War Lessons," *Cavalry Journal* 48, no. 5 (September–October 1939): 371.
18. David C. Evans and Mark R. Peattie, *Kaigun: Strategy, Tactics, and Technology in the Imperial Japanese Navy, 1887–1941* (Annapolis: Naval Institute Press, 1997): 347–52.
19. Colonel Masanobu Tsuji, *Japan's Greatest Victory, Britain's Worst Defeat*, ed. H. V. Howe, trans. Margaret E. Lake (New York: Sarpedon Books, 1993): 1–18.

Table 13   Stage at Which Innovations Were Detected

	Speculation	Experimentation	Implementation
Failure			
Japanese Carrier Aviation			X
German Rocketry			
British Integrated Air Defenses			X
Partial Success			
Japanese Surface Warfare			X
German Tactical Aviation			X
Success			
Japanese Amphibious Warfare		X	X
British Armored Warfare	X	X	X
German Armored Warfare	X	X	X
British Tank Experiments	X	X	X

nize it because of prevailing assumptions about the character and conduct of warfare. Yet the barriers to uncovering foreign innovation are not insurmountable. Innovation is a process that unfolds over years or decades in discrete phases, each with unique indicators. To be successful, intelligence agencies need to be receptive to evidence of innovation.

The United States today sits at the apex of the international military hierarchy. The U.S. armed forces have repeatedly demonstrated the ability to project power rapidly across the globe and to wage high-intensity military operations when they arrive, a capability currently beyond the means of even its most proficient allies. It would be dangerous, however, to assume that for the foreseeable future no other power will be able to devise effective methods to challenge the U.S. armed forces. Indeed, such hubris could breed disaster in a future conflict.

In recent years, various scholars have argued that the growth and diffusion of information technology will radically alter the character and conduct of war.[20] Over the next several decades, the armed forces of states across the globe will incorporate advanced information pro-

20. See, for example, Eliot A. Cohen, "A Revolution in Warfare," *Foreign Affairs* 75, no. 2 (March/April 1996); James R. FitzSimonds, and Jan M. van Tol, "Revolutions in Military Affairs," *Joint Force Quarterly* no. 4 (spring 1994); and Andrew F. Krepinevich, "Cavalry to Computer: The Patterns of Military Revolutions," *The National Interest* no. 37 (fall 1994).

cessing, precision-strike systems, and stealth technology. Some military services will develop novel concepts and doctrine in an attempt to use these new weapons to overcome strategic and operational challenges.

The first decades of the new millennium may thus witness the emergence of new warfare areas as well as the doctrine and organizations necessary to carry them out. One concept is that long-range precision-strike weapons, combined with effective sensors and command and control systems, will dominate the future battlefield. Rather than closing with an adversary, these systems will make it possible to destroy him at a distance. Another concept is that information technology will dramatically improve the ability of military forces to collect, process, and disseminate information. The ability to degrade, destroy, or disrupt an adversary's information system while protecting one's own will thus be an important component of future military operations. Other concepts may appear as well.

Americans have not been alone in arguing that the information revolution is transforming warfare. Russian analysts have argued that future conflicts will be characterized by the dominance of aerospace and information warfare over traditional ground combat.[21] Moreover, despite fiscal stringency, Russia is investing considerable resources to develop and to field advanced weapons.[22] Chinese defense analysts have echoed the belief that the world is experiencing a period of military transformation. Chinese military publications have accorded increased attention to emerging warfare areas such as information operations.[23] India, Israel, and Australia are interested in pursuing new ways of war as well.[24]

Foreign military theorists are unlikely to agree on a single vision of future warfare. Rather, discrete schools of thought will emerge. In his study of Russian lessons of the Gulf War, for example, Stuart Kaufman identified three views of future warfare.[25] Michael Pillsbury, for his part, has delineated Chinese schools of thought regarding the emerg-

---

21. Mary C. FitzGerald, *The New Revolution in Russian Military Affairs* (London: RUSI, 1994).

22. Martin Sieff, "Cash-Strapped Russian Forces Increase R&D Spending Sixfold," *The Washington Times,* May 14, 1997: A8.

23. Michael Pillsbury, ed., *Chinese Views of Future Warfare* (Washington, D.C.: National Defense University Press, 1997).

24. National Intelligence Council, *Buck Rogers or Rock Throwers?*, Conference Report 2000–03 (April 2000); Eliot A. Cohen, Michael J. Eisenstadt, and Andrew J. Bacevich, "Israel's Revolution in Strategic Affairs," *Survival* 40, no. 1 (spring 1998).

25. Stuart Kaufman, "Lessons from the 1991 Gulf War and Russian Military Doctrine," *Journal of Slavic Military Studies* 6, no. 3 (September 1993): 375–96.

ing Revolution in Military Affairs (RMA).[26] Identifying these perspectives and tracking the debate among them is fundamental to understanding foreign innovation, because it illuminates the context within which it will occur. Developing an appreciation of the culture of foreign military services may be similarly useful, since this too may help determine the form that innovation will take.

Although some states may emulate U.S. military practices, others are likely to develop innovative approaches to achieve their political objectives. Strategies designed to negate the effectiveness or to exploit the weaknesses of high-technology forces may be especially appealing to states lacking the means to compete head-to-head with the United States. Some may, for example, develop ways to deny the United States and its allies the ability to project power into their spheres of influence.[27] Others may challenge the United States in space or in the information spectrum.[28] Some adversaries may also invest heavily in high-technology niche capabilities to counter the United States, much as North Vietnam acquired a sophisticated air defense system to limit the effectiveness of U.S. air power.

One side effect of the development of new combat methods will be that assessing military balances will become progressively more difficult. Measures of military power have traditionally focused on the quantity and quality of weaponry to the exclusion of qualitative factors such as intelligence, command and control, doctrine, training, leadership, and morale. In the past, this has produced wildly inaccurate predictions of combat outcomes. This problem is likely to grow in coming years as the United States, its allies, and adversaries incorporate information technology into their armed forces. As the number of states entering the information age expands, the possibility of strategic surprise will grow dramatically.

The United States is today blessed with capabilities and burdened with liabilities it lacked during the interwar period. We have a broad array of sophisticated airborne and space-based reconnaissance and surveillance platforms. These systems offer previously unavailable opportunities to detect experimentation by foreign militaries. They also complicate a potential adversary's attempts at denial and deception.

26. Michael Pillsbury, "China and the Revolution in Military Affairs," report for the Office of Net Assessment, n.d. See also June Teufel Dreyer, *The PLA and the Kosovo Conflict* (Carlisle, Penn.: U.S. Army War College, 2000).

27. Thomas G. Mahnken, "Deny U.S. Access?" *U.S. Naval Institute Proceedings* 124, no. 9 (September 1998).

28. National Defense Panel, *Transforming Defense: National Security in the 21st Century* (Washington, D.C.: Government Printing Office, 1997): 12–14.

Yet it would be wrong to conclude that the development of technical collection methods has eliminated the possibility of surprise. Although airborne and space-based systems allow intelligence organizations to gather an increasing volume of information, they do not eliminate the need to decide what to collect. Nor do they solve the more formidable problem of how to interpret data. The failure of U.S. intelligence to detect preparations for India's May 1998 nuclear weapons test and the substantial U.S. underestimation of North Korea's development of long-range ballistic missiles provide a sobering antidote to the belief that technology has solved the problem of surprise.[29] As the case studies of Japan, Germany, and Great Britain illustrate, preconceptions about the character of warfare and the competence of foreign militaries may limit the type and amount of information that intelligence organizations collect. The dearth of data on foreign developments may, in turn, lead analysts to overlook instances of innovation.

The expansive scope of U.S. engagement makes the early detection and recognition of foreign innovation all the more important. During the interwar period, America's insularity, combined with a policy of unilateralism, allowed the U.S. armed forces to observe foreign conflicts and to respond to new approaches to warfare once they appeared on the battlefield. We are unlikely to enjoy such a luxury in the future. As the sole superpower, we set the standard by which others measure their armed forces. Moreover, we face adversaries that span the spectrum from terrorist groups to sophisticated regional powers. The deployment of U.S. forces across the globe limits our opportunity to observe and to adapt before becoming involved in a conflict. To avoid surprise, we will need to anticipate new combat methods before they appear on the battlefield.

Several trends may make it especially difficult to understand foreign innovation in coming years. First, the very nature of the information revolution complicates attempts to assess innovation. The increasing use of information technology in military systems implies that the characteristics of individual weapon platforms may be less important than the way military organizations integrate weapons, sensors, and command and control systems. Understanding command and control systems is difficult, and assessing how different command and control systems may interact in wartime is even more challenging.

Second, the increasing use of modeling and simulation by military organizations across the globe may limit opportunities to observe at-

29. Robert D. Walpole, national intelligence officer for strategic and nuclear programs, speech at the Carnegie Endowment for International Peace, September 17, 1998, at http://www.odci.gov/cia/public_affairs/speeches/walpole_speech_091798.html.

tempts to experiment with new technology and new doctrine. In the past, a service interested in procuring a new weapon system would build and test prototypes, an act that often provided the first concrete evidence of innovation. Similarly, a service that perceived the need to modify its doctrine and organization would hold maneuvers to test the effectiveness of the changes. Many once-observable activities traditionally associated with innovation can, however, now be performed by computer. As a result, it may be increasingly difficult for U.S. intelligence organizations to observe foreign innovation.

Third, the increasing overlap between civilian and military technology will complicate assessment. As armed forces come to rely on commercial technology, it will become increasingly difficult to identify their military research and development activities. This will further limit opportunities to detect foreign innovation.

This book suggests that three types of innovation should be particularly difficult to detect. First, intelligence organizations tend to overlook the development of new military technology. The U.S. armed forces, for example, are conducting research and development on a number of advanced technologies, including unmanned air vehicles, robotics, microelectromechanical systems, directed-energy weapons, and high-energy density explosives.[30] To the extent that intelligence organizations focus on current weapon systems, they may miss the emergence of new ways of war. Moreover, new technology is increasingly emerging from the civilian sector rather than from traditional military research and development centers. To make matters worse, intelligence agencies often lack analysts with skills in cutting-edge technologies because they cannot compete with private-sector pay scales.[31] As a result, the agencies may miss potentially important technological developments.

Second, warfare areas that have yet to be demonstrated on the battlefield may surprise intelligence organizations. The United States and other militaries are exploiting new ways of war, including long-range precision-strike warfare, sophisticated information operations, and space warfare. Although the U.S. armed forces enjoy a lead in these warfare areas, the durability of that lead is uncertain. Moreover, potential adversaries appear to be developing innovative capabilities, such

30. See, for example, statement by Frank Fernandez, director, Defense Advanced Research Projects Agency (DARPA), before the Senate Armed Services Committee, Emerging Threats and Capabilities Subcommittee, April 20, 1999.

31. Scientific and Technical Intelligence Committee, *The Health of Scientific and Technical Intelligence: A Study Conducted by the Scientific and Technical Intelligence Committee,* STIC 98–001 (Washington, D.C.: National Intelligence Council, April 1998).

as those needed to blunt power projection forces.[32] This book suggests that collecting intelligence regarding these areas may be a real challenge. To be successful, the United States will have to resist the ever-present temptation of *hubris*.

A third likely blind spot involves technologies and concepts that the United States has not explored or has abandoned. For example, Iraq surprised the U.S. intelligence community by using calutrons—based on technology the United States had long since abandoned—to produce weapons-grade uranium prior to the Gulf War. Similar surprises are likely in the future. The U.S. armed forces must resist the temptation to dismiss foreign developments based on the assumption of U.S. technological superiority.

The United States can improve its ability to detect and to recognize foreign innovation in several ways. One way to increase our knowledge of foreign doctrinal debates is to make a systematic effort to analyze open sources such as military newspapers, professional journals, and books, as well as semi-open sources such as doctrinal publications. In many cases, they may offer the first indication that a foreign service is studying new warfare areas. During the Cold War, analysis of doctrinal publications gave the U.S. military valuable insight into Soviet thinking regarding nuclear and conventional operations.[33] More recently, analysts have looked to open sources for a glimpse into Chinese views of future warfare.[34]

Because states have historically pursued innovative approaches to warfare to overcome strategic or operational challenges that defy conventional solutions, much can be learned by trying to understand the strategic and operational challenges that may force potential adversaries to innovate. By determining the problems that drive states to innovate, intelligence services may be able to identify the innovations that the states may adopt. Countering the qualitative advantages of U.S. power projection forces, for example, dictates that the states identify and exploit vulnerabilities in our systems and concepts.

32. Mahnken, "Deny U.S. Access?"

33. William R. Kintner, ed., and Harriet Fast Scott, trans., *The Nuclear Revolution in Soviet Military Affairs* (Norman: University of Oklahoma Press, 1968); Harriet Fast Scott and William F. Scott, eds., *The Soviet Art of War: Doctrine, Strategy, and Tactics* (Boulder, Colo.: Westview Press, 1982); Ghulam Dastagir Wardak, comp., *The Voroshilov Lectures: Materials from the Soviet General Staff Academy*, 3 vols. (Washington, D.C.: National Defense University Press, 1989–1992).

34. Pillsbury, ed., *Chinese Views of Future Warfare*. Of note is that the articles in this book were collected not by a U.S. government agency but by a private citizen.

A complementary approach would be to establish multidisciplinary research centers to examine selected countries of interest. During the Cold War, for example, a number of think tanks studied Soviet military concepts and doctrine. Similar efforts could help the U.S. government understand potential future competitors. What lessons, for example, are they drawing from contemporary conflicts? How do they view U.S. forces? Are they attempting to emulate or to counter U.S. technology and doctrine?

Information gathered by defense attachés, liaison officers, and students at foreign military schools can play an important role in detecting and characterizing foreign military innovation. Defense attachés often have the opportunity to work closely with their foreign counterparts. They may also be able to monitor doctrinal debates. If appropriately trained and tasked, human intelligence sources can provide tremendous insight into foreign innovation. The services should strengthen their foreign area officer programs, with emphasis on regions that are likely to be of increasing interest to the United States, such as Asia.

An effort to identify and to track innovators may further illuminate the scope, pace, and emphasis of foreign efforts. During the 1930s, for example, U.S. attachés in Germany followed Guderian's writings, mining them for clues to German armored doctrine. A dedicated effort to identify and to track foreign individuals and institutions associated with innovation efforts could prove similarly useful. How do they portray future conflicts? Who, if anyone, within their armed forces pays attention to their ideas? Are their ideas used in war games and exercises? Are they incorporated in doctrine?

Developing relationships with foreign professional military education institutions also may be worthwhile. During the 1920s and 1930s, for example, the Marine Corps schools at Quantico, Virginia, were responsible for writing amphibious doctrine, while the Naval War College was the hub of that service's thinking regarding carrier aviation. It would be worthwhile to determine whether foreign armed forces are founding new doctrinal and educational institutions. Who is being assigned to their professional military education institutions? Where are they going after these assignments?

Some states considering innovative approaches to warfare may move beyond speculation to begin experimenting with new operational concepts and organizations. An examination of foreign exercises may offer important clues regarding new technology and doctrine. Attempts to explore innovative weapons and concepts should, for example, lead to a change in the observable pattern of exercises. An in-depth study of foreign exercises may reveal attempts to develop new approaches to combat.

[181]

It is unlikely that the world will see a major interstate war for many years to come. The participants will look and fight much differently from the superpowers during the Cold War. As the experience of the U.S. intelligence community during the years between the two world wars shows, understanding new ways of war requires a long-term, focused effort. It is thus incumbent on the United States to begin now to concentrate on foreign attempts to develop new approaches to warfare.

Index

CORNELL STUDIES IN SECURITY AFFAIRS

A series edited by

Robert J. Art
Robert Jervis
Stephen M. Walt

Reputation and International Politics by Jonathan Mercer

Undermining the Kremlin: America's Strategy to Subvert the Soviet Bloc, 1947–1956 by Gregory Mitrovich

Report to JFK: The Skybolt Crisis in Perspective by Richard E. Neustadt

The Sacred Cause: Civil-Military Conflict over Soviet National Security, 1917–1992 by Thomas M. Nichols

Liberal Peace, Liberal War: American Politics and International Security by John M. Owen IV

Bombing to Win: Air Power and Coercion in War by Robert A. Pape

A Question of Loyalty: Military Manpower in Multiethnic States by Alon Peled

Inadvertent Escalation: Conventional War and Nuclear Risks by Barry R. Posen

The Sources of Military Doctrine: France, Britain, and Germany between the World Wars by Barry Posen

Dilemmas of Appeasement: British Deterrence and Defense, 1934–1937 by Gaines Post Jr.

Crucible of Beliefs: Learning, Alliances, and World Wars by Dan Reiter

Eisenhower and the Missile Gap by Peter J. Roman

The Domestic Bases of Grand Strategy edited by Richard Rosecrance and Arthur Stein

Societies and Military Power: India and Its Armies by Stephen Peter Rosen

Winning the Next War: Innovation and the Modern Military by Stephen Peter Rosen

Fighting to a Finish: The Politics of War Termination in the United States and Japan, 1945 by Leon V. Sigal

Alliance Politics by Glenn H. Snyder

The Ideology of the Offensive: Military Decision Making and the Disasters of 1914 by Jack Snyder

Myths of Empire: Domestic Politics and International Ambition by Jack Snyder

The Militarization of Space: U.S. Policy, 1945–1984 by Paul B. Stares

The Nixon Administration and the Making of U.S. Nuclear Strategy by Terry Terriff

The Ethics of Destruction: Norms and Force in International Relations by Ward Thomas

Causes of War: Power and the Roots of Conflict by Stephen Van Evera

Mortal Friends, Best Enemies: German-Russian Cooperation after the Cold War by Celeste A. Wallander

The Origins of Alliances by Stephen M. Walt

Revolution and War by Stephen M. Walt

The Tet Offensive: Intelligence Failure in War by James J. Wirtz

The Elusive Balance: Power and Perceptions during the Cold War by William Curti Wohlforth

Deterrence and Strategic Culture: Chinese-American Confrontations, 1949–1958 by Shu Guang Zhang